What You Can Learn About Your Baby *Now*

Discover your child's Moon sign and understand why:

- a Moon in Libra child needs to be actively encouraged to express his or her emotions;
- a Moon in Scorpio child needs time to be alone;
- a Moon in Sagittarius child needs challenge and adventure;
- teeth and bones are weak spots in the body of the Moon in Capricorn child;
- a Moon in Aquarius child is prone to be a daredevil;
- it's very hard for a child with a Moon in Pisces to separate from his or her mother;
- a Moon in Leo child is prone to exaggeration.

Read on and discover the keys to your child's heart and mind. . . .

Also by Debbie Frank

Birth Signs

BABY SIGNS

How to Discover Your Child's Personality Through the Stars

DEBBIE FRANK

POCKET BOOKS
New York London Toronto Sydney Tokyo Singapore

Astrological tables provided by Magic Space Promotions.

An *Original* Publication of POCKET BOOKS

POCKET BOOKS, a division of Simon & Schuster Inc.
1230 Avenue of the Americas, New York, NY 10020

First published in Great Britain by Vermilion Arrow

ISBN: 0-671-50258-1

First Pocket Books printing June 1996

10 9 8 7 6 5 4 3 2 1

Front cover illustration by Punz Wolff

Printed in the U.S.A.

This book is for all children everywhere,
including those that remain inside every adult.

Contents

Introduction

When you gaze at a newborn baby for the first time, a question springs to mind—who is here? The parents are gardeners who have accepted delivery of some seeds, but there are no instructions as to what kind of flower, tree, or plant the child will become. There is no picture on the front of the packet to show what the end result might be, or in which part of the garden the seed might flourish.

Is your baby a potential oak tree that needs to be planted with a lot of room to grow? Or perhaps a climbing rose that must be planted against the security of the house in order to thrive? Does this seed prefer sunshine or shade, hard or soft soil? Is your baby a hardy annual or a fragile orchid? Knowing the Sun and Moon signs of your baby will give you an insight into the answers.

The baby is at the seedling stage of his or her life's purpose, whatever its unique offering may be. Knowing the Sun and Moon signs of your baby will give you some idea of just what might be in the packet, and the right conditions that are needed for him to become who he is meant to be and to realize his full potential.

Discovering the Moon Sign

You can discover the Moon sign of your child by simply looking up his or her date and time of birth in the tables at the front of the Moon section. The tables cover the years from 1985 to 2001. Once you have found the Moon sign, you will have the key to your child's early years, because at that stage in his development he is more likely to express his Moon sign than his Sun sign.

The Moon represents our early nurturing and instinctive nature. In the Moon sign section you will learn how your baby perceives his or her mother (because the maternal instinct is rules by the Moon) and the type of feeding and sleeping patterns he might have. The Moon also describes how a baby is fed both emotionally and physically during the early years, and points toward our reactions in later life—do we reach for a cookie when things get difficult, do we want to be alone or with other people? The Moon sign will reveal how we learn to handle our feelings from babyhood onward.

Knowing the Moon sign of your child will show you what he or she needs in order to feel safe and secure and how he is likely to express his feelings. Because the Moon is unconscious and instinctual, it describes how your child naturally reacts and responds to situations—whether he is fussy, shy, lively, easygoing, or demanding. The Moon sign describes the baby, the child, and the inner, private person, and as adults, we continue to need whatever our Moon sign requires. The Moon is the chief significator of childhood conditioning, and it continues to influence our future throughout our lives.

Learning about the Sun Sign

The Sun sign begins to make its influence felt around the age of six months, when a baby first realizes that he or she is actually a separate being and not still fused with the mother. Therefore the Sun describes the potential qualities that are present in the child, even though they will begin to operate more fully as he learns to stand on his own two feet.

When you look up your child's Sun sign, you will read about the special qualities he or she possesses. These are all potentials that are available to him, and you can help him develop and express them so that he can tap into his strengths. This is followed by a section indicating how girls and boys may express their Sun signs in different ways. In the sections headed At School and At Play, you will see how the different Sun signs experience their school years and also how the various signs all behave differently at play.

Finally, you can read how your own Sign gets on with that of your child. As a mother or father, your energies and qualities will influence and be influenced by those of your child, and this section aims to help you understand the cross-currents and connections between you.

The child is a kernel of all that he or she will be in the future. Being a parent offers an opportunity to allow these qualities to unfold and come to life so that your child can grow into the unique person that only he or she can be.

—Debbie Frank
London, 1993

Note: Some sections of this book refer specifically to boys and girls or male and female. In all other instances, however, the words "he" and "she" are interchangeable.

Moon Tables

How to Use These Tables to Find Your Child's Moon Sign

Hopefully, these tables won't send you into a state of confusion. The process of finding your child's moon sign does involve making a small calculation, but if you follow this step-by-step guide, it should be a simple process. The Moon sign tables are produced for Greenwich Mean Time (GMT), which is the time system used by astrologers all over the world, so the American birth time needs to be converted to GMT. Here is how you do it.

1. Winter Time or Summer Time Birth?

First you need to know if your child was born in normal standard Winter Time, or was born when the clocks are one hour forward in the summer. Summer Time (Daylight Savings Time) is uniformly observed throughout the United States between the first Sunday in April and the last Sunday in October, changing at 2:00 A.M. (Note: If you live an in area that does not observe Daylight Savings Time, you will have to take this into account in your calculations.)

Summer Time Chart

1985	4/7–10/27	1991	4/7–10/27	1997	4/6–10/26
1986	4/6–10/26	1992	4/6–10/25	1998	4/5–10/25
1987	4/5–10/25	1993	4/4–10/31	1999	4/4–10/31
1988	4/3–10/30	1994	4/3–10/30	2000	4/2–10/29
1989	4/2–10/29	1995	4/2–10/29	2001	4/1–10/28
1990	4/1–10/28	1996	4/7–10/27		

2. Time Zone Calculation

Look up the time zone in which your child was born, either in wintertime or summertime, and add on the number of hours shown to your child's American birth time.

Example A: If your child was born in Winter Time in a place within the Eastern Time Zone, you will need to add on 5 hours to get the GMT. If your child was born during Summer Time in the Eastern Time Zone, you will need to add on only 4 hours to get the GMT.

Example B: If your child was born in Winter Time in a place within the Central Time Zone, you will need to add on 6 hours to get the GMT. If your child was born during Summer Time in the Central Time Zone, you will need to add on only 5 hours to get the GMT.

Time Zone Chart

Time Zone	*Winter Birth*	*Summer Birth*
Eastern Time Zone	Add 5 hours	Add 4 hours
Central Time Zone	Add 6 hours	Add 5 hours
Mountain Time Zone	Add 7 hours	Add 6 hours
Pacific Time Zone	Add 8 hours	Add 7 hours
Yukon Time Zone	Add 9 hours	Add 8 hours
Alaska-Hawaii Time Zone	Add 10 hours	Add 9 hours
Atlantic Time Zone	Add 4 hours	Add 3 hours

(Your child's day of birth might also change if the hours to add on take you into the next day.)

3. Find the Moon Sign

Next, look up at the page that gives Moon sign tables for the year in which your child was born. You will see that not every date is mentioned. This is because the Moon changes signs only every 2 to 3 days, and so only the dates that have a change of sign are given with the exact time in which the Moon entered a new sign.

If your child's birthday is given, then the Moon will be changing signs at the time printed alongside the date. If your child was born before this time (GMT), then the Moon sign will be the one listed for the previous date. If your child was born on or after the time given, the Moon sign will be the one given on that line.

If your child's date is not given, then look up the date previous to his or her birthday. Your child will have the Moon in the sign given for this date, as it will not have moved into another sign for his or her birthday.

1985 Moon Signs	All times are GMT (Greenwich Mean Time) 24-hour clock system	1985 Summer Time
The Moon's Sign of the Zodiac changes every 2–3 days at the time indicated	Examples: 21:17 = 9:17 P.M. 11:03 = 11:03 A.M.	Subtract 1 hour from your child's birth time between April 28 at 2:00 A.M. and October 27 at 2:00 A.M. for time correction to GMT

Jan. 1 Taurus	0:37	Mar. 12 Sagittarius	1:31	May 22 Cancer	11:03
Jan. 3 Gemini	11:57	Mar. 14 Capricorn	5:58	May 24 Leo	19:53
Jan. 5 Cancer	20:16	Mar. 16 Aquarius	13:15	May 27 Virgo	2:06
Jan. 8 Leo	1:28	Mar. 18 Pisces	22:52	May 29 Libra	5:39
Jan. 10 Virgo	4:40	Mar. 21 Aries	10:22	May 31 Scorpio	7:07
Jan. 12 Libra	7:15	Mar. 23 Taurus	23:07	June 2 Sagittarius	7:35
Jan. 14 Scorpio	10:10	Mar. 26 Gemini	12:01	June 4 Capricorn	8:38
Jan. 16 Sagittarius	13:50	Mar. 28 Cancer	23:14	June 6 Aquarius	11:58
Jan. 18 Capricorn	18:31	Mar. 31 Leo	6:47	June 8 Pisces	18:51
Jan. 21 Aquarius	0:39	Apr. 2 Virgo	10:20	June 11 Aries	5:27
Jan. 23 Pisces	9:06	Apr. 4 Libra	10:52	June 13 Taurus	18:12
Jan. 25 Aries	20:07	Apr. 6 Scorpio	10:13	June 16 Gemini	6:44
Jan. 28 Taurus	8:53	Apr. 8 Sagittarius	10:23	June 18 Cancer	17:20
Jan. 30 Gemini	21:00	Apr. 10 Capricorn	13:03	June 21 Leo	1:32
Feb. 2 Cancer	5:55	Apr. 12 Aquarius	19:08	June 23 Virgo	7:31
Feb. 4 Leo	10:58	Apr. 15 Pisces	4:33	June 25 Libra	11:46
Feb. 6 Virgo	13:08	Apr. 17 Aries	16:20	June 27 Scorpio	14:36
Feb. 8 Libra	14:12	Apr. 20 Taurus	5:13	June 29 Sagittarius	16:31
Feb. 10 Scorpio	15:52	Apr. 22 Gemini	18:00	July 1 Capricorn	18:24
Feb. 12 Sagittarius	19:12	Apr. 25 Cancer	5:24	July 3 Aquarius	21:38
Feb. 15 Capricorn	0:28	Apr. 27 Leo	14:06	July 6 Pisces	3:44
Feb. 17 Aquarius	7:39	Apr. 29 Virgo	19:22	July 8 Aries	13:25
Feb. 19 Pisces	16:41	May 1 Libra	21:21	July 11 Taurus	1:45
Feb. 22 Aries	3:44	May 3 Scorpio	21:17	July 13 Gemini	14:22
Feb. 24 Taurus	16:28	May 5 Sagittarius	20:58	July 16 Cancer	0:54
Feb. 27 Gemini	5:10	May 7 Capricorn	22:14	July 18 Leo	8:23
Mar. 1 Cancer	15:19	May 10 Aquarius	2:41	July 20 Virgo	13:28
Mar. 3 Leo	21:27	May 12 Pisces	11:01	July 22 Libra	17:10
Mar. 5 Virgo	23:43	May 14 Aries	22:27	July 24 Scorpio	20:17
Mar. 7 Libra	23:48	May 17 Taurus	11:24	July 26 Sagittarius	23:13
Mar. 9 Scorpio	23:48	May 20 Gemini	0:02	July 29 Capricorn	2:22

July 31 Aquarius	6:29	Sept. 21 Capricorn	13:54	Nov. 13 Sagittarius	5:54
Aug. 2 Pisces	12:39	Sept. 23 Aquarius	19:15	Nov. 15 Capricorn	5:58
Aug. 4 Aries	21:45	Sept. 26 Pisces	2:53	Nov. 17 Aquarius	8:32
Aug. 7 Taurus	9:43	Sept. 28 Aries	12:46	Nov. 19 Pisces	14:48
Aug. 9 Gemini	22:32	Oct. 1 Taurus	0:36	Nov. 22 Aries	0:44
Aug. 12 Cancer	9:25	Oct. 3 Gemini	13:37	Nov. 24 Taurus	13:08
Aug. 14 Leo	16:54	Oct. 6 Cancer	1:59	Nov. 27 Gemini	2:09
Aug. 16 Virgo	21:14	Oct. 8 Leo	11:29	Nov. 29 Cancer	14:22
Aug. 18 Libra	23:45	Oct. 10 Virgo	17:06	Dec. 2 Leo	1:00
Aug. 21 Scorpio	1:52	Oct. 12 Libra	19:10	Dec. 4 Virgo	9:11
Aug. 23 Sagittarius	4:38	Oct. 14 Scorpio	19:13	Dec. 6 Libra	14:30
Aug. 25 Capricorn	8:27	Oct. 16 Sagittarius	19:08	Dec. 8 Scorpio	16:54
Aug. 27 Aquarius	13:35	Oct. 18 Capricorn	20:38	Dec. 10 Sagittarius	17:13
Aug. 29 Pisces	20:27	Oct. 21 Aquarius	0:56	Dec. 12 Capricorn	17:02
Sept. 1 Aries	5:45	Oct. 23 Pisces	8:32	Dec. 14 Aquarius	18:20
Sept. 3 Taurus	17:30	Oct. 25 Aries	18:50	Dec. 16 Pisces	22:52
Sept. 6 Gemini	6:26	Oct. 28 Taurus	7:01	Dec. 19 Aries	7:41
Sept. 8 Cancer	18:08	Oct. 30 Gemini	20:00	Dec. 21 Taurus	19:42
Sept. 11 Leo	2:26	Nov. 2 Cancer	8:29	Dec. 24 Gemini	8:45
Sept. 13 Virgo	6:50	Nov. 4 Leo	19:02	Dec. 26 Cancer	20:44
Sept. 15 Libra	8:33	Nov. 7 Virgo	2:17	Dec. 29 Leo	6:43
Sept. 17 Scorpio	9:19	Nov. 9 Libra	5:49	Dec. 31 Virgo	14:45
Sept. 19 Sagittarius	10:44	Nov. 11 Scorpio	6:30		

1986 Moon Signs

The Moon's Sign of the Zodiac changes every 2–3 days at the time indicated

All Times are GMT (Greenwich Mean Time) 24-hour clock system

Examples:
21:17 = 9:17 P.M.
11:03 = 11:03 A.M.

1986 Summer Time

Subtract 1 hour from your child's birth time between April 27 at 2:00 A.M. and October 26 at 2:00 A.M. for time correction to GMT

Jan. 2 Libra	20:45	Feb. 7 Aquarius	14:38	Mar. 16 Gemini	8:24
Jan. 5 Scorpio	0:44	Feb. 9 Pisces	18:36	Mar. 18 Cancer	21:04
Jan. 7 Sagittarius	2:47	Feb. 12 Aries	1:23	Mar. 21 Leo	7:35
Jan. 9 Capricorn	3:43	Feb. 14 Taurus	11:42	Mar. 23 Virgo	14:36
Jan. 11 Aquarius	5:05	Feb. 17 Gemini	0:18	Mar. 25 Libra	18:21
Jan. 13 Pisces	8:45	Feb. 19 Cancer	12:37	Mar. 27 Scorpio	20:06
Jan. 15 Aries	16:09	Feb. 21 Leo	22:25	Mar. 29 Sagittarius	21:22
Jan. 18 Taurus	3:15	Feb. 24 Virgo	4:56	Mar. 31 Capricorn	23:26
Jan. 20 Gemini	36:12	Feb. 26 Libra	9:06	Apr. 3 Aquarius	3:13
Jan. 23 Cancer	4:14	Feb. 28 Scorpio	2:06	Apr. 5 Pisces	9:07
Jan. 25 Leo	13:45	Mar. 2 Sagittarius	14:53	Apr. 7 Aries	17:15
Jan. 27 Virgo	20:51	Mar. 4 Capricorn	17:57	Apr. 10 Taurus	3:38
Jan. 30 Libra	2:10	Mar. 6 Aquarius	21:44	Apr. 12 Gemini	15:52
Feb. 1 Scorpio	6:19	Mar. 9 Pisces	2:50	Apr. 15 Cancer	4:42
Feb. 3 Sagittarius	9:31	Mar. 11 Aries	10:08	Apr. 17 Leo	16:07
Feb. 5 Capricorn	12:02	Mar. 13 Taurus	20:06	Apr. 20 Virgo	0:24

MOON TABLES

Apr. 22 Libra	4:48	July 17 Sagittarius	12:32	Oct. 11 Aquarius	11:48
Apr. 24 Scorpio	6:15	July 19 Capricorn	13:10	Oct. 13 Pisces	16:07
Apr. 26 Sagittarius	6:18	July 21 Aquarius	13:21	Oct. 15 Aries	22:15
Apr. 28 Capricorn	6:45	July 23 Pisces	15:05	Oct. 18 Taurus	6:38
Apr. 30 Aquarius	9:11	July 25 Aries	20:07	Oct. 20 Gemini	17:18
May 2 Pisces	14:35	July 28 Taurus	5:14	Oct. 23 Cancer	5:38
May 4 Aries	23:02	July 30 Gemini	17:21	Oct. 25 Leo	18:01
May 7 Taurus	10:01	Aug. 2 Cancer	6:03	Oct. 28 Virgo	4:18
May 9 Gemini	22:27	Aug. 4 Leo	17:25	Oct. 30 Libra	11:00
May 12 Cancer	11:18	Aug. 7 Virgo	2:44	Nov. 1 Scorpio	14:16
May 14 Leo	23:16	Aug. 9 Libra	10:03	Nov. 3 Sagittarius	15:19
May 17 Virgo	8:41	Aug. 11 Scorpio	15:34	Nov. 5 Capricorn	15:51
May 19 Libra	14:36	Aug. 13 Sagittarius	19:16	Nov. 7 Aquarius	17:33
May 21 Scorpio	16:59	Aug. 15 Capricorn	21:23	Nov. 9 Pisces	21:32
May 23 Sagittarius	16:56	Aug. 17 Aquarius	22:45	Nov. 12 Aries	4:17
May 25 Capricorn	16:18	Aug. 20 Pisces	0:54	Nov. 14 Taurus	13:28
May 27 Aquarius	17:05	Aug. 22 Aries	5:32	Nov. 17 Gemini	0:27
May 29 Pisces	20:58	Aug. 24 Taurus	13:42	Nov. 19 Cancer	12:47
June 1 Aries	4:46	Aug. 27 Gemini	1:01	Nov. 22 Leo	1:26
June 3 Taurus	15:48	Aug. 29 Cancer	13:39	Nov. 24 Virgo	12:43
June 6 Gemini	4:27	Sept. 1 Leo	1:09	Nov. 26 Libra	20:57
June 8 Cancer	17:16	Sept. 3 Virgo	10:03	Nov. 29 Scorpio	1:13
June 11 Leo	5:11	Sept. 5 Libra	16:32	Dec. 1 Sagittarius	2:08
June 13 Virgo	15:15	Sept. 7 Scorpio	21:12	Dec. 3 Capricorn	1:30
June 15 Libra	22:38	Sept. 10 Sagittarius	0:41	Dec. 5 Aquarius	1:25
June 18 Scorpio	2:35	Sept. 12 Capricorn	3:29	Dec. 7 Pisces	3:52
June 20 Sagittarius	3:35	Sept. 14 Aquarius	6:09	Dec. 9 Aries	9:54
June 22 Capricorn	3:01	Sept. 16 Pisces	9:30	Dec. 11 Taurus	9:13
June 24 Aquarius	2:53	Sept. 18 Aries	14:38	Dec. 14 Gemini	6:43
June 26 Pisces	5:18	Sept. 20 Taurus	22:27	Dec. 16 Cancer	19:10
June 28 Aries	11:41	Sept. 23 Gemini	9:16	Dec. 19 Leo	7:44
June 30 Taurus	21:56	Sept. 25 Cancer	21:45	Dec. 21 Virgo	19:30
July 3 Gemini	10:33	Sept. 28 Leo	9:37	Dec. 24 Libra	5:02
July 5 Cancer	23:20	Sept. 30 Virgo	18:55	Dec. 26 Scorpio	11:01
July 8 Leo	10:54	Oct. 3 Libra	1:03	Dec. 28 Sagittarius	13:16
July 10 Virgo	20:49	Oct. 5 Scorpio	4:35	Dec. 30 Capricorn	12:54
July 13 Libra	4:39	Oct. 7 Sagittarius	6:48		
July 15 Scorpio	9:55	Oct. 9 Capricorn	8:55		

1987 Moon Signs

All times are GMT (Greenwich Mean Time) 24-hour clock system

1987 Summer Time

The Moon's Sign of the Zodiac changes every 2–3 days at the time indicated

Examples:
21:17 = 9:17 P.M.
11:03 = 11:03 A.M.

Subtract 1 hour from our child's birth time between April 5 at 2:00 A.M. and October 25 at 2:00 A.M. for time correction to GMT

Jan. 1 Aquarius	11:58	Jan. 5 Aries	16:57	Jan. 10 Gemini	12:42
Jan. 3 Pisces	12:43	Jan. 8 Taurus	1:14	Jan. 13 Cancer	1:19

Jan. 15 Leo	13:45
Jan. 18 Virgo	1:15
Jan. 20 Libra	11:07
Jan. 22 Scorpio	18:28
Jan. 24 Sagittarius	22:35
Jan. 26 Capricorn	23:43
Jan. 28 Aquarius	23:18
Jan. 30 Pisces	23:25
Feb. 2 Aries	2:12
Feb. 4 Taurus	8:59
Feb. 6 Gemini	19:26
Feb. 9 Cancer	7:56
Feb. 11 Leo	20:21
Feb. 14 Virgo	7:25
Feb. 16 Libra	16:43
Feb. 19 Scorpio	0:05
Feb. 21 Sagittarius	5:07
Feb. 23 Capricorn	7:55
Feb. 25 Aquarius	9:09
Feb. 27 Pisces	10:10
Mar. 1 Aries	12:43
Mar. 3 Taurus	18:16
Mar. 6 Gemini	3:29
Mar. 8 Cancer	15:26
Mar. 11 Leo	3:54
Mar. 13 Virgo	14:53
Mar. 15 Libra	23:35
Mar. 18 Scorpio	5:56
Mar. 20 Sagittarius	10:31
Mar. 22 Capricorn	13:48
Mar. 24 Aquarius	16:19
Mar. 26 Pisces	18:47
Mar. 28 Aries	22:14
Mar. 31 Taurus	3:49
Apr. 2 Gemini	12:21
Apr. 4 Cancer	24:34
Apr. 7 Leo	12:03
Apr. 9 Virgo	23:28
Apr. 12 Libra	8:02
Apr. 14 Scorpio	13:38
Apr. 16 Sagittarius	17:01
Apr. 18 Capricorn	19:22
Apr. 20 Aquarius	21:46
Apr. 23 Pisces	1:03
Apr. 25 Aries	5:43
Apr. 27 Taurus	12:10
Apr. 29 Gemini	20:45
May 2 Cancer	7:42
May 4 Leo	20:07
May 7 Virgo	8:05
May 9 Libra	17:25
May 11 Scorpio	23:09
May 14 Sagittarius	1:41
May 16 Capricorn	2:38
May 18 Aquarius	3:45
May 20 Pisces	6:28
May 22 Aries	11:27
May 24 Taurus	18:42
May 27 Gemini	3:57
May 29 Cancer	15:02
June 1 Leo	3:26
June 3 Virgo	15:55
June 6 Libra	2:23
June 8 Scorpio	9:01
June 10 Sagittarius	11:49
June 12 Capricorn	12:04
June 14 Aquarius	11:48
June 16 Pisces	13:00
June 18 Aries	17:01
June 21 Taurus	0:10
June 23 Gemini	9:57
June 25 Cancer	21:24
June 28 Leo	9:53
June 30 Virgo	22:35
July 3 Libra	9:51
July 5 Scorpio	17:59
July 7 Sagittarius	22:04
July 9 Capricorn	22:44
July 11 Aquarius	21:50
July 13 Pisces	21:38
July 16 Aries	0:01
July 18 Taurus	6:09
July 20 Gemini	15:36
July 23 Cancer	3:14
July 25 Leo	15:51
July 28 Virgo	4:26
July 30 Libra	15:58
Aug. 2 Scorpio	1:09
Aug. 4 Sagittarius	6:43
Aug. 6 Capricorn	8:48
Aug. 8 Aquarius	8:37
Aug. 10 Pisces	8:05
Aug. 12 Aries	9:16
Aug. 14 Taurus	3:45
Aug. 16 Gemini	22:01
Aug. 19 Cancer	9:21
Aug. 21 Leo	21:59
Aug. 24 Virgo	10:23
Aug. 26 Libra	21:35
Aug. 29 Scorpio	6:47
Aug. 31 Sagittarius	13:20
Sept. 2 Capricorn	17:01
Sept. 4 Aquarius	18:21
Sept. 6 Pisces	18:38
Sept. 8 Aries	19:37
Sept. 10 Taurus	22:59
Sept. 13 Gemini	5:59
Sept. 15 Cancer	16:25
Sept. 18 Leo	4:51
Sept. 20 Virgo	17:12
Sept. 23 Libra	3:57
Sept. 25 Scorpio	12:28
Sept. 27 Sagittarius	18:48
Sept. 29 Capricorn	23:09
Oct. 2 Aquarius	1:52
Oct. 4 Pisces	3:40
Oct. 6 Aries	5:37
Oct. 8 Taurus	9:02
Oct. 10 Gemini	15:09
Oct. 13 Cancer	0:32
Oct. 15 Leo	12:36
Oct. 18 Virgo	1:06
Oct. 20 Libra	11:47
Oct. 22 Scorpio	19:40
Oct. 25 Sagittarius	0:58
Oct. 27 Capricorn	4:33
Oct. 29 Aquarius	7:28
Oct. 31 Pisces	10:21
Nov. 2 Aries	13:42
Nov. 4 Taurus	18:05
Nov. 7 Gemini	0:17
Nov. 9 Cancer	9:14
Nov. 11 Leo	20:47
Nov. 14 Virgo	9:28
Nov. 16 Libra	20:47
Nov. 19 Scorpio	4:44
Nov. 21 Sagittarius	9:14
Nov. 23 Capricorn	11:32
Nov. 25 Aquarius	13:15
Nov. 27 Pisces	15:44
Nov. 19 Aries	19:38
Dec. 2 Taurus	1:07
Dec. 4 Gemini	8:17
Dec. 6 Cancer	17:23
Dec. 9 Leo	4:42
Dec. 11 Virgo	17:30
Dec. 14 Libra	5:38
Dec. 16 Scorpio	14:36
Dec. 18 Sagittarius	19:30
Dec. 20 Capricorn	21:07
Dec. 22 Aquarius	21:21
Dec. 24 Pisces	22:12
Dec. 27 Aries	1:07
Dec. 29 Taurus	6:40
Dec. 31 Gemini	14:32

MOON TABLES

1988 Moon Signs

The Moon's Sign of the Zodiac changes every 2–3 days at the time indicated

All Times Are GMT (Greenwich Mean Time) 24-hour clock system

Examples:
21:17 = 9:17 PM.
11:03 = 11:03 A.M.

1988 Summer Time

Subtract 1 hour from your child's birth time between April 3 at 2:00 A.M. and October 30 at 2:00 A.M. for time correction to GMT

Jan. 3 Cancer	0:18	Apr. 3 Scorpio	18:24	July 3 Pisces	8:36
Jan. 5 Leo	11:50	Apr. 6 Sagittarius	2:28	July 5 Aries	10:41
Jan. 8 Virgo	0:36	Apr. 8 Capricorn	8:18	July 7 Taurus	14:31
Jan. 10 Libra	13:15	Apr. 10 Aquarius	12:08	July 9 Gemini	10:19
Jan. 12 Scorpio	23:40	Apr. 12 Pisces	14:24	July 12 Cancer	4:11
Jan. 15 Sagittarius	5:54	Apr. 14 Aries	15:48	July 14 Leo	14:15
Jan. 17 Capricorn	8:12	Apr. 16 Taurus	17:34	July 17 Virgo	2:18
Jan. 19 Aquarius	8:02	Apr. 18 Gemini	21:13	July 19 Libra	15:21
Jan. 21 Pisces	7:30	Apr. 21 Cancer	4:08	July 22 Scorpio	3:12
Jan. 23 Aries	8:37	Apr. 23 Leo	14:38	July 24 Sagittarius	11:37
Jan. 25 Taurus	12:42	Apr. 26 Virgo	3:16	July 26 Capricorn	16:03
Jan. 27 Gemini	20:05	Apr. 28 Libra	15:36	July 28 Aquarius	17:24
Jan. 30 Cancer	6:14	May 1 Scorpio	1:39	July 30 Pisces	17:24
Feb. 1 Leo	18:08	May 3 Sagittarius	8:50	Aug. 1 Aries	17:56
Feb. 4 Virgo	6:55	May 5 Capricorn	13:53	Aug. 3 Taurus	20:27
Feb. 6 Libra	19:36	May 7 Aquarius	17:37	Aug. 6 Gemini	1:45
Feb. 9 Scorpio	6:39	May 9 Pisces	20:39	Aug. 8 Cancer	9:56
Feb. 11 Sagittarius	14:31	May 11 Aries	23:24	Aug. 10 Leo	20:28
Feb. 13 Capricorn	18:33	May 14 Taurus	2:23	Aug. 13 Virgo	8:47
Feb. 15 Aquarius	19:24	May 16 Gemini	6:35	Aug. 15 Libra	21:52
Feb. 17 Pisces	18:45	May 18 Cancer	13:11	Aug. 18 Scorpio	10:09
Feb. 19 Aries	18:39	May 20 Leo	22:53	Aug. 20 Sagittarius	19:53
Feb. 21 Taurus	20:54	May 23 Virgo	11:14	Aug. 23 Capricorn	1:48
Feb. 24 Gemini	2:45	May 25 Libra	23:50	Aug. 25 Aquarius	4:03
Feb. 26 Cancer	12:16	May 28 Scorpio	10:02	Aug. 27 Pisces	4:02
Feb. 29 Leo	0:13	May 30 Sagittarius	16:54	Aug. 29 Aries	3:31
Mar. 2 Virgo	13:07	June 1 Capricorn	20:58	Aug. 31 Taurus	4:26
Mar. 5 Libra	1:32	June 3 Aquarius	23:34	Sept. 2 Gemini	8:17
Mar. 7 Scorpio	12:25	June 6 Pisces	2:02	Sept. 4 Cancer	15:42
Mar. 9 Sagittarius	20:58	June 8 Aries	5:06	Sept. 7 Leo	2:16
Mar. 12 Capricorn	2:30	June 10 Taurus	9:05	Sept. 9 Virgo	14:49
Mar. 14 Aquarius	5:06	June 12 Gemini	14:18	Sept. 12 Libra	3:51
Mar. 16 Pisces	5:42	June 14 Cancer	21:21	Sept. 14 Scorpio	16:06
Mar. 18 Aries	5:48	June 17 Leo	7:01	Sept. 17 Sagittarius	2:25
Mar. 20 Taurus	7:10	June 19 Virgo	19:05	Sept. 19 Capricorn	9:41
Mar. 22 Gemini	11:28	June 22 Libra	7:56	Sept. 21 Aquarius	13:39
Mar. 24 Cancer	19:31	June 24 Scorpio	18:56	Sept. 23 Pisces	14:49
Mar. 27 Leo	6:56	June 27 Sagittarius	2:17	Sept. 25 Aries	14:31
Mar. 29 Virgo	19:49	June 29 Capricorn	5:58	Sept. 27 Taurus	14:33
Apr. 1 Libra	8:04	July 1 Aquarius	7:30	Sept. 29 Gemini	16:49

MOON TABLES

Oct. 1 Cancer	22:41	Nov. 3 Virgo	4:03	Dec. 5 Scorpio	12:48
Oct. 4 Leo	8:35	Nov. 5 Libra	17:03	Dec. 7 Sagittarius	21:55
Oct. 6 Virgo	21:02	Nov. 8 Scorpio	4:45	Dec. 10 Capricorn	4:06
Oct. 9 Libra	10:03	Nov. 10 Sagittarius	14:04	Dec. 12 Aquarius	8:25
Oct. 11 Scorpio	21:58	Nov. 12 Capricorn	21:12	Dec. 14 Pisces	11:53
Oct. 14 Sagittarius	7:56	Nov. 15 Aquarius	2:36	Dec. 16 Aries	15:04
Oct. 16 Capricorn	15:42	Nov. 17 Pisces	6:33	Dec. 18 Taurus	18:12
Oct. 18 Aquarius	21:04	Nov. 19 Aries	9:12	Dec. 20 Gemini	21:44
Oct. 20 Pisces	23:59	Nov. 21 Taurus	11:03	Dec. 23 Cancer	2:37
Oct. 23 Aries	1:00	Nov. 23 Gemini	13:16	Dec. 25 Leo	10:02
Oct. 25 Taurus	1:24	Nov. 25 Cancer	17:25	Dec. 27 Virgo	20:30
Oct. 27 Gemini	2:59	Nov. 28 Leo	0:53	Dec. 30 Libra	9:10
Oct. 29 Cancer	7:34	Nov. 30 Virgo	12:03		
Oct. 31 Leo	16:08	Dec. 3 Libra	0:56		

1989 Moon Signs	All times are GMT (Greenwich Mean Time) 24-hour clock system	1989 Summer Time
The Moon's Sign of the Zodiac changes every 2–3 days at the time indicated	Examples: 21:17 = 9:17 P.M. 11:03 = 11:03 A.M.	Subtract 1 hour from your child's birth time between April 2 at 2:00 A.M. and October 29 at 2:00 A.M. for time correction to GMT

Jan. 1 Scorpio	21:33	Feb. 28 Sagittarius	0:30	Apr. 25 Capricorn	22:15
Jan. 4 Sagittarius	7:08	Mar. 2 Capricorn	8:53	Apr. 28 Aquarius	5:31
Jan. 6 Capricorn	13:10	Mar. 4 Aquarius	13:32	Apr. 30 Pisces	10:00
Jan. 8 Aquarius	16:29	Mar. 6 Pisces	14:56	May 2 Aries	11:48
Jan. 10 Pisces	18:32	Mar. 8 Aries	4:37	May 4 Taurus	11:56
Jan. 12 Aries	20:37	Mar. 10 Taurus	14:30	May 6 Gemini	12:08
Jan. 14 Taurus	23:37	Mar. 12 Gemini	16:22	May 8 Cancer	14:26
Jan. 17 Gemini	3:59	Mar. 14 Cancer	21:30	May 10 Leo	20:52
Jan. 19 Cancer	10:01	Mar. 17 Leo	6:16	May 13 Virgo	6:33
Jan. 21 Leo	18:06	Mar. 19 Virgo	17:42	May 15 Libra	19:08
Jan. 24 Virgo	4:35	Mar. 22 Libra	6:25	May 18 Scorpio	7:47
Jan. 26 Libra	17:03	Mar. 24 Scorpio	19:11	May 20 Sagittarius	18:51
Jan. 29 Scorpio	5:47	Mar. 27 Sagittarius	6:52	May 23 Capricorn	3:53
Jan. 31 Sagittarius	16:27	Mar. 29 Capricorn	16:23	May 25 Aquarius	10:59
Feb. 2 Capricorn	23:30	Mar. 31 Aquarius	22:45	May 27 Pisces	16:11
Feb. 5 Aquarius	2:50	Apr. 3 Pisces	1:37	May 29 Aries	19:25
Feb. 7 Pisces	3:53	Apr. 5 Aries	1:51	May 31 Taurus	21:00
Feb. 9 Aries	4:20	Apr. 7 Taurus	1:09	June 2 Gemini	22:04
Feb. 11 Taurus	5:49	Apr. 9 Gemini	1:33	June 5 Cancer	0:18
Feb. 13 Gemini	9:27	Apr. 11 Cancer	5:03	June 7 Leo	5:33
Feb. 15 Cancer	15:44	Apr. 13 Leo	12:37	June 9 Virgo	14:34
Feb. 18 Leo	0:34	Apr. 15 Virgo	23:40	June 12 Libra	2:32
Feb. 20 Virgo	11:37	Apr. 18 Libra	12:32	June 14 Scorpio	15:10
Feb. 23 Libra	0:06	Apr. 21 Scorpio	1:14	June 17 Sagittarius	2:12
Feb. 25 Scorpio	12:56	Apr. 23 Sagittarius	12:37	June 19 Capricorn	10:39

June 21 Aquarius	16:56	Aug. 25 Cancer	22:15	Oct. 31 Sagittarius	15:22
June 23 Pisces	21:36	Aug. 28 Leo	5:15	Nov. 3 Capricorn	2:46
June 26 Aries	1:07	Aug. 30 Virgo	14:33	Nov. 5 Aquarius	12:06
June 28 Taurus	3:46	Sept. 2 Libra	1:49	Nov. 7 Pisces	18:22
June 30 Gemini	6:10	Sept. 4 Scorpio	14:24	Nov. 9 Aries	21:07
July 2 Cancer	9:23	Sept. 7 Sagittarius	2:50	Nov. 11 Taurus	21:09
July 4 Leo	14:43	Sept. 9 Capricorn	13:09	Nov. 13 Gemini	20:21
July 6 Virgo	23:06	Sept. 11 Aquarius	19:59	Nov. 15 Cancer	20:55
July 9 Libra	10:32	Sept. 13 Pisces	23:08	Nov. 18 Leo	0:47
July 11 Scorpio	23:10	Sept. 15 Aries	23:39	Nov. 20 Virgo	8:59
July 14 Sagittarius	10:28	Sept. 17 Taurus	23:23	Nov. 22 Libra	20:27
July 16 Capricorn	18:59	Sept. 20 Gemini	0:17	Nov. 25 Scorpio	9:13
July 19 Aquarius	0:36	Sept. 22 Cancer	3:54	Nov. 27 Sagittarius	21:30
July 21 Pisces	4:07	Sept. 24 Leo	10:49	Nov. 30 Capricorn	8:25
July 23 Aries	6:41	Sept. 26 Virgo	20:34	Dec. 2 Aquarius	17:41
July 25 Taurus	9:12	Sept. 29 Libra	8:17	Dec. 5 Pisces	0:48
July 27 Gemini	12:18	Oct. 1 Scorpio	20:54	Dec. 7 Aries	5:09
July 29 Cancer	16:35	Oct. 4 Sagittarius	9:29	Dec. 9 Taurus	6:58
July 31 Leo	22:43	Oct. 6 Capricorn	20:44	Dec. 11 Gemini	7:16
Aug. 3 Virgo	7:23	Oct. 9 Aquarius	5:04	Dec. 13 Cancer	7:54
Aug. 5 Libra	18:30	Oct. 11 Pisces	9:33	Dec. 15 Leo	10:48
Aug. 8 Scorpio	7:05	Oct. 13 Aries	10:39	Dec. 17 Virgo	17:25
Aug. 10 Sagittarius	19:01	Oct. 15 Taurus	9:54	Dec. 20 Libra	3:47
Aug. 13 Capricorn	4:14	Oct. 17 Gemini	9:25	Dec. 22 Scorpio	16:19
Aug. 15 Aquarius	9:55	Oct. 19 Cancer	11:16	Dec. 25 Sagittarius	4:36
Aug. 17 Pisces	12:44	Oct. 21 Leo	16:53	Dec. 27 Capricorn	15:09
Aug. 19 Aries	14:00	Oct. 24 Virgo	2:17	Dec. 29 Aquarius	23:38
Aug. 21 Taurus	15:13	Oct. 26 Libra	14:13		
Aug. 23 Gemini	17:42	Oct. 29 Scorpio	2:57		

1990 Moon Signs

The Moon's Sign of the Zodiac changes every 2–3 days at the time indicated

All times are GMT (Greenwich Mean Time) 24-hour clock system

Examples:
21:17 = 9:17 P.M.
11:03 = 11:03 A.M.

1990 Summer Time

Subtract 1 hour from your child's birth time between April 1 at 2:00 A.M. and October 28 at 2:00 A.M. for time correction to GMT

Jan. 1 Pisces	6:09	Jan. 23 Capricorn	23:28	Feb. 15 Scorpio	8:36
Jan. 3 Aries	10:55	Jan. 26 Aquarius	7:23	Feb. 17 Sagittarius	21:07
Jan. 5 Taurus	14:03	Jan. 28 Pisces	12:49	Feb. 20 Capricorn	8:27
Jan. 7 Gemini	16:02	Jan. 30 Aries	16:34	Feb. 22 Aquarius	16:49
Jan. 9 Cancer	17:54	Feb. 1 Taurus	19:28	Feb. 24 Pisces	21:49
Jan. 11 Leo	21:05	Feb. 3 Gemini	22:13	Feb. 27 Aries	0:17
Jan. 14 Virgo	3:00	Feb. 6 Cancer	1:28	Mar. 1 Taurus	1:44
Jan. 16 Libra	12:22	Feb. 8 Leo	5:55	Mar. 3 Gemini	3:40
Jan. 19 Scorpio	0:17	Feb. 10 Virgo	12:18	Mar. 5 Cancer	7:06
Jan. 21 Sagittarius	12:42	Feb. 12 Libra	21:11	Mar. 7 Leo	12:28

Mar. 9 Virgo	19:50	June 18 Taurus	16:40	Sept. 26 Capricorn	18:36
Mar. 12 Libra	5:11	June 20 Gemini	17:14	Sept. 29 Aquarius	5:51
Mar. 14 Scorpio	16:27	June 22 Cancer	17:12	Oct. 1 Pisces	13:37
Mar. 17 Sagittarius	4:56	June 24 Leo	18:29	Oct. 3 Aries	17:39
Mar. 19 Capricorn	17:00	June 26 Virgo	22:44	Oct. 5 Taurus	19:06
Mar. 22 Aquarius	2:30	June 29 Libra	6:51	Oct. 7 Gemini	19:49
Mar. 24 Pisces	8:04	July 1 Scorpio	18:03	Oct. 9 Cancer	21:31
Mar. 26 Aries	10:13	July 4 Sagittarius	6:36	Oct. 12 Leo	1:18
Mar. 28 Taurus	10:27	July 6 Capricorn	18:39	Oct. 14 Virgo	7:24
Mar. 30 Gemini	10:46	July 9 Aquarius	5:05	Oct. 16 Libra	15:30
Apr. 1 Cancer	12:55	July 11 Pisces	13:27	Oct. 19 Scorpio	1:25
Apr. 3 Leo	17:54	July 13 Aries	19:35	Oct. 21 Sagittarius	13:12
Apr. 6 Virgo	1:43	July 15 Taurus	23:29	Oct. 24 Capricorn	2:03
Apr. 8 Libra	11:47	July 18 Gemini	1:32	Oct. 26 Aquarius	14:11
Apr. 10 Scorpio	23:19	July 20 Cancer	2:45	Oct. 28 Pisces	23:22
Apr. 13 Sagittarius	11:49	July 22 Leo	4:32	Oct. 31 Aries	4:12
Apr. 16 Capricorn	0:15	July 24 Virgo	8:23	Nov. 2 Taurus	5:30
Apr. 18 Aquarius	10:48	July 26 Libra	15:24	Nov. 4 Gemini	5:08
Apr. 20 Pisces	17:53	July 29 Scorpio	1:40	Nov. 6 Cancer	5:11
Apr. 22 Aries	20:57	July 31 Sagittarius	14:00	Nov. 8 Leo	7:29
Apr. 24 Taurus	21:02	Aug. 3 Capricorn	2:09	Nov. 10 Virgo	12:53
Apr. 26 Gemini	20:14	Aug. 5 Aquarius	12:16	Nov. 12 Libra	21:11
Apr. 28 Cancer	20:43	Aug. 7 Pisces	19:53	Nov. 15 Scorpio	7:42
May 1 Leo	0:09	Aug. 10 Aries	1:13	Nov. 17 Sagittarius	19:41
May 3 Virgo	7:22	Aug. 12 Taurus	4:55	Nov. 20 Capricorn	8:32
May 5 Libra	17:31	Aug. 14 Gemini	7:42	Nov. 22 Aquarius	21:07
May 8 Scorpio	5:24	Aug. 16 Cancer	10:14	Nov. 25 Pisces	7:28
May 10 Sagittarius	17:57	Aug. 18 Leo	13:14	Nov. 27 Aries	14:01
May 13 Capricorn	6:21	Aug. 20 Virgo	17:36	Nov. 29 Taurus	16:34
May 15 Aquarius	17:28	Aug. 23 Libra	0:18	Dec. 1 Gemini	16:22
May 18 Pisces	1:53	Aug. 25 Scorpio	10:00	Dec. 3 Cancer	15:31
May 20 Aries	6:28	Aug. 27 Sagittarius	21:58	Dec. 5 Leo	16:06
May 22 Taurus	7:40	Aug. 30 Capricorn	10:21	Dec. 7 Virgo	19:43
May 24 Gemini	7:01	Sept. 1 Aquarius	20:50	Dec. 10 Libra	3:03
May 26 Cancer	6:38	Sept. 4 Pisces	4:06	Dec. 12 Scorpio	13:31
May 28 Leo	8:36	Sept. 6 Aries	8:21	Dec. 15 Sagittarius	1:45
May 30 Virgo	14:14	Sept. 8 Taurus	10:56	Dec. 17 Capricorn	14:35
June 1 Libra	23:32	Sept. 10 Gemini	13:07	Dec. 20 Aquarius	2:59
June 4 Scorpio	11:23	Sept. 12 Cancer	15:55	Dec. 22 Pisces	13:45
June 7 Sagittarius	0:00	Sept. 14 Leo	19:54	Dec. 24 Aries	21:44
June 9 Capricorn	12:11	Sept. 17 Virgo	1:20	Dec. 27 Taurus	2:08
June 11 Aquarius	23:10	Sept. 19 Libra	8:38	Dec. 29 Gemini	3:25
June 14 Pisces	7:57	Sept. 21 Scorpio	18:09	Dec. 31 Cancer	3:04
June 16 Aries	13:51	Sept. 24 Sagittarius	5:54		

MOON TABLES

1991 Moon Signs

The Moon's Sign of the Zodiac changes every 2–3 days at the time indicated

All times are GMT (Greenwich Mean Time) 24-hour clock system

Examples:
21:17 = 9:17 P.M.
11:03 = 11:03 A.M.

1991 Summer Time

Subtract 1 hour from your child's birth time between April 7 at 2:00 A.M. and October 27 at 2:00 A.M. for time correction to GMT

Jan. 2 Leo	2:57	Apr. 5 Capricorn	20:21	July 8 Gemini	12:38
Jan. 4 Virgo	5:02	Apr. 8 Aquarius	8:58	July 10 Cancer	13:02
Jan. 6 Libra	10:40	Apr. 10 Pisces	19:15	July 12 Leo	12:38
Jan. 8 Scorpio	20:02	Apr. 13 Aries	1:49	July 14 Virgo	13:17
Jan. 11 Sagittarius	8:08	Apr. 15 Taurus	5:05	July 16 Libra	16:40
Jan. 13 Capricorn	21:01	Apr. 17 Gemini	6:42	July 18 Scorpio	23:47
Jan. 16 Aquarius	9:03	Apr. 19 Cancer	8:20	July 21 Sagittarius	10:20
Jan. 18 Pisces	19:22	Apr. 21 Leo	11:08	July 23 Capricorn	22:56
Jan. 21 Aries	3:27	Apr. 23 Virgo	15:33	July 26 Aquarius	11:48
Jan. 23 Taurus	8:58	Apr. 25 Libra	21:38	July 28 Pisces	23:35
Jan. 25 Gemini	12:04	Apr. 28 Scorpio	5:37	July 31 Aries	9:18
Jan. 27 Cancer	13:23	Apr. 30 Sagittarius	15:45	Aug. 2 Taurus	16:29
Jan. 29 Leo	14:06	May 3 Capricorn	3:56	Aug. 4 Gemini	20:53
Jan. 31 Virgo	15:49	May 5 Aquarius	16:50	Aug. 6 Cancer	22:47
Feb. 2 Libra	20:06	May 8 Pisces	4:02	Aug. 8 Leo	23:10
Feb. 5 Scorpio	4:05	May 10 Aries	11:29	Aug. 10 Virgo	23:36
Feb. 7 Sagittarius	15:26	May 12 Taurus	15:04	Aug. 13 Libra	1:54
Feb. 10 Capricorn	7:16	May 14 Gemini	16:01	Aug. 15 Scorpio	7:39
Feb. 12 Aquarius	16:15	May 16 Cancer	16:16	Aug. 17 Sagittarius	17:15
Feb. 15 Pisces	1:59	May 18 Leo	17:34	Aug. 20 Capricorn	5:35
Feb. 17 Aries	9:10	May 20 Virgo	21:03	Aug. 22 Aquarius	18:26
Feb. 19 Taurus	14:23	May 23 Libra	3:10	Aug. 25 Pisces	5:50
Feb. 21 Gemini	18:10	May 25 Scorpio	11:45	Aug. 27 Aries	14:59
Feb. 23 Cancer	20:57	May 27 Sagittarius	22:23	Aug. 29 Taurus	22:00
Feb. 25 Leo	23:14	May 30 Capricorn	10:42	Sept. 1 Gemini	3:02
Feb. 28 Virgo	1:52	June 1 Aquarius	23:42	Sept. 3 Cancer	6:19
Mar. 2 Libra	6:07	June 4 Pisces	11:33	Sept. 5 Leo	8:13
Mar. 4 Scorpio	13:14	June 6 Aries	20:23	Sept. 7 Virgo	9:38
Mar. 6 Sagittarius	23:36	June 9 Taurus	1:12	Sept. 9 Libra	11:57
Mar. 9 Capricorn	12:14	June 11 Gemini	2:36	Sept. 11 Scorpio	16:48
Mar. 12 Aquarius	0:31	June 13 Cancer	2:18	Sept. 14 Sagittarius	1:16
Mar. 14 Pisces	10:07	June 15 Leo	2:13	Sept. 16 Capricorn	13:06
Mar. 16 Aries	16:35	June 17 Virgo	4:07	Sept. 19 Aquarius	1:58
Mar. 18 Taurus	20:40	June 19 Libra	9:07	Sept. 21 Pisces	13:18
Mar. 20 Gemini	23:38	June 21 Scorpio	17:22	Sept. 23 Aries	21:55
Mar. 23 Cancer	2:29	June 24 Sagittarius	4:18	Sept. 26 Taurus	3:59
Mar. 25 Leo	5:45	June 26 Capricorn	16:51	Sept. 28 Gemini	8:25
Mar. 27 Virgo	9:44	June 29 Aquarius	5:47	Sept. 30 Cancer	11:58
Mar. 29 Libra	14:53	July 1 Pisces	17:50	Oct. 2 Leo	14:59
Mar. 31 Scorpio	22:03	July 4 Aries	3:32	Oct. 4 Virgo	17:46
Apr. 3 Sagittarius	8:02	July 6 Taurus	9:47	Oct. 6 Libra	21:02

MOON TABLES

Oct. 9	Scorpio	2:02
Oct. 11	Sagittarius	10:03
Oct. 13	Capricorn	21:12
Oct. 16	Aquarius	10:04
Oct. 18	Pisces	21:52
Oct. 21	Aries	6:30
Oct. 23	Taurus	11:53
Oct. 25	Gemini	15:08
Oct. 27	Cancer	17:38
Oct. 29	Leo	20:22
Oct. 31	Virgo	23:48
Nov. 3	Libra	4:15
Nov. 5	Scorpio	10:13
Nov. 7	Sagittarius	18:25
Nov. 10	Capricorn	5:19
Nov. 12	Aquarius	18:07
Nov. 15	Pisces	6:31
Nov. 17	Aries	16:04
Nov. 19	Taurus	21:48
Nov. 22	Gemini	0:23
Nov. 24	Cancer	1:26
Nov. 26	Leo	2:39
Nov. 28	Virgo	5:15
Nov. 20	Libra	9:51
Dec. 2	Scorpio	16:37
Dec. 5	Sagittarius	1:34
Dec. 7	Capricorn	12:44
Dec. 10	Aquarius	1:27
Dec. 12	Pisces	14:18
Dec. 15	Aries	1:06
Dec. 17	Taurus	8:05
Dec. 19	Gemini	11:18
Dec. 21	Cancer	11:54
Dec. 23	Leo	11:41
Dec. 25	Virgo	12:29
Dec. 27	Libra	15:43
Dec. 29	Scorpio	22:05

1992 Moon Signs

The Moon's Sign of the Zodiac changes every 2–3 days at the time indicated

All times are GMT
(Greenwich Mean Time)
24-hour clock system

Examples:
21:17 = 9:17 A.M.
11:03 = 11:03 A.M.

1992 Summer Time

Subtract 1 hour from your child's birth time between April 5 at 2:00 A.M. and October 25 at 2:00 A.M. for time correction to GMT

Jan. 1	Sagittarius	7:33
Jan. 3	Capricorn	19:11
Jan. 6	Aquarius	8:00
Jan. 8	Pisces	20:52
Jan. 11	Aries	8:20
Jan. 13	Taurus	16:57
Jan. 15	Gemini	21:54
Jan. 17	Cancer	23:27
Jan. 19	Leo Leo	22:57
Jan. 21	Virgo	22:24
Jan. 23	Libra	23:43
Jan. 26	Scorpio	4:36
Jan. 28	Sagittarius	13:24
Jan. 31	Capricorn	1:08
Feb. 2	Aquarius	14:09
Feb. 5	Pisces	2:51
Feb. 7	Aries	14:13
Feb. 9	Taurus	23:36
Feb. 12	Gemini	6:05
Feb. 14	Cancer	9:27
Feb. 16	Leo	10:14
Feb. 18	Virgo	9:49
Feb. 20	Libra	10:10
Feb. 22	Scorpio	13:18
Feb. 24	Sagittarius	20:30
Feb. 27	Capricorn	7:36
Feb. 29	Aquarius	20:35
Mar. 3	Pisces	9:10
Mar. 5	Aries	20:06
Mar. 8	Taurus	5:04
Mar. 10	Gemini	12:01
Mar. 12	Cancer	16:47
Mar. 14	Leo	19:20
Mar. 16	Virgo	20:14
Mar. 18	Libra	20:57
Mar. 20	Scorpio	23:21
Mar. 23	Sagittarius	5:18
Mar. 25	Capricorn	15:13
Mar. 28	Aquarius	3:45
Mar. 30	Pisces	16:22
Apr. 2	Aries	3:03
Apr. 4	Taurus	11:16
Apr. 6	Gemini	17:32
Apr. 8	Cancer	22:19
Apr. 11	Leo	1:46
Apr. 13	Virgo	4:10
Apr. 15	Libra	6:13
Apr. 17	Scorpio	9:15
Apr. 19	Sagittarius	14:46
Apr. 21	Capricorn	23:42
Apr. 24	Aquarius	11:40
Apr. 27	Pisces	0:20
Apr. 29	Aries	11:10
May 1	Taurus	19:08
May 4	Gemini	0:29
May 6	Cancer	4:10
May 8	Leo	7:08
May 10	Virgo	9:58
May 12	Libra	13:08
May 14	Scorpio	17:18
May 16	Sagittarius	23:23
May 19	Capricorn	8:17
May 21	Aquarius	19:45
May 24	Pisces	8:25
May 26	Aries	19:51
May 29	Taurus	4:14
May 31	Gemini	9:16
June 2	Cancer	11:57
June 4	Leo	13:36
June 6	Virgo	15:31
June 8	Libra	18:36
June 10	Scorpio	23:28
June 13	Sagittarius	6:32
June 15	Capricorn	15:53
June 18	Aquarius	3:20
June 20	Pisces	16:00
June 23	Aries	4:02
June 25	Taurus	13:24

June 27 Gemini	19:11
June 29 Cancer	21:42
July 1 Leo	22:16
July 3 Virgo	22:39
July 6 Libra	0:29
July 8 Scorpio	4:57
July 10 Sagittarius	12:22
July 12 Capricorn	22:17
July 15 Aquarius	10:05
July 17 Pisces	22:45
July 20 Aries	11:06
July 22 Taurus	21:35
July 25 Gemini	4:41
July 27 Cancer	8:05
July 29 Leo	8:38
July 31 Virgo	8:04
Aug. 2 Libra	8:22
Aug. 4 Scorpio	11:23
Aug. 6 Sagittarius	18:02
Aug. 9 Capricorn	4:02
Aug. 11 Aquarius	16:08
Aug. 14 Pisces	4:52
Aug. 16 Aries	17:11
Aug. 19 Taurus	4:09
Aug. 21 Gemini	12:32
Aug. 23 Cancer	17:33
Aug. 25 Leo	19:13
Aug. 27 Virgo	18:47
Aug. 29 Libra	18:14
Aug. 31 Scorpio	19:43
Sept. 3 Sagittarius	0:52
Sept. 5 Capricorn	10:10
Sept. 7 Aquarius	22:09
Sept. 10 Pisces	10:56
Sept. 12 Aries	23:03
Sept. 15 Taurus	9:46
Sept. 17 Gemini	18:38
Sept. 20 Cancer	0:59
Sept. 22 Leo	4:17
Sept. 24 Virgo	5:08
Sept. 26 Libra	4:58
Sept. 28 Scorpio	5:49
Sept. 30 Sagittarius	9:40
Oct. 2 Capricorn	17:34
Oct. 5 Aquarius	4:55
Oct. 7 Pisces	17:38
Oct. 10 Aries	5:35
Oct. 12 Taurus	15:47
Oct. 15 Gemini	0:09
Oct. 17 Cancer	6:34
Oct. 19 Leo	10:59
Oct. 21 Virgo	13:26
Oct. 23 Libra	14:41
Oct. 25 Scorpio	16:08
Oct. 27 Sagittarius	19:33
Oct. 30 Capricorn	2:20
Nov. 1 Aquarius	12:47
Nov. 4 Pisces	1:13
Nov. 6 Aries	13:17
Nov. 8 Taurus	23:20
Nov. 11 Gemini	6:48
Nov. 13 Cancer	12:18
Nov. 15 Leo	16:23
Nov. 17 Virgo	19:28
Nov. 19 Libra	22:04
Nov. 22 Scorpio	0:53
Nov. 24 Sagittarius	5:04
Nov. 26 Capricorn	11:43
Nov. 28 Aquarius	21:21
Dec. 1 Pisces	9:25
Dec. 3 Aries	21:49
Dec. 6 Taurus	8:13
Dec. 8 Gemini	15:34
Dec. 10 Cancer	20:05
Dec. 12 Leo	22:48
Dec. 15 Virgo	0:57
Dec. 17 Libra	3:35
Dec. 19 Scorpio	7:23
Dec. 21 Sagittarius	12:46
Dec. 23 Capricorn	20:07
Dec. 26 Aquarius	5:46
Dec. 28 Pisces	17:30
Dec. 31 Aries	6:06

1993 Moon Signs

The Moon's Sign of the Zodiac changes every 2–3 days at the time indicated

All times are GMT (Greenwich Mean Time) 24-hour clock system

Examples:
21:17 = 9:17 P.M.
11:03 = 11:03 A.M.

1993 Summer Time

Subtract 1 hour from your child's birth time between April 4 at 2:00 A.M. and October 31 at 2:00 A.M. for time correction to GMT

Jan. 2 Taurus	17:28
Jan. 5 Gemini	1:41
Jan. 7 Cancer	6:08
Jan. 9 Leo	7:49
Jan. 11 Virgo	8:23
Jan. 13 Libra	9:35
Jan. 15 Scorpio	12:47
Jan. 17 Sagittarius	18:34
Jan. 20 Capricorn	2:48
Jan 22 Aquarius	13:03
Jan. 25 Pisces	0:48
Jan. 27 Aries	13:28
Jan. 30 Taurus	1:37
Feb. 1 Gemini	11:10
Feb. 3 Cancer	16:52
Feb. 5 Leo	18:49
Feb. 7 Virgo	18:29
Feb. 9 Libra	18:02
Feb. 11 Scorpio	19:28
Feb. 14 Sagittarius	0:09
Feb. 16 Capricorn	8:24
Feb. 18 Aquarius	19:07
Feb. 21 Pisces	7:13
Feb. 23 Aries	19:51
Feb. 26 Taurus	8:10
Feb. 28 Gemini	18:50
Mar. 3 Cancer	2:15
Mar. 5 Leo	5:37
Mar. 7 Virgo	5:51
Mar. 9 Libra	4:49
Mar. 11 Scorpio	4:44
Mar. 13 Sagittarius	7:40
Mar. 15 Capricorn	14:33
Mar. 18 Aquarius	0:53
Mar. 20 Pisces	13:12
Mar. 23 Aries	1:52

Mar. 25 Taurus	13:59	June 28 Scorpio	16:40	Oct. 2 Taurus	16:14
Mar. 28 Gemini	0:48	June 30 Sagittarius	20:30	Oct. 5 Gemini	4:26
Mar. 30 Cancer	9:10	July 3 Capricorn	1:50	Oct. 7 Cancer	14:39
Apr. 1 Leo	14:17	July 5 Aquarius	9:18	Oct. 9 Leo	21:32
Apr. 3 Virgo	16:08	July 7 Pisces	19:12	Oct. 12 Virgo	0:36
Apr. 5 Libra	15:55	July 10 Aries	7:12	Oct. 14 Libra	0:48
Apr. 7 Scorpio	15:36	July 12 Taurus	19:37	Oct. 16 Scorpio	0:02
Apr. 9 Sagittarius	17:16	July 15 Gemini	6:04	Oct. 18 Sagittarius	0:24
Apr. 11 Capricorn	22:26	July 17 Cancer	13:03	Oct. 20 Capricorn	3:46
Apr. 14 Aquarius	7:40	July 19 Leo	16:45	Oct. 22 Aquarius	10:54
Apr. 16 Pisces	19:34	July 21 Virgo	18:24	Oct. 24 Pisces	21:19
Apr. 19 Aries	8:14	July 23 Libra	19:41	Oct. 27 Aries	9:40
Apr. 21 Taurus	20:08	July 25 Scorpio	22:02	Oct. 29 Taurus	22:21
Apr. 24 Gemini	6:26	July 28 Sagittarius	2:15	Nov. 1 Gemini	10:12
Apr. 26 Cancer	14:43	July 30 Capricorn	8:30	Nov. 3 Cancer	20:24
Apr. 28 Leo	20:38	Aug. 1 Aquarius	16:40	Nov. 6 Leo	4:05
May 1 Virgo	0:01	Aug. 4 Pisces	2:45	Nov. 8 Virgo	8:44
May 3 Libra	1:21	Aug. 6 Aries	14:41	Nov. 10 Libra	10:40
May 5 Scorpio	1:59	Aug. 9 Taurus	3:23	Nov. 12 Scorpio	11:01
May 7 Sagittarius	3:38	Aug. 11 Gemini	14:44	Nov. 14 Sagittarius	11:25
May 9 Capricorn	7:57	Aug. 13 Cancer	22:46	Nov. 16 Capricorn	13:40
May 11 Aquarius	15:49	Aug. 16 Leo	2:42	Nov. 18 Aquarius	19:12
May 14 Pisces	2:52	Aug. 18 Virgo	3:41	Nov. 21 Pisces	4:30
May 16 Aries	15:24	Aug. 20 Libra	7:37	Nov. 23 Aries	16:32
May 19 Taurus	3:16	Aug. 22 Scorpio	4:31	Nov. 26 Taurus	5:14
May 21 Gemini	13:05	Aug. 24 Sagittarius	7:50	Nov. 28 Gemini	16:46
May 23 Cancer	20:38	Aug. 26 Capricorn	14:02	Dec. 1 Cancer	2:17
May 26 Leo	2:02	Aug. 28 Aquarius	22:43	Dec. 3 Leo	9:31
May 28 Virgo	5:46	Aug. 21 Pisces	9:21	Dec. 5 Virgo	14:41
May 20 Libra	8:18	Sept. 2 Aries	21:22	Dec. 7 Libra	18:03
June 1 Scorpio	10:24	Sept. 5 Taurus	10:09	Dec. 9 Scorpio	20:05
June 3 Sagittarius	13:05	Sept. 7 Gemini	22:16	Dec. 11 Sagittarius	21:40
June 5 Capricorn	17:30	Sept. 10 Cancer	7:32	Dec. 14 Capricorn	0:07
June 8 Aquarius	0:41	Sept. 12 Leo	12:46	Dec. 16 Aquarius	4:56
June 10 Pisces	11:00	Sept. 14 Virgo	14:17	Dec. 18 Pisces	13:04
June 12 Aries	23:15	Sept. 16 Libra	13:45	Dec. 21 Aries	0:20
June 15 Taurus	11:17	Sept. 18 Scorpio	13:19	Dec. 23 Taurus	13:04
June 17 Gemini	21:11	Sept. 20 Sagittarius	14:59	Dec. 26 Gemini	0:46
June 20 Cancer	4:04	Sept. 22 Capricorn	19:58	Dec. 28 Cancer	9:43
June 22 Leo	8:25	Sept. 25 Aquarius	4:21	Dec. 30 Leo	1557
June 24 Virgo	11:18	Sept. 27 Pisces	15:15		
June 26 Libra	13:47	Sept. 30 Aries	3:30		

MOON TABLES

1994 Moon Signs

The Moon's Sign of the Zodiac changes every 2–3 days at the time indicated

All times are GMT (Greenwich Mean Time) 24-hour clock system

Examples:
21:17 = 9:17 P.M.
11:03 = 11:03 A.M.

1994 Summer Time

Subtract 1 hour from your child's birth time between April 3 at 2:00 A.M. and October 30 at 2:00 A.M. for time correction to GMT

Jan. 1 Virgo	20:15	Apr. 4 Aquarius	9:50	July 7 Cancer	14:15
Jan. 3 Libra	23:32	Apr. 6 Pisces	18:54	July 9 Leo	22:44
Jan. 6 Scorpio	2:30	Apr. 9 Aries	6:11	July 12 Virgo	4:48
Jan. 8 Sagittarius	5:36	Apr. 11 Taurus	18:49	July 14 Libra	9:14
Jan. 10 Capricorn	9:19	Apr. 14 Gemini	7:48	July 16 Scorpio	12:34
Jan. 12 Aquarius	14:29	Apr. 16 Cancer	19:40	July 18 Sagittarius	15:10
Jan. 14 Pisces	22:06	Apr. 19 Leo	4:42	July 20 Capricorn	17:32
Jan. 17 Aries	8:45	Apr. 21 Virgo	9:53	July 22 Aquarius	20:41
Jan. 19 Taurus	21:23	Apr. 23 Libra	11:37	July 25 Pisces	1:58
Jan. 22 Gemini	9:32	Apr. 25 Scorpio	11:19	July 27 Aries	10:36
Jan. 24 Cancer	18:52	Apr. 27 Sagittarius	10:53	July 29 Taurus	22:14
Jan. 27 Leo	0:39	Apr. 29 Capricorn	12:11	Aug. 1 Gemini	11:04
Jan. 29 Virgo	3:39	May 1 Aquarius	16:40	Aug. 3 Cancer	22:22
Jan. 31 Libra	5:35	May 4 Pisces	0:48	Aug. 6 Leo	6:28
Feb. 2 Scorpio	7:52	May 6 Aries	12:04	Aug. 8 Virgo	11:40
Feb. 4 Sagittarius	11:18	May 9 Taurus	0:51	Aug. 10 Libra	15:07
Feb. 6 Capricorn	16:05	May 11 Gemini	13:43	Aug. 12 Scorpio	17:57
Feb. 8 Aquarius	22:18	May 14 Cancer	1:27	Aug. 14 Sagittarius	20:54
Feb. 11 Pisces	6:26	May 16 Leo	10:55	Aug. 17 Capricorn	0:19
Feb. 13 Aries	16:53	May 18 Virgo	17:28	Aug. 19 Aquarius	4:36
Feb. 16 Taurus	5:21	May 20 Libra	20:54	Aug. 21 Pisces	10:32
Feb. 18 Gemini	18:04	May 22 Scorpio	21:51	Aug. 23 Aries	18:58
Feb. 21 Cancer	4:25	May 24 Sagittarius	21:44	Aug. 26 Taurus	6:16
Feb. 23 Leo	10:43	May 26 Capricorn	22:19	Aug. 28 Gemini	19:08
Feb. 25 Virgo	13:24	May 29 Aquarius	1:21	Aug. 31 Cancer	6:57
Feb. 27 Libra	14:07	May 31 Pisces	8:09	Sept. 2 Leo	15:33
Mar. 1 Scorpio	14:47	June 2 Aries	18:34	Sept. 4 Virgo	20:32
Mar. 3 Sagittarius	16:58	June 5 Taurus	7:15	Sept. 6 Libra	22:57
Mar. 5 Capricorn	21:26	June 7 Gemini	20:03	Sept. 9 Scorpio	0:27
Mar. 8 Aquarius	4:17	June 10 Cancer	7:20	Sept. 11 Sagittarius	2:27
Mar. 10 Pisces	13:13	June 12 Leo	16:27	Sept. 13 Capricorn	5:47
Mar. 12 Aries	24:00	June 14 Virgo	23:17	Sept. 15 Aquarius	10:46
Mar. 15 Taurus	12:29	June 17 Libra	3:47	Sept. 17 Pisces	17:34
Mar. 18 Gemini	1:29	June 19 Scorpio	6:19	Sept. 20 Aries	2:32
Mar. 20 Cancer	12:50	June 21 Sagittarius	7:33	Sept. 22 Taurus	13:50
Mar. 22 Leo	20:37	June 23 Capricorn	8:40	Sept. 25 Gemini	2:42
Mar. 25 Virgo	0:15	June 25 Aquarius	11:15	Sept. 27 Cancer	15:09
Mar. 27 Libra	0:47	June 27 Pisces	16:50	Sept. 30 Leo	0:55
Mar. 29 Scorpio	0:16	June 20 Aries	2:09	Oct. 2 Virgo	6:36
Mar. 31 Sagittarius	0:43	July 2 Taurus	14:25	Oct. 4 Libra	8:54
Apr. 2 Capricorn	3:41	July 5 Gemini	3:12	Oct. 6 Scorpio	9:23

Oct. 8 Sagittarius	9:51	Nov. 6 Capricorn	20:05	Dec. 6 Aquarius	7:58
Oct. 10 Capricorn	11:49	Nov. 8 Aquarius	22:50	Dec. 8 Pisces	12:31
Oct. 12 Aquarius	16:14	Nov. 11 Pisces	5:08	Dec. 10 Aries	21:06
Oct. 14 Pisces	23:20	Nov. 13 Aries	14:47	Dec. 13 Taurus	8:58
Oct. 17 Aries	8:59	Nov. 16 Taurus	2:45	Dec. 15 Gemini	22:01
Oct. 19 Taurus	20:36	Nov. 18 Gemini	15:42	Dec. 18 Cancer	10:24
Oct. 22 Gemini	9:28	Nov. 21 Cancer	4:21	Dec. 20 Leo	21:13
Oct. 24 Cancer	22:16	Nov. 23 Leo	15:31	Dec. 23 Virgo	5:59
Oct. 27 Leo	9:01	Nov. 26 Virgo	0:10	Dec. 25 Libra	12:24
Oct. 29 Virgo	16:17	Nov. 28 Libra	5:20	Dec. 27 Scorpio	16:15
Oct. 31 Libra	19:44	Nov. 30 Scorpio	7:19	Dec. 29 Sagittarius	17:44
Nov. 2 Scorpio	20:19	Dec. 2 Sagittarius	7:13	Dec. 31 Capricorn	17:59
Nov. 4 Sagittarius	19:48	Dec. 4 Capricorn	6:46		

1995 Moon Signs

All times are GMT (Greenwich Mean Time) 24-hour clock system

1995 Summer Time

The Moon's Sign of the Zodiac changes every 2–3 days at the time indicated

Examples:
21:17 = 9:17 P.M.
11:03 = 11:03 A.M.

Subtract 1 hour from your child's birth tiime between April 2 at 2:00 A.M, and October 29 at 2:00 A.M. for time correction to GMT

Jan. 2 Aquarius	18:42	Mar. 5 Taurus	8:55	May 6 Leo	12:5
Jan. 4 Pisces	21:52	Mar. 7 Gemini	20:57	May 8 Virgo	22:3
Jan. 7 Aries	5:01	Mar. 10 Cancer	9:39	May 11 Libra	4:2
Jan. 9 Taurus	16:01	Mar. 12 Leo	20:27	May 13 Scorpio	6:51
Jan. 12 Gemini	4:58	Mar. 15 Virgo	3:53	May 15 Sagittarius	6:5
Jan. 14 Cancer	17:19	Mar. 17 Libra	8:16	May 17 Capricorn	6:3
Jan. 17 Leo	3:36	Mar. 19 Scorpio	10:52	May 19 Aquarius	7:4
Jan. 19 Virgo	11:38	Mar. 21 Sagittarius	12:59	May 21 Pisces	11:4
Jan. 21 Libra	17:53	Mar. 23 Capricorn	15:34	May 23 Aries	19:1
Jan. 23 Scorpio	22:33	Mar. 25 Aquarius	19:12	May 26 Taurus	5:4
Jan. 26 Sagittarius	1:37	Mar. 28 Pisces	0:19	May 28 Gemini	18:0
Jan. 28 Capricorn	3:27	Mar. 30 Aries	7:29	May 31 Cancer	7:0
Jan. 30 Aquarius	5:06	Apr. 1 Taurus	17:02	June 2 Leo	19:1
Feb. 1 Pisces	28:10	Apr. 4 Gemini	4:51	June 5 Virgo	5:4
Feb. 3 Aries	14:19	Apr. 6 Cancer	17:40	June 7 Libra	13:0
Feb. 6 Taurus	0:10	Apr. 9 Leo	5:13	June 9 Scorpio	17:0
Feb. 8 Gemini	12:45	Apr. 11 Virgo	13:34	June 11 Sagittarius	17:4
Feb. 11 Cancer	1:17	Apr. 13 Libra	18:18	June 13 Capricorn	17:0
Feb. 13 Leo	11:28	Apr. 15 Scorpio	20:13	June 15 Aquarius	16:5
Feb. 15 Virgo	18:50	Apr. 17 Sagittarius	20:53	June 17 Pisces	19:1
Feb. 18 Libra	0:01	Apr. 19 Capricorn	21:55	June 20 Aries	1:3
Feb. 20 Scorpio	3:56	Apr. 22 Aquarius	0:39	June 22 Taurus	11:3
Feb. 22 Sagittarius	7:13	Apr. 24 Pisces	5:54	June 25 Gemini	0:0
Feb. 24 Capricorn	10:12	Apr. 26 Aries	13:45	June 27 Cancer	12:5
Feb. 26 Aquarius	13:16	Apr. 28 Taurus	23:54	June 30 Leo	1:0
Feb. 28 Pisces	17:19	May 1 Gemini	11:55	July 2 Virgo	11:3
Mar. 2 Aries	23:31	May 4 Cancer	0:46	July 4 Libra	19:5

July 7 Scorpio	1:19	Sept. 5 Aquarius	21:48	Nov. 6 Taurus	3:38
July 9 Sagittarius	3:37	Sept. 8 Pisces	0:09	Nov. 8 Gemini	13:58
July 11 Capricorn	3:44	Sept. 10 Aries	4:18	Nov. 11 Cancer	1:58
July 13 Aquarius	3:23	Sept. 12 Taurus	11:27	Nov. 13 Leo	14:37
July 15 Pisces	4:42	Sept. 14 Gemini	21:50	Nov. 16 Virgo	2:02
July 17 Aries	9:30	Sept. 17 Cancer	10:16	Nov. 18 Libra	10:13
July 19 Taurus	18:24	Sept. 19 Leo	22:20	Nov. 20 Scorpio	14:36
July 22 Gemini	6:25	Sept. 22 Virgo	7:59	Nov. 22 Sagittarius	15:55
July 24 Cancer	19:16	Sept. 24 Libra	14:47	Nov. 24 Capricorn	15:50
July 27 Leo	7:06	Sept. 26 Scorpio	19:20	Nov. 26 Aquarius	16:20
July 29 Virgo	17:11	Sept. 28 Sagittarius	22:31	Nov. 28 Pisces	19:03
Aug. 1 Libra	1:24	Oct. 1 Capricorn	1:11	Dec. 1 Aries	0:52
Aug. 3 Scorpio	7:27	Oct. 3 Aquarius	4:01	Dec. 3 Taurus	9:43
Aug. 5 Sagittarius	11:11	Oct. 5 Pisces	7:38	Dec. 5 Gemini	20:36
Aug. 7 Capricorn	12:51	Oct. 7 Aries	12:46	Dec. 8 Cancer	8:46
Aug. 9 Aquarius	13:30	Oct. 9 Taurus	20:08	Dec. 10 Leo	21:25
Aug. 11 Pisces	14:51	Oct. 12 Gemini	6:13	Dec. 13 Virgo	9:25
Aug. 13 Aries	18:46	Oct. 14 Cancer	18:21	Dec. 15 Libra	19:07
Aug. 16 Taurus	2:28	Oct. 17 Leo	6:45	Dec. 18 Scorpio	1:07
Aug. 18 Gemini	13:43	Oct. 19 Virgo	17:09	Dec. 20 Sagittarius	3:12
Aug. 21 Cancer	2:24	Oct. 22 Libra	0:16	Dec. 22 Capricorn	2:47
Aug. 23 Leo	14:11	Oct. 24 Scorpio	4:06	Dec. 24 Aquarious	1:54
Aug. 25 Virgo	23:51	Oct. 26 Sagittarius	5:57	Dec. 26 Pisces	2:48
Aug. 28 Libra	7:14	Oct. 28 Capricorn	7:17	Dec. 28 Aries	7:12
Aug. 30 Scorpio	12:50	Oct. 30 Aquarius	9:27	Dec. 30 Taurus	15:25
Sept. 1 Sagittarius	16:56	Nov. 1 Pisces	13:22		
Sept. 3 Capricorn	19:45	Nov. 3 Aries	19:24		

1996 Moon Signs

The Moon's Sign of the Zodiac changes every 2–3 days at the time indicated

All times are GMT (Greenwich Mean Time) 24-hour clock system

Examples:
21:17 = 9:17 P.M.
11:03 = 11:03 A.M.

1996 Summer Time

Subtract 1 hour from your child's birth time between April 7 at 2:00 A.M. and October 27 at 2:00 A.M. for time correction to GMT

Jan. 2 Gemini	2:31	Jan. 31 Cancer	21:12	Mar. 1 Leo	16:47
Jan. 4 Cancer	14:57	Feb. 3 Leo	9:46	Mar. 4 Virgo	4:12
Jan. 7 Leo	3:31	Feb. 5 Virgo	21:23	Mar. 6 Libra	13:39
Jan. 9 Virgo	15:29	Feb. 8 Libra	7:28	Mar. 8 Scorpio	21:05
Jan. 12 Libra	1:55	Feb. 10 Scorpio	15:33	Mar. 1 Sagittarius	2:32
Jan. 14 Scorpio	9:26	Feb. 12 Sagittarius	20:57	Mar. 13 Capricorn	6:07
Jan. 16 Sagittarius	13:20	Feb. 14 Capricorn	23:30	Mar. 15 Aquarius	8:15
Jan. 18 Capricorn	14:05	Feb. 17 Aquarius	0:01	Mar. 17 Pisces	9:53
Jan. 20 Aquarius	13:17	Feb. 19 Pisces	0:10	Mar. 19 Aries	12:20
Jan. 22 Pisces	13:08	Feb. 21 Aries	2:01	Mar. 21 Taurus	17:04
Jan. 24 Aries	15:44	Feb. 23 Taurus	7:14	Mar. 24 Gemini	1:01
Jan. 26 Taurus	22:19	Feb. 25 Gemini	16:18	Mar. 26 Cancer	12:09
Jan. 29 Gemini	8:46	Feb. 28 Cancer	4:12	Mar. 29 Leo	0:38

MOON TABLES

Mar. 31 Virgo	12:12	July 2 Aquarius	12:07	Oct. 3 Cancer	13:19
Apr. 2 Libra	21:26	July 4 Pisces	12:12	Oct. 6 Leo	1:13
Apr. 5 Scorpio	3:56	July 6 Aries	14:48	Oct. 8 Virgo	13:48
Apr. 7 Sagittarius	8:21	July 8 Taurus	20:46	Oct. 11 Libra	1:01
Apr. 9 Capricorn	11:30	July 11 Gemini	5:55	Oct. 13 Scorpio	9:43
Apr. 11 Aquarius	14:11	July 13 Cancer	17:10	Oct. 16 Sagittarius	16:06
Apr. 13 Pisces	17:02	July 16 Leo	5:33	Oct. 17 Capricorn	20:37
Apr. 15 Aries	20:45	July 18 Virgo	18:17	Oct. 19 Aquarius	23:52
Apr. 18 Taurus	2:08	July 21 Libra	6:12	Oct. 22 Pisces	2:23
Apr. 20 Gemini	9:59	July 23 Scorpio	15:39	Oct. 24 Aries	4:52
Apr. 22 Cancer	20:27	July 25 Sagittarius	21:22	Oct. 26 Taurus	8:15
Apr. 25 Leo	8:45	July 27 Capricorn	23:18	Oct. 28 Gemini	13:40
Apr. 27 Virgo	20:48	July 29 Aquarius	22:48	Oct. 30 Cancer	21:59
Apr. 30 Libra	6:24	July 31 Pisces	22:03	Nov. 2 Leo	9:18
May 2 Scorpio	12:39	Aug. 2 Aries	23:07	Nov. 4 Virgo	21:58
May 4 Sagittarius	16:03	Aug. 5 Taurus	3:37	Nov. 7 Libra	9:26
May 6 Capricorn	17:54	Aug. 7 Gemini	11:53	Nov. 9 Scorpio	17:59
May 8 Aquarius	19:41	Aug. 9 Cancer	22:59	Nov. 11 Sagittarius	23:27
May 10 Pisces	22:31	Aug. 12 Leo	11:30	Nov. 14 Capricorn	2:44
May 13 Aries	3:02	Aug. 15 Virgo	0:08	Nov. 16 Aquarius	5:15
May 15 Taurus	9:28	Aug. 17 Libra	11:54	Nov. 18 Pisces	8:02
May 17 Gemini	17:51	Aug. 19 Scorpio	21:50	Nov. 20 Aries	11:36
May 20 Cancer	4:18	Aug. 22 Sagittarius	4:46	Nov. 22 Taurus	16:15
May 22 Leo	16:29	Aug. 24 Capricorn	8:18	Nov. 24 Gemini	22:21
May 25 Virgo	4:58	Aug. 26 Aquarius	9:09	Nov. 27 Cancer	6:41
May 27 Libra	15:30	Aug. 28 Pisces	8:51	Nov. 29 Leo	17:33
May 29 Scorpio	22:30	Aug. 30 Aries	9:21	Dec. 2 Virgo	6:11
June 1 Sagittarius	1:43	Sept. 1 Taurus	12:26	Dec. 4 Libra	18:22
June 3 Capricorn	2:30	Sept. 3 Gemini	19:13	Dec. 7 Scorpio	3:37
June 5 Aquarius	2:47	Sept. 6 Cancer	5:32	Dec. 9 Sagittarius	8:55
June 7 Pisces	4:23	Sept. 8 Leo	17:55	Dec. 11 Capricorn	11:13
June 9 Aries	8:28	Sept. 11 Virgo	6:28	Dec. 13 Aquarius	12:16
June 11 Taurus	15:15	Sept. 13 Libra	17:50	Dec. 15 Pisces	13:48
June 14 Gemini	0:17	Sept. 16 Scorpio	3:19	Dec. 17 Aries	16:59
June 16 Cancer	11:11	Sept. 18 Sagittarius	10:28	Dec. 19 Taurus	22:11
June 18 Leo	23:23	Sept. 20 Capricorn	15:10	Dec. 22 Gemini	5:20
June 21 Virgo	12:06	Sept. 22 Aquarius	17:38	Dec. 24 Cancer	14:17
June 23 Libra	23:38	Sept. 24 Pisces	18:44	Dec. 27 Leo	1:10
June 26 Scorpio	7:49	Sept. 26 Aries	19:48	Dec. 29 Virgo	13:46
June 28 Sagittarius	11:56	Sept. 28 Taurus	22:26		
June 30 Capricorn	12:45	Oct. 1 Gemini	4:05		

MOON TABLES

1997 Moon Signs

The Moon's Sign of the Zodiac changes every 2–3 days at the time indicated

All times are GMT
(Greenwich Mean Time)
24-hour clock system

Examples:
21:17 = 9:17 P.M.
11:02 = 11:03 A.M.

1997 Summer Time

Subtract 1 hour from your child's birth time between April 6 at 2:00 A.M. and October 26 at 2:00 A.M. for time correction to GMT

Jan. 1 Libra	2:32	Apr. 4 Pisces	5:42	July 6 Leo	3:48
Jan. 3 Scorpio	12:57	Apr. 6 Aries	6:21	July 8 Virgo	15:24
Jan. 5 Sagittarius	19:24	Apr. 8 Taurus	7:25	July 11 Libra	4:21
Jan. 7 Capricorn	21:54	Apr. 10 Gemini	10:34	July 13 Scorpio	16:18
Jan. 9 Aquarius	22:00	Apr. 12 Cancer	17:09	July 16 Sagittarius	1:02
Jan. 11 Pisces	21:53	Apr. 15 Leo	3:24	July 18 Capricorn	5:43
Jan. 13 Aries	23:23	Apr. 17 Virgo	16:01	July 20 Aquarius	7:28
Jan. 16 Taurus	3:43	Apr. 20 Libra	4:36	July 22 Pisces	8:02
Jan. 18 Gemini	10:57	Apr. 22 Scorpio	15:17	July 24 Aries	9:07
Jan. 20 Cancer	20:31	Apr. 24 Sagittarius	23:33	July 26 Taurus	11:58
Jan. 23 Leo	7:52	Apr. 27 Capricorn	5:32	July 28 Gemini	17:08
Jan. 25 Virgo	20:28	Apr. 29 Aquarius	9:49	July 31 Cancer	0:40
Jan. 28 Libra	9:21	May 1 Pisces	12:50	Aug. 2 Leo	10:30
Jan. 30 Scorpio	20:47	May 3 Aries	15:00	Aug. 4 Virgo	22:17
Feb. 2 Sagittarius	4:48	May 5 Taurus	17:07	Aug. 7 Libra	11:17
Feb. 4 Capricorn	8:40	May 7 Gemini	20:24	Aug. 9 Scorpio	23:51
Feb. 6 Aquarius	9:20	May 10 Cancer	2:15	Aug. 12 Sagittarius	9:41
Feb. 8 Pisces	8:36	May 12 Leo	11:38	Aug. 14 Capricorn	15:38
Feb. 10 Aries	8:35	May 14 Virgo	23:45	Aug. 16 Aquarius	17:56
Feb. 12 Taurus	11:03	May 17 Libra	12:25	Aug. 18 Pisces	18:01
Feb. 14 Gemini	16:58	May 19 Scorpio	23:12	Aug. 20 Aries	17:48
Feb. 17 Cancer	2:14	May 22 Sagittarius	6:49	Aug. 22 Taurus	19:01
Feb. 19 Leo	13:55	May 24 Capricorn	11:50	Aug. 24 Gemini	22:58
Feb. 22 Virgo	2:39	May 26 Aquarius	15:20	Aug. 27 Cancer	6:14
Feb. 24 Libra	15:23	May 28 Pisces	18:19	Aug. 29 Leo	16:22
Feb. 27 Scorpio	2:56	May 30 Aries	21:19	Sept. 1 Virgo	4:29
Mar. 1 Sagittarius	11:57	June 2 Taurus	0:40	Sept. 3 Libra	17:30
Mar. 3 Capricorn	17:35	June 4 Gemini	4:57	Sept. 6 Scorpio	6:09
Mar. 5 Aquarius	19:53	June 6 Cancer	11:07	Sept. 8 Sagittarius	16:52
Mar. 7 Pisces	19:57	June 8 Leo	20:01	Sept. 11 Capricorn	0:24
Mar. 9 Aries	19:35	June 11 Virgo	7:45	Sept. 13 Aquarius	4:08
Mar. 11 Taurus	20:41	June 13 Libra	20:36	Sept. 15 Pisces	4:59
Mar. 14 Gemini	0:50	June 16 Scorpio	7:48	Sept. 17 Aries	4:27
Mar. 16 Cancer	8:56	June 18 Sagittarius	15:35	Sept. 19 Taurus	4:25
Mar. 18 Leo	20:10	June 20 Capricorn	20:01	Sept. 21 Gemini	6:44
Mar. 21 Virgo	9:00	June 22 Aquarius	22:21	Sept. 23 Cancer	12:39
Mar. 23 Libra	21:36	June 25 Pisces	0:10	Sept. 25 Leo	22:14
Mar. 26 Scorpio	8:40	June 27 Aries	2:40	Sept. 28 Virgo	10:29
Mar. 28 Sagittarius	17:38	June 29 Taurus	6:26	Sept. 30 Libra	23:33
Mar. 31 Capricorn	0:08	July 1 Gemini	11:39	Oct. 3 Scorpio	11:56
Apr. 2 Aquarius	3:58	July 3 Cancer	18:36	Oct. 5 Sagittarius	22:43

Oct. 8 Capricorn	7:01	Nov. 6 Aquarius	18:32	Dec. 6 Pisces	4:08
Oct. 10 Aquarius	12:25	Nov. 8 Pisces	22:35	Dec. 8 Aries	7:24
Oct. 12 Pisces	14:57	Nov. 11 Aries	0:44	Dec. 10 Taurus	10:01
Oct. 14 Aries	15:25	Nov. 13 Taurus	1:46	Dec. 12 Gemini	12:38
Oct. 16 Taurus	15:19	Nov. 15 Gemini	3:08	Dec. 14 Cancer	16:30
Oct. 18 Gemini	16:32	Nov. 17 Cancer	6:38	Dec. 16 Leo	22:59
Oct. 20 Cancer	20:49	Nov. 19 Leo	3:44	Dec. 19 Virgo	9:04
Oct. 23 Leo	5:14	Nov. 22 Virgo	0:34	Dec. 21 Libra	21:36
Oct. 25 Virgo	17:02	Nov. 24 Libra	13:30	Dec. 24 Scorpio	10:05
Oct. 28 Libra	6:05	Nov. 27 Scorpio	1:43	Dec. 26 Sagittarius	20:06
Oct. 30 Scorpio	18:15	Nov. 29 Sagittarius	11:26	Dec. 29 Capricorn	2:48
Nov. 2 Sagittarius	4:26	Dec. 1 Capricorn	18:37		
Nov. 4 Capricorn	12:29	Dec. 3 Aquarius	23:59		

1998 Moon Signs

The Moon's Sign of the Zodiac changes every 2–3 days at the time indicated

All times are GMT (Greenwich Mean Time) 24-hour clock system

Examples:
21:17 = 9:17 P.M.
11:03 = 11:03 A.M.

1998 Summer Times

Subtract 1 hour from your child's birth time between April 5 at 2:00 A.M. and October 25 at 2:00 A.M for time correction to GMT

Jan. 2 Pisces	9:57	Mar. 4 Gemini	7:20	May 4 Virgo	19:50
Jan. 4 Aries	12:45	Mar. 6 Cancer	12:32	May 7 Libra	8:20
Jan. 6 Taurus	15:54	Mar. 8 Leo	20:48	May 9 Scorpio	21:11
Jan. 8 Gemini	19:44	Mar. 11 Virgo	7:38	May 12 Sagittarius	8:47
Jan. 11 Cancer	0:44	Mar. 13 Libra	19:59	May 14 Capricorn	18:38
Jan. 13 Leo	7:50	Mar. 16 Scorpio	8:51	May 17 Aquarius	2:30
Jan. 15 Virgo	17:35	Mar. 18 Sagittarius	20:56	May 19 Pisces	8:01
Jan. 18 Libra	5:46	Mar. 21 Capricorn	6:40	May 21 Aries	11:03
Jan. 20 Scorpio	18:34	Mar. 23 Aquarius	12:57	May 23 Taurus	12:06
Jan. 23 Sagittarius	5:23	Mar. 25 Pisces	15:39	May 25 Gemini	12:28
Jan. 25 Capricorn	12:35	Mar. 27 Aries	15:48	May 27 Cancer	14:04
Jan. 27 Aquarius	16:25	Mar. 29 Taurus	15:09	May 29 Leo	18:43
Jan. 29 Pisces	18:09	Mar. 31 Gemini	15:43	June 1 Virgo	3:24
Jan. 31 Aries	19:23	Apr. 2 Cancer	19:14	June 3 Libra	15:19
Feb. 2 Taurus	21:27	Apr. 5 Leo	2:38	June 6 Scorpio	4:05
Feb. 5 Gemini	1:11	Apr. 7 Virgo	13:29	June 8 Sagittarius	15:33
Feb. 7 Cancer	7:01	Apr. 10 Libra	2:06	June 11 Capricorn	0:51
Feb. 9 Leo	15:01	Apr. 12 Scorpio	14:56	June 13 Aquarius	8:02
Feb. 12 Virgo	1:11	Apr. 15 Sagittarius	2:52	June 15 Pisces	13:30
Feb. 14 Libra	13:19	Apr. 17 Capricorn	13:02	June 17 Aries	17:22
Feb. 17 Scorpio	2:13	Apr. 19 Aquarius	20:40	June 19 Taurus	19:48
Feb. 19 Sagittarius	13:53	Apr. 22 Pisces	1:06	June 21 Gemini	21:27
Feb. 21 Capricorn	22:29	Apr. 24 Aries	2:30	June 23 Cancer	23:40
Feb. 24 Aquarius	3:09	Apr. 26 Taurus	2:10	June 26 Leo	4:08
Feb. 26 Pisces	4:42	Apr. 28 Gemini	1:58	June 28 Virgo	12:00
Feb. 28 Aries	4:44	Apr. 30 Cancer	4:01	June 30 Libra	23:06
Mar. 2 Taurus	5:04	May 2 Leo	9:56	July 3 Scorpio	11:45

MOON TABLES

July 5 Sagittrius	23:24	Sept. 5 Pisces	12:45	Nov. 5 Gemini	10:15
July 8 Capricorn	8:25	Sept. 7 Aries	13:52	Nov. 7 Cancer	10:46
July 10 Aquarius	14:50	Sept. 9 Taurus	14:19	Nov. 9 Leo	14:40
July 12 Pisces	19:22	Sept. 11 Gemini	15:45	Nov. 11 Virgo	22:39
July 14 Aries	22:45	Sept. 13 Cancer	19:24	Nov. 14 Libra	10:00
July 17 Taurus	1:34	Sept. 16 Leo	1:50	Nov. 16 Scorpio	22:42
July 19 Gemini	4:20	Sept. 18 Virgo	10:55	Nov. 19 Sagittarius	11:13
July 21 Cancer	7:46	Sept. 20 Libra	21:59	Nov. 21 Capricorn	22:46
July 23 Leo	12:53	Sept. 23 Scorpio	10:23	Nov. 24 Aquarius	8:41
July 25 Virgo	20:37	Sept. 25 Sagittarius	23:05	Nov. 26 Pisces	16:11
July 28 Libra	7:17	Sept. 28 Capricorn	10:27	Nov. 28 Aries	20:32
July 30 Scorpio	19:45	Sept. 30 Aquarius	18:51	Nov. 30 Taurus	21:52
Aug. 2 Sagittarius	7:46	Oct. 2 Pisces	23:24	Dec. 2 Gemini	21:31
Aug. 4 Capricorn	17:15	Oct. 5 Aries	0:33	Dec. 4 Cancer	21:30
Aug. 6 Aquarius	23:32	Oct. 6 Taurus	23:58	Dec. 6 Leo	23:57
Aug. 9 Pisces	3:04	Oct. 8 Gemini	23:45	Dec. 9 Virgo	6:27
Aug. 11 Aries	5:11	Oct. 11 Cancer	1:51	Dec. 11 Libra	16:47
Aug. 13 Taurus	7:07	Oct. 13 Leo	7:30	Dec. 14 Scorpio	5:17
Aug. 15 Gemini	9:49	Oct. 15 Virgo	16:36	Dec. 16 Sagittarius	17:47
Aug. 17 Cancer	13:59	Oct. 18 Libra	4:04	Dec. 19 Capricorn	4:55
Aug. 19 Leo	20:03	Oct. 20 Scorpio	16:38	Dec. 21 Aquarius	14:15
Aug. 22 Virgo	4:24	Oct. 23 Sagittarius	5:16	Dec. 23 Pisces	21:45
Aug. 24 Libra	15:05	Oct. 25 Capricorn	17:04	Dec. 26 Aries	3:03
Aug. 27 Scorpio	3:26	Oct. 28 Aquarius	2:43	Dec. 28 Taurus	6:04
Aug. 29 Sagittarius	15:54	Oct. 30 Pisces	8:54	Dec. 30 Gemini	7:22
Sept. 1 Capricorn	2:22	Nov. 1 Aries	11:23		
Sept. 3 Aquarius	9:17	Nov. 3 Taurus	11:12		

1999 Moon Signs

The Moon's Sign of the Zodiac changes every 2–3 days at the time indicated

All times are GMT (Greenwich Mean Time) 24-hour clock system

Examples:
21:17 = 9:17 P.M.
11:03 = 11:03 A.M.

1999 Summer Time

Subtract 1 hour from your child's birth time between April 4 at 2:00 A.M. and October 31 at 2:00 A.M. for time correction to GMT

Jan. 1 Cancer	8:18	Jan. 30 Leo	20:18	Mar. 1 Virgo	10:09
Jan. 3 Leo	10:37	Feb. 2 Virgo	1:40	Mar. 3 Libra	18:37
Jan. 5 Virgo	15:55	Feb. 4 Libra	10:00	Mar. 6 Scorpio	5:24
Jan. 8 Libra	0:54	Feb. 6 Scorpio	21:08	Mar. 8 Sagittarius	17:47
Jan. 10 Scorpio	12:51	Feb. 9 Sagittarius	9:38	Mar. 11 Capricorn	5:52
Jan. 13 Sagittarius	1:24	Feb. 11 Capricorn	21:10	Mar. 13 Aquarius	15:28
Jan. 15 Capricorn	12:26	Feb. 14 Aquarius	5:55	Mar. 15 Pisces	21:29
Jan. 17 Aquarius	21:11	Feb. 16 Pisces	11:37	Mar. 18 Aries	0:14
Jan. 20 Pisces	3:40	Feb. 18 Aries	15:06	Mar. 20 Taurus	1:10
Jan. 22 Aries	8:24	Feb. 20 Taurus	17:30	Mar. 22 Gemini	2:07
Jan. 24 Taurus	11:52	Feb. 22 Gemini	19:55	Mar. 24 Cancer	4:37
Jan. 26 Gemini	14:30	Feb. 24 Cancer	23:10	Mar. 26 Leo	9:27
Jan. 28 Cancer	16:59	Feb. 27 Leo	3:47	Mar. 28 Virgo	16:38

MOON TABLES

Mar. 31 Libra	1:51	July 3 Pisces	4:33	Oct. 3 Leo	17:17
Apr. 2 Scorpio	12:51	July 5 Aries	11:18	Oct. 5 Virgo	22:41
Apr. 5 Sagittarius	1:09	July 7 Taurus	15:19	Oct. 8 Libra	5:55
Apr. 7 Capricorn	13:38	July 9 Gemini	16:59	Oct. 10 Scorpio	15:05
Apr. 10 Aquarius	0:25	July 11 Cancer	17:29	Oct. 13 Sagittarius	2:20
Apr. 12 Pisces	7:30	July 13 Leo	18:29	Oct. 15 Capricorn	15:04
Apr. 14 Aries	10:42	July 15 Virgo	21:42	Oct. 18 Aquarius	3:16
Apr. 16 Taurus	11:07	July 18 Libra	4:23	Oct. 20 Pisces	12:28
Apr. 18 Gemini	10:42	July 20 Scorpio	14:34	Oct. 22 Aries	17:38
Apr. 10 Cancer	11:33	July 23 Sagittarius	2:49	Oct. 24 Taurus	19:24
Apr. 22 Leo	15:12	July 25 Capricorn	15:08	Oct. 26 Gemini	19:35
Apr. 24 Virgo	22:06	July 28 Aquarius	1:54	Oct. 28 Cancer	20:12
Apr. 27 Libra	7:49	July 30 Pisces	10:25	Oct. 30 Leo	22:49
Apr. 29 Scorpio	19:14	Aug. 1 Aries	16:45	Nov. 2 Virgo	4:10
May 2 Sagittarius	7:37	Aug. 3 Taurus	21:08	Nov. 4 Libra	12:00
May 4 Capricorn	20:12	Aug. 5 Gemini	23:58	Nov. 6 Scorpio	21:47
May 7 Aquarius	7:38	Aug. 8 Cancer	1:54	Nov. 9 Sagittarius	9:17
May 9 Pisces	16:12	Aug. 10 Leo	3:58	Nov. 11 Capricorn	22:01
May 11 Aries	20:51	Aug. 12 Virgo	7:26	Nov. 14 Aquarius	10:44
May 13 Taurus	21:56	Aug. 14 Libra	13:30	Nov. 16 Pisces	21:20
May 15 Gemini	21:08	Aug. 16 Scorpio	22:42	Nov. 19 Aries	3:55
May 17 Cancer	20:43	Aug. 19 Sagittarius	10:33	Nov. 21 Taurus	6:23
May 19 Leo	22:39	Aug. 21 Capricorn	23:00	Nov. 23 Gemini	6:14
May 22 Virgo	4:19	Aug. 24 Aquarius	9:46	Nov. 25 Cancer	5:32
May 24 Libra	13:33	Aug. 26 Pisces	17:48	Nov. 27 Leo	6:24
May 27 Scorpio	1:06	Aug. 28 Aries	23:10	Nov. 29 Virgo	10:17
May 29 Sagittarius	13:38	Aug. 31 Taurus	2:41	Dec. 1 Libra	17:33
June 1 Capricorn	2:06	Sept. 2 Gemini	5:26	Dec. 4 Scorpio	3:37
June 3 Aquarius	13:35	Sept. 4 Cancer	8:11	Dec. 6 Sagittarius	15:29
June 5 Pisces	23:01	Sept. 6 Leo	11:32	Dec. 9 Capricorn	4:15
June 8 Aries	5:05	Sept. 8 Virgo	16:00	Dec. 11 Aquarius	16:59
June 10 Taurus	7:41	Sept. 10 Libra	22:18	Dec. 14 Pisces	4:16
June 12 Gemini	7:48	Sept. 13 Scorpio	7:12	Dec. 16 Aries	12:25
June 14 Cancer	7:17	Sept. 15 Sagittarius	18:37	Dec. 18 Taurus	16:41
June 16 Leo	8:13	Sept. 18 Capricorn	7:13	Dec. 20 Gemini	17:37
June 18 Virgo	12:19	Sept. 20 Aquarius	18:36	Dec. 22 Cancer	16:54
June 20 Libra	20:14	Sept. 23 Pisces	2:50	Dec. 24 Leo	16:36
June 23 Scorpio	7:20	Sept. 25 Aries	7:31	Dec. 26 Virgo	18:39
June 25 Sagittarius	19:52	Sept. 27 Taurus	9:50	Dec. 29 Libra	0:16
June 28 Capricorn	8:11	Sept. 29 Gemini	11:23	Dec. 31 Scorpio	9:41
June 30 Aquarius	19:19	Oct. 1 Cancer	13:35		

MOON TABLES

2000 Moon Signs

The Moon's Sign of the Zodiac changes every 2–3 days at the time indicated

All times are GMT (Greenwich Mean Time) 24-hour clock system

Examples:
21:17 = 9:17 P.M.
11:03 = 11:03 A.M.

2000 Summer Time

Subtract 1 hour from your child's birth time between April 2 at 2:00 A.M. and October 29 at 2:00 A.M. for time correction to GMT

Jan. 2 Sagittarius	21:33	Apr. 5 Taurus	19:28	July 7 Libra	6:52
Jan. 5 Capricorn	10:24	Apr. 7 Gemini	21:59	July 9 Scorpio	13:54
Jan. 7 Aquarius	22:54	Apr. 10 Cancer	0:17	July 12 Sagittarius	0:07
Jan. 10 Pisces	9:57	Apr. 12 Leo	3:18	July 14 Capricorn	12:29
Jan. 12 Aries	18:47	Apr. 14 Virgo	7:21	July 17 Aquarius	1:27
Jan. 15 Taurus	0:38	Apr. 16 Libra	12:39	July 19 Pisces	13:43
Jan. 17 Gemini	3:24	Apr. 18 Scorpio	19:38	July 22 Aries	0:10
Jan. 19 Cancer	4:01	Apr. 21 Sagittarius	5:01	July 24 Taurus	7:40
Jan. 21 Leo	4:01	Apr. 23 Capricorn	16:50	July 26 Gemini	11:58
Jan. 23 Virgo	5:12	Apr. 26 Aquarius	5:41	July 28 Cancer	13:28
Jan. 25 Libra	9:16	Apr. 28 Pisces	17:03	July 30 Leo	13:25
Jan. 27 Scorpio	17:06	May 1 Aries	0:55	Aug. 1 Virgo	13:32
Jan. 30 Sagittarius	4:20	May 3 Taurus	4:52	Aug. 3 Libra	15:38
Feb. 1 Capricorn	17:10	May 5 Gemini	6:24	Aug. 5 Scorpio	21:08
Feb. 4 Aquarius	5:30	May 7 Cancer	7:16	Aug. 8 Sagittarius	6:34
Feb. 6 Pisces	16:00	May 9 Leo	9:05	Aug. 10 Capricorn	18:46
Feb. 9 Aries	0:18	May 11 Virgo	12:45	Aug. 13 Aquarius	7:43
Feb. 11 Taurus	6:19	May 13 Libra	18:30	Aug. 15 Pisces	19:41
Feb. 13 Gemini	10:21	May 16 Scorpio	2:19	Aug. 18 Aries	5:42
Feb. 15 Cancer	12:44	May 18 Sagittarius	12:13	Aug. 20 Taurus	13:29
Feb. 17 Leo	14:13	May 21 Capricorn	0:02	Aug. 22 Gemini	18:53
Feb. 19 Virgo	15:57	May 23 Aquarius	13:01	Aug. 24 Cancer	22:00
Feb. 21 Libra	19:25	May 26 Pisces	1:08	Aug. 26 Leo	23:18
Feb. 24 Scorpio	2:00	May 28 Aries	10:03	Aug. 28 Virgo	23:56
Feb. 26 Sagittarius	12:14	May 30 Taurus	14:58	Aug. 31 Libra	1:35
Feb. 29 Capricorn	0:46	June 1 Gemini	16:33	Sept. 2 Scorpio	6:01
Mar. 2 Aquarius	13:13	June 3 Cancer	16:31	Sept. 4 Sagittarius	14:14
Mar. 4 Pisces	23:31	June 5 Leo	16:49	Sept. 7 Capricorn	1:48
Mar. 7 Aries	6:52	June 7 Virgo	19:01	Sept. 9 Aquarius	14:44
Mar. 9 Taurus	12:00	June 9 Libra	24:00	Sept. 12 Pisces	2:34
Mar. 11 Gemini	15:46	June 15 Scorpio	7:59	Sept. 14 Aries	11:58
Mar. 13 Cancer	18:52	June 14 Sagittarius	18:21	Sept. 16 Taurus	19:05
Mar. 15 Leo	21:44	June 17 Capricorn	6:28	Sept. 19 Gemini	0:23
Mar. 18 Virgo	0:50	June 19 Aquarius	19:27	Sept. 21 Cancer	4:16
Mar. 20 Libra	5:00	June 22 Pisces	7:50	Sept. 23 Leo	7:00
Mar. 22 Scorpio	11:23	June 24 Aries	17:53	Sept. 25 Virgo	9:03
Mar. 24 Sagittarius	20:46	June 27 Taurus	0:19	Sept. 27 Libra	11:26
Mar. 27 Capricorn	8:52	June 29 Gemini	2:59	Sept. 29 Scorpio	15:35
Mar. 29 Aquarius	21:35	July 1 Cancer	3:10	Oct. 1 Sagittarius	22:52
Apr. 1 Pisces	8:09	July 3 Leo	2:40	Oct. 4 Capricorn	9:46
Apr. 3 Aries	15:19	July 5 Virgo	3:23	Oct. 6 Aquarius	22:34

Oct. 9 Pisces	10:34	Nov. 8 Aries	5:00	Dec. 7 Taurus	21:25
Oct. 11 Aries	19:50	Nov. 10 Taurus	11:08	Dec. 10 Gemini	0:51
Oct. 14 Taurus	2:06	Nov. 12 Gemini	14:26	Dec. 12 Cancer	1:49
Oct. 16 Gemini	6:19	Nov. 14 Cancer	16:22	Dec. 14 Leo	2:10
Oct. 18 Cancer	9:38	Nov. 16 Leo	18:21	Dec. 16 Virgo	3:33
Oct. 20 Leo	12:43	Nov. 18 Virgo	21:17	Dec. 18 Libra	7:06
Oct. 22 Virgo	15:54	Nov. 21 Libra	1:37	Dec. 20 Scorpio	13:16
Oct. 24 Libra	19:32	Nov. 23 Scorpio	7:37	Dec. 22 Sagittarius	21:59
Oct. 27 Scorpio	0:25	Nov. 25 Sagittarius	15:37	Dec. 25 Capricorn	8:57
Oct. 29 Sagittarius	7:45	Nov. 28 Capricorn	1:59	Dec. 27 Aquarius	21:27
Oct. 31 Capricorn	18:05	Nov. 30 Aquarius	14:28	Dec. 30 Pisces	10:27
Nov. 3 Aquarius	6:42	Dec. 3 Pisces	3:22		
Nov. 5 Pisces	19:12	Dec. 5 Aries	14:13		

2001 Moon Signs

The Moon's Sign of the Zodiac changes every 2–3 days at the time indicated

All times are GMT (Greenwich Mean Time) 24-hour clock system

Examples:
21:17 = 9:17 P.M.
11:03 = 11:03 A.M.

2001 Summer Time

Subtract 1 hour from your child's birth time between April 1 at 2:00 A.M. and October 28 at 2:00 A.M. for time correction to GMT

Jan. 1 Aries	22:14	Mar. 4 Cancer	8:21	May 4 Libra	4:52
Jan. 4 Taurus	6:53	Mar. 6 Leo	10:28	May 6 Scorpio	8:04
Jan. 6 Gemini	11:39	Mar. 8 Virgo	10:45	May 8 Sagittarius	13:11
Jan. 8 Cancer	13:06	Mar. 10 Libra	10:52	May 10 Capricorn	21:13
Jan. 10 Leo	12:45	Mar. 12 Scorpio	12:50	May 13 Aquarius	8:23
Jan. 12 Virgo	12:30	Mar. 14 Sagittarius	18:22	May 15 Pisces	21:02
Jan. 14 Libra	14:12	Mar. 17 Capricorn	4:05	May 18 Aries	8:39
Jan. 16 Scorpio	19:07	Mar. 19 Aquarius	16:38	May 20 Taurus	17:27
Jan. 19 Sagittarius	3:38	Mar. 22 Pisces	5:28	May 22 Gemini	23:13
Jan. 21 Capricorn	14:59	Mar. 24 Aries	16:42	May 25 Cancer	2:43
Jan. 24 Aquarius	3:44	Mar. 27 Taurus	1:51	May 27 Leo	5:13
Jan. 26 Pisces	16:39	Mar. 29 Gemini	8:59	May 29 Virgo	7:40
Jan. 29 Aries	4:34	Mar. 31 Cancer	14:21	May 31 Libra	10:44
Jan. 31 Taurus	14:18	Apr. 2 Leo	17:53	June 2 Scorpio	14:59
Feb. 2 Gemini	20:54	Apr. 4 Virgo	1947	June 4 Sagittarius	21:00
Feb. 5 Cancer	0:01	Apr. 6 Libra	20:58	June 7 Capricorn	5:26
Feb. 7 Leo	0:22	Apr. 8 Scorpio	23:03	June 9 Aquarius	16:22
Feb. 8 Virgo	23:36	Apr. 11 Sagittarius	3:51	June 12 Pisces	4:54
Feb. 10 Libra	23:47	Apr. 13 Capricorn	12:26	June 14 Aries	17:02
Feb. 13 Scorpio	2:55	Apr. 16 Aquarius	0:12	June 17 Taurus	2:38
Feb. 15 Sagittarius	10:08	Apr. 18 Pisces	12:59	June 19 Gemini	8:39
Feb. 17 Capricorn	21:01	Apr. 21 Aries	0:19	June 21 Cancer	11:39
Feb. 20 Aquarius	9:54	Apr. 23 Taurus	8:54	June 23 Leo	12:55
Feb. 22 Pisces	22:46	Apr. 25 Gemini	15:10	June 25 Virgo	14:01
Feb. 25 Aries	10:18	Apr. 27 Cancer	19:49	June 27 Libra	16:15
Feb. 27 Taurus	20:05	Apr. 29 Leo	23:26	June 29 Scorpio	20:31
Mar. 2 Gemini	3:35	May 2 Virgo	2:17	July 2 Sagittraius	3:16

MOON TABLES

July 4 Capricorn	12:25
July 6 Aquarius	23:34
July 9 Pisces	12:06
July 12 Aries	0:37
July 14 Taurus	11:09
July 16 Gemini	18:22
July 18 Cancer	21:56
July 20 Leo	22:43
July 22 Virgo	22:30
July 24 Libra	23:09
July 27 Scorpio	2:20
July 29 Sagittarius	8:49
July 31 Capricorn	18:19
Aug. 3 Aquarius	5:55
Aug. 5 Pisces	18:31
Aug. 8 Aries	7:05
Aug. 10 Taurus	18:22
Aug. 13 Gemini	2:57
Aug. 15 Cancer	7:51
Aug. 17 Leo	9:23
Aug. 19 Virgo	8:54
Aug. 21 Libra	8:24
Aug. 23 Scorpio	9:57
Aug. 25 Sagittarius	15:06
Aug. 28 Capricorn	0:03
Aug. 30 Aquarius	11:50
Sept. 2 Pisces	0:33
Sept. 4 Aries	12:58
Sept. 7 Taurus	0:19
Sept. 9 Gemini	9:38
Sept. 11 Cancer	16:06
Sept. 13 Leo	19:14
Sept. 15 Virgo	19:39
Sept. 17 Libra	19:02
Sept. 19 Scorpio	19:31
Sept. 21 Sagittarius	23:04
Sept. 24 Capricorn	6:53
Sept. 26 Aquarius	18:07
Sept. 29 Pisces	6:50
Oct. 1 Aries	19:08
Oct. 4 Taurus	6:00
Oct. 6 Gemini	15:11
Oct. 8 Cancer	22:19
Oct. 11 Leo	2:54
Oct. 13 Virgo	4:57
Oct. 15 Libra	5:28
Oct. 17 Scorpio	6:07
Oct. 19 Sagittarius	8:53
Oct. 21 Capricorn	15:17
Oct. 24 Aquarius	1:28
Oct. 26 Pisces	13:56
Oct. 29 Aries	2:15
Oct. 31 Taurus	12:46
Nov. 2 Gemini	21:12
Nov. 5 Cancer	3:44
Nov. 7 Leo	8:33
Nov. 9 Virgo	11:48
Nov. 11 Libra	13:53
Nov. 13 Scorpio	15:47
Nov. 15 Sagittarius	18:55
Nov. 18 Capricorn	0:41
Nov. 20 Aquarius	9:59
Nov. 22 Pisces	21:54
Nov. 25 Aries	10:20
Nov. 27 Taurus	21:05
Nov. 30 Gemini	5:02
Dec. 2 Cancer	10:28
Dec. 4 Leo	14:15
Dec. 6 Virgo	17:12
Dec. 8 Libra	19:58
Dec. 10 Scorpio	23:10
Dec. 13 Sagittarius	3:32
Dec. 15 Capricorn	9:53
Dec. 17 Aquarius	18:46
Dec. 20 Pisces	6:11
Dec. 22 Aries	18:45
Dec. 25 Taurus	6:10
Dec. 27 Gemini	14:35
Dec. 29 Cancer	19:38
Dec. 31 Leo	22:09

Abbrev.	Time Zone	Hours from Greenwich
GMT	Greenwich Mean Time	0
ADT	Atlantic Daylight Time	- 3
AST	Atlantic Standard Time	- 4
EDT	Eastern Daylight Time	- 4
EST	Eastern Standard Time	- 5
CDT	Central Daylight Time	- 5
CST	Central Standard Time	- 5
MDT	Mountain Daylight Time	- 6
MST	Mountain Standard Time	- 7
PDT	Pacific Daylight Time	- 7
PST	Pacific Standard Time	- 8
YDT	Yukon Daylight Time	- 8
YST	Yukon Standard Time	- 9
HST	Hawaiian Standard Time	-10
AHDT	Alaska-Hawaii Daylight Time	- 9
AHST	Alaska-Hawaii Standard Time	-10

Credit for tables of Moon Signs 1985–2001

Magic Space Promotions
England

SECTION I

Moon Signs

Moon in Aries

THE BABY BORN WITH THE MOON IN ARIES WILL ALWAYS LET you know exactly how he or she feels. This baby cannot wait easily for his needs to be met, and his quick body reactions dictate his emotional well-being to such an extent that you're always running around after him. At least he is straightforward and easy to read, because he is not concerned with trying to please you but simply with ensuring that you know what he wants and can supply it as quickly as possible. Your Moon in Aries child is demonstrative and needs plenty of action and bodily contact.

How Moon in Aries Feels About Mother

The pattern that is usually set in early infancy is one of constant activity. The child with the Moon in Aries appreciates a buzz in his or her surroundings, and the early environment usually provides plenty of stimulation. The mother is seen by the baby as a "doer," someone with energy and get-up-and-go, and the child learns early on that relationships can express fire at their core. This position of the Moon suggests the "immediate gratification" concept—if I want something, I need it *now*. The mother is seen as strong and capable unless aspects from Neptune (the planet of diffusion) in her natal chart soften this image.

In fact, people born with the Moon in Aries often find that they share the same goals in life as their mothers. The baby perceives the mother as pushy, striving to get on in life. Even if she is not ambitious for herself in the outside world, the mother of the Moon in Aries baby projects the qualities of drive and independence onto him or her, and unconsciously the child tunes in to them and acts accordingly.

The Body: Feeding and Sleeping Patterns

The Moon in Aries child tends to be very direct and vocal. This baby is not a regressive type but is constantly pushing forward—and therefore can seem quite grown up for his or her age. He is demanding about food and quite determined to have what he wants when he wants it—something that can turn into a battle of wills between parent and child. It is a good idea to negotiate and reach compromises so he learns not to panic when he doesn't get his own way. Later issues with this Moon placement can revolve around impulsive spending and eating.

Possessing natural vitality and high spirits, children with the Moon in Aries can get by on very little sleep. They find it hard to relax or wind down, and therefore they are usually either rushing around or zonked out completely. Because they push themselves very hard, they may not even realize when they are overtired. It is important that children with the Moon in Aries are encouraged to recognize the limits of their bodies and find ways to enjoy resting.

What Moon in Aries Needs to Feel Safe and Secure

Security for this Moon placement involves inviting a certain amount of challenge into life. The Moon sign indicates what we need in order to feel truly at peace with ourselves, and paradoxically, because Aries is the sign of action, this child needs excitement, stimulation, and to be busy, sometimes even to be pushed to the limit, in order to experience a rush of well-being.

Moon in Aries is happiest when he is in the midst of things—as long as there is plenty to do, he feels engaged in life. Being in the midst of a hurly-burly atmosphere suits him best, and he needs an honest and direct exchange of feelings. Moon in Aries cannot handle emotional games and nebulous undercurrents. Instead, he needs to know simply that he is loved, because this charges his own emotional batteries with the fire that is his element. Demonstrative, passionate relationships in later life are related to the amount of straightforward emotional feeding the Moon in Aries child received in the early years. This is the child who demands to be told the truth rather than the little white lie.

How Moon in Aries Expresses Feelings

The key word for the emotional life of Moon in Aries is *dynamic.* His impulsiveness and tendency to rush in where angels fear to tread reflects a trailblazing quality that is evident in infancy. The child tends to take an immediate like or dislike to people. There is tremendous spontaneity in his or her ability to respond to others with a warmth that can take them by surprise. However, he can blow hot and cold, and his instant gut reactions can produce some aggressive outbursts and tantrums.

How Moon in Aries Reacts to the Environment

Moon in Aries is a natural leader, and therefore quickly decides what he or she needs to do in any situation in order to take control of it. He tends to rush ahead and jump into new experiences without a great deal of forethought, spurred on by the thrill of excitement and his natural enthusiasm.

Essentially, Moon in Aries likes to dominate his surroundings, particularly at home. He is decisive and dynamic, and is certainly not one to hide in the shadows domestically. He has the sort of energy that can be felt the minute he enters a room. As an adult, Moon in Aries lives by his ability to read any situation instantly and react by taking charge. He is apt to push others into action and motivate them to get things done.

Moon in Taurus

THE CHILD WITH THE MOON IN TAURUS ENJOYS HIS OR HER creature comforts, and as long as there is a plentiful supply of food, affection, and security, he or she is on cloud nine. But if this sense of security is threatened, he will turn obstinate. *Adaptability* is not a word associated with Taurus, and therefore any change of timetable can bring out the worst in this Moon sign. Where other babies might draw comfort from the stimulation of new sights and sounds, this child is miserable without a routine.

How Moon in Taurus Feels About Mother

Usually, the moon in Taurus baby forms a very strong link with his or her mother, yet this bond extends beyond a purely personal relationship and becomes intertwined with the rituals of family life. There is an incredibly strong instinctive need for order, stability, and security on the home front with this Moon sign, and as a baby, Moon in Taurus latches on to the mother as the chief provider of these requirements. Unless there are difficult aspects to the Moon, the baby bull wallows in the protection and nurturing that radiates from the mother.

The image the Moon in Taurus baby forms of his mother is rather traditional—she is regarded as patient, reliable, and practical, whether or not that is really the case. She may not fit into the traditional maternal stereotype at all, but the Moon in Taurus baby will be concentrating on the food and the quality of physical contact that she supplies. As long as these needs are constantly met, the child will feel completely secure. This is because the placement of the Moon is subjective and reveals what the baby tunes into from his surroundings rather than the objective facts.

The Body: Feeding and Sleeping Patterns

It is hard for Moon in Taurus to separate love from the provision of food. Even as an adult, unconsciously this Moon sign feels that to love is to feed or be fed by someone. Taurus is a physical sign, and therefore feelings of love can easily be translated into physicality rather than emotion. Touch and food assume the greatest importance with the Moon in Taurus as the barometer of emotional well-being.

Moon in Taurus can become absorbed in his or her body and particularly in the indulgence of it. Basically, this Moon sign needs pampering on a physical level and, when a baby, responds through the senses of taste, touch, and smell. Because Taurus is such a sensual sign, the skin is highly sensitive and can be irritated by manmade fibers. A Moon in Taurus baby really likes to be kept wrapped up in a 100 percent cotton comfort zone. One of the natural gifts of this Moon sign is the ability to relax, and sleep usually comes easily and readily, provided there is enough comfort and routine.

What Moon in Taurus Needs to Feel Safe and Secure

Taurus needs roots and a solid foundation. Without a stable home life, these people feel rudderless in the outside world. Therefore, what is forged in the very early years continues to provide a source of security in later life. When young, children with the Moon in Taurus need to be encouraged to value their ability to see something through from beginning to end. This placement is the opposite of the birdbrain or butterfly mind, and he or she enjoys seeing things grow and develop over a period of time.

In the early years, building and making things puts children with the Moon in Taurus in touch with their practical abilities. This sign appreciates the simple, earthy things in life, such as planting seeds and watching them grow, making (and eating) cookies, and playing with a pet—Moon in Taurus likes to touch, feel, and taste.

How Moon in Taurus Expresses Feelings

Children with the Moon in Taurus are demonstrative and affectionate. They are generally placid and easygoing, yet the bull that lurks within them expresses itself in a tenaciousness that can make them especially stubborn. It can be really hard to persuade Moon in Taurus to change his mind, or let go of something he has set his heart on, and occasionally a real rage can ensure when he does not get his own way.

One of the words associated with Taurus is *attachment.* As a child, Moon in Taurus will invest great emotional security in particular possessions and rituals, so if these things are not available to him at a particular time and place, it can seem very threatening. This is when the parents of a Moon in Taurus child realize to what extent he or she holds on to things in his or her mind, and how difficult it can be to let them go.

How Moon in Taurus Reacts to the Environment

Moon in Taurus is cautious—the tortoise rather than the hare. This child is not a great risk taker or raring to experiment with life. Confidence is built up slowly, and Moon in Taurus likes to take one step at a time and won't enjoy being pushed into new situations. In fact, it can be surprisingly easy to gauge in advance this child's reaction to just about anything because his or her nature tends toward constancy rather than unpredictability.

Changes need to be brought about gradually and within a framework of the past so that Moon in Taurus sees life as a continuum. However, too little risk and movement in the early years can keep Moon in Taurus stuck in a rut later on. These people will cling to a pattern of taking the easy way out and putting up with relationships and situations that have had their day because they are too afraid to strike out into the unknown. It is therefore important for Moon in Taurus children to learn to accept gentle challenges from an early age.

Moon in Gemini

THE MOON IN GEMINI BABY POSSESSES A NATURAL CURIOSITY about life and revels in plenty of stimulation. This is the baby who thrives on plenty of comings and goings around him and enjoys as much contact with other people as possible. The reason for this is that Gemini is a naturally sociable sign and has a very low threshold of boredom. The Moon in Gemini baby would rather that you took him or her with you to a party or restaurant to be cooed over and passed around rather than left him or her safely tucked in at home.

How Moon in Gemini Feels About Mother

Since Gemini is the sign of duality, it frequently happens that there is more than one main care-giver for this child in the early years. Moon in Gemini learns early on to adapt to more than one familiar pair of hands. Gemini is also a sign linked with the mind, and therefore, from a very young age, this baby is aware of more than just the realm of the body and feelings. He or she is alert, mentally attuned to the mother and trying to communicate even in the early weeks.

Children with the Moon in Gemini tend to have an inner restlessness that has first been perceived in the mother. Gemini tends to have many things going on at once, and the baby with the Moon in this sign soon realizes that he can survive without his mother's undivided attention. This is not to say that the quality of mothering is less nurturing, just that the baby notices and accepts a certain busyness about the mother. As Moon in Gemini grows up, he is instinctively comfortable with changing circumstances and enjoys movement around himself rather than routine.

The Body: Feeding and Sleeping Patterns

The Moon in Gemini baby tends to be more interested in what is going on around him rather than focused on his own body. His attention is easily distracted from feeding, and his alertness and mental curiosity can keep him awake at night. Certainly, as a young child, Moon in Gemini enjoys talking rather than eating, and it can be hard to get him to stand still, which takes an enormous toll on his nervous system.

If Moon in Gemini is encouraged to relax in childhood, then he can really make the best of his appetite for life, but if he is allowed to live out his butterfly tendencies, it can set up a pattern that is hard to break. He will always be on the run, on the go, and his mind will never switch off long enough for him to recharge his batteries.

A strong indication of the Moon in Gemini baby's being overtired is when his mind is running riot, he is incessantly chattering, and moving constantly from one activity to the next without completing anything. Because Moon in Gemini is naturally blessed with an alert and active mind, his early years are vital in blending his mental curiosity with respect for his body.

What Moon in Gemini Needs to Feel Safe and Secure

It is a paradox that the person with the Moon in Gemini almost feels most secure when things are changing around him or her. In other words, perhaps more than any other sign, this placement enjoys learning something new and adapting to different situations. Moon in Gemini is in his or her element when making journeys, visits, and short trips, or doing anything else that stretches the mind.

What comes naturally to this Moon placement is communication, so it is important that this child comes into frequent contact with people and begins to form opinions and ideas, and is encouraged to express them, from an early age. Moon in Gemini is easily stifled by a cloistered environment and needs to mix with different types of people and develop many interests. He enjoys games that stimulate his mental skills and train his hungry mind. This moon sign is the quintessential questioner.

How Moon in Gemini Expresses Feelings

Moon in Gemini is a changeable child. One minute he or she is occupied, the next bored. And his inconsistency means that one can never be sure exactly what will catch his interest. His feelings also appear to change rapidly. This means that he is not one to hold grudges, or sulk—his feelings pass through him and move on. His chief emotional need is to talk about how he feels; he can talk about his feelings even at a young age.

However, this ability to communicate can be misleading. It means that as a child, Moon in Gemini can be treated as an adult, and because he operates so easily on this level, all appears to be well. Yet if he gets caught up in rationalizing and talking about his feelings rather than just experiencing them, he can grow up to be an adult with an emotionally paralyzed child trapped inside himself. He will discount his anger, his pain, or his joy and be able to explain it all to himself while suppressing his actual feelings.

How Moon in Gemini Reacts to the Environment

The child with the Moon in Gemini reacts to the minutest change in his or her environment—it is always foremost on his mind. He notices everything and tries to understand it all. Basically, Moon in Gemini wants to build up as much knowledge as possible, because life is seen as an enormous question, and he must keep constantly on the move if he is to discover the answers.

It is hard for Moon in Gemini to concentrate on one particular activity or subject because his mind is always racing ahead—he will be thinking about doing the next thing while still doing the first one. Such a high level of curiosity means that, as a toddler, Moon in Gemini can never leave things alone and is into everything. His entire existence seems to revolve around the question "Why?" In a sense, Moon in Gemini never loses this childlike openness to learning, and this is what keeps him mentally alive.

Moon in Cancer

THE MOON IN CANCER BABY IS EMOTIONALLY ATTUNED TO his or her mother and surroundings from the word *go.* In fact, it is probably true to say that Moon in Cancer feels more comfortable in babyhood than at any other time in his life. This is because Cancer is the sign of the mother and is associated with the breast and nurturing, so a baby with this Moon sign feels naturally at home being merged with his mother.

How Moon in Cancer Feels About Mother

A very strong bond is formed between a mother and her Moon in Cancer baby. Psychologically, any baby in the early months of its life cannot differentiate between itself and its mother because the baby is not aware of having a separate identity. When the Moon is in the sign of Cancer, this merging with the mother can last a lifetime. The baby tends almost to swallow the whole essence of its mother and is attuned to all her feelings. A baby with the Moon in Cancer can have a smothering mother who pours everything into her child, endlessly filling him up with her own emotions, and this can create a real psychic sickness. Yet if the Moon in Cancer child is lacking a truly devoted bond with his or her mother, the resulting emotional emptiness will be equally devastating.

In some instances, the child is so responsive to the mother that his or her whole world revolves around her. Later in life, Moon in Cancer can become very emotionally dependent on other people because there is such a strong sense of comfort to be derived from being completely intertwined with another person. Moon in Cancer is always sensitive to other people's feelings—this is a gift that is brought into being initially through his or her ability to tune into the feelings of the mother and the mother's ability to connect emotionally with her baby.

The Body: Feeding and Sleeping Patterns

Cancer is a water sign, and therefore the health of someone born with the Moon in this sign will be dictated by his or her emotional well-being. A Moon in Cancer baby will feed and sleep according to his or her level of emotional tranquillity. This sign needs to release the emotions and is highly sensitive to changes in the environment. The baby will also pick up any emotional currents in the atmosphere, so although nothing appears to be wrong on the surface, the Moon in Cancer baby will sense if the mother is slightly tense and will feel anxious as a result.

Basically, Moon in Cancer babies need to be held for both physical and emotional comfort. The need for emotional closeness is ever present, both at the baby stage and throughout later life, and the degree to which this need is satisfied will be reflected in the person's health. Eating disorders can sometimes be associated with a poorly nurtured Moon in Cancer, and certainly, if the child does not receive enough emotional feeding in the early years, then the adult can try to compensate for this by becoming obsessive about his or her food intake.

What Moon in Cancer Needs to Feel Safe and Secure

The Moon in Cancer infant needs to have a sense of belonging. Initially this is with the family, which will remain the prime source of comfort and nurturing. The home will always be the central reference point for someone with this Moon sign.

Yet in order for the person with the Moon in Cancer to find his feet, he or she needs to be able to reach out and find this sense of belonging outside the home and family. Because Moon in Cancer is such a sensitive type, the slightest rocking of the boat can produce great anxiety. While other Moon signs can ride over a few emotional waves, the Cancerian Moon will feel as if his world has plunged into chaos.

Therefore, it is important for the parent of a child with the Moon in Cancer to encourage him or her to find an inner sense of security and use it whenever life seems threatening. Although this sign will always look for evidence of a sympatico atmosphere before trusting people and places, he can learn that others will respond benignly to him if he can always trust himself.

How Moon in Cancer Expresses Feelings

Loving feelings are translated into a flow of caring and protection by Moon in Cancer. As a child, he or she can be encouraged to show this nurturing, nourishing energy to suitable objects and people, whether that is a younger brother or sister, a pet, or a doll. It is when Moon in Cancer is feeling unhappy or uncomfortable that he or she clams up and retreats into a shell for self-protection. In fact, because Moon in Cancer lives life to such a large extent on an emotional level, his or her moods can shift constantly. As long as Moon in Cancer's feelings are taken seriously, accepted, and allowed to be expressed, this sign feels secure.

How Moon in Cancer Reacts to the Environment

There is a shyness with Moon in Cancer that tends to turn the feelings inward. An important pointer to the emotional well-being of a child of this sign is the amount of clingyness he or she shows. Although the Moon in Cancer child is deeply attached to the mother, a complete reluctance to be held by other people or engage in any other relationship will show that something is badly wrong. Retreat is the natural expression of anxiety with this sign, and even adult Cancer Moons will sometimes experience an overwhelming desire to go home when they feel challenged or threatened.

Moon in Cancer seldom forces himself on anyone or anything. His emotional waveband is set on receive rather than transmit, and his antennae are so sensitive that he picks up all the vibrations in the atmosphere and decides whether it feels safe or not to be himself. This acute sensitivity is a gift that enables him to tune into other people and "read" them. Yet, Moon in Cancer can be oversensitive, flooded with impressions and experiences that do not belong to him at all. Sometimes he needs to tune out. If he can always learn to ask himself what he is feeling, rather than what others are feeling, it will help him to be true to himself.

Moon in Leo

This is an exuberant placing for the Moon. Because Leo is the sign that is most in touch with the playful child, Leo Moon is able to express himself with all the spontaneity of a child who believes he is the center of his own universe. Dramatic, captivating, and impish by turns, Leo Moon attracts attention and leaves others in no doubt as to what is going on inside him or her.

How Moon in Leo Feels About Mother

When the Moon is in the sign of Leo, the child tends to perceive the mother as someone who radiates life. She is seen to be confident—someone who gets noticed. And in the psychological scheme of things, if the mother is the one who draws a great deal of attention, then the child has to work harder to attract recognition. However, Leo pours out warmth, and the child usually feels that he is able to bask in the light and heat generated by his mother, even if he is reflecting her glory rather than revealing his own. The baby soaks up this special atmosphere and soon learns that an ability to turn heads provides him with the attention he needs to feel secure.

When young, Moon in Leo is often applauded and admired simply for being a child. The mother is particularly proud of her creative achievement in producing this child, and thus he or she is seen as something unique and precious. The person with the Moon in Leo never loses the wonder of being able to perform with the naturalness of a child.

The Body: Feeding and Sleeping Patterns

Because the child with the Moon in Leo responds like a dream to anything that makes him or her feel special, food can often be packaged to cater to this need. This child delights in creating an imaginative fantasy world around his or her everyday life. It is wise to keep a few tricks up one's sleeve to sweep the Moon in Leo child away from fractiousness and into a sense of fun.

Moon in Leo children have a secret belief that they are actually little princes and princesses, and their bedrooms are their castles. They are fiery and willful, and full of energy, romping around until they drop. As babies there can be a real sense of their crying for attention when it is time for them to go to sleep and testing you to see if they are still number one in your affections once the lights are out! Moon in Leo children are vibrant, with plenty of healthy energy, and have strong recuperative powers. Even when tiny, they also possess a healing energy that works on other people. They are carriers of the spirit of life.

What Moon in Leo Needs to Feel Safe and Secure

Catching other people's attention is a big issue for this Moon sign, and he can almost feel as if he ceases to exist if you are not looking at him. Moon in Leo needs to impress, to get a reaction, to be praised, and if such rewards are not forthcoming from the parents, the child can grow up into an adult who has a desperate craving to be noticed, with the stakes getting higher and higher.

However, since Moon in Leo is a natural performer, it is almost impossible not to fix your attention on this child. He or she will demand it and need it in order to feel safe and secure—"Yes, I am still Mommy's special child." This needs to be internalized. With maturity, the adult can recognize his or her own worth and value, but, when a child, the parental mirror must contain the vital sense of validation.

How Moon in Leo Expresses Feelings

Moon in Leo needs room to play, to be himself, to dance, sing, invent, dramatize, or draw. All creativity is an important vehicle for this sign's self-expression. This child is unfailingly generous with his feelings, with his warmth, his sunshine ... and, on the other end of the scale, the odd tirade or two. Moon in Leo is known for exaggeration—the volume of this child's feelings is set permanently on high.

This child finds it hard to sit things out or wait and see—he feels something and wants to act it out immediately. Trying to control his or her exuberance can lead to an almighty sulk, a pouting game that is guaranteed to draw attention anyway. Mainly, though, Leo reflects its ruling planet, the Sun, in a relatively sunny disposition, and certainly people with this Moon sign can make you feel the sun has come out whenever they smile.

How Moon in Leo Reacts to the Environment

Moon in Leo tends to act on, rather than react to, his environment. He is a great one for making things happen around him, as he is a natural leader and loves to take center stage. Whether he is in the school play or clowning around at home, he thrives on entertaining others.

He enjoys showing off, yet can be crushed to pieces by indifference. To safeguard against fading into the background, and therefore not feeling loved, this child will take the initiative in creating a relationship with you. Someone with the Moon in Leo can act precociously when young, and in later life, if he is not receiving enough attention, he can easily revert to childish behavior. However, the bubbly nature and sparkle of Moon in Leo creates a great impact on others. Even as a baby, the power of his energy is enough to draw people to him like a magnet. Somehow, a Leo Moon can stop others in their tracks.

Moon in Virgo

THE MOON IN VIRGO CHILD IS GENTLE, YET CONSTANTLY ALERT and observant. Even though Virgo is an earth sign, its affinity with the planet Mercury (which rules this sign) makes itself felt with a strong emphasis on the mind. With the Moon in Virgo, nothing will go unnoticed, and this sign is very quick on the uptake without having to shout about it.

How Moon in Virgo Feels About Mother

When the Moon is in an earth sign such as Virgo, the mother is seen as being primarily concerned with practical matters. Because Virgo is the sign of order and routine, the mother has usually instilled a distinct pattern into the life of her baby right from the start. This is where the child with Moon in Virgo learns to feel comfortable with efficiency, because as a baby there is a certain predictability to his day, and he needs to retain a measure of consistency throughout his life in order to feel good.

The baby with the Moon in Virgo perceives his or her mother as someone who organizes the rhythm of life and makes it run smoothly. This Moon sign tends toward duty, perhaps noticing the dutiful mother. There is an emphasis on hygiene, cleanliness, and precision—a sort of "everything in its place" philosophy. In fact, practical matters take priority over feelings. The mother of a Moon in Virgo baby may notice the rash rather than the discomfort that preceded it, but she is good at taking care of her child.

Sometimes, Moon in Virgo has a rather critical mother who is constantly casting her eye about for faults, so the Moon in Virgo child never feels good enough to match up to her high standards. Usually, though, there is the steadiness in the early home life that is found in the earth signs and that provides grounding and stability.

The Body: Feeding and Sleeping Patterns

Virgo is associated with digestion—the mental capacity to pigeonhole and compartmentalize everything is reflected in the health of the stomach. Chewing things over, both in the mind and the body, comes naturally to the Moon in Virgo, and the stomach is constantly busy breaking down food and generally working overtime. Many Moon in Virgo adults develop ulcers literally stewing over their worries and food, and in childhood this Moon sign can suffer from digestive problems that are emotional in origin. Little Moon in Virgo needs to be fed little and often when he or she is feeling anxious.

On the subject of food, Moon in Virgo can be a real fusspot at the table, smelling everything before eating it as if you are trying to poison him. The slightest hint of anything not 100 percent wholesome and hygienic will put him off his food. Yesterday's leftovers simply will not do! Generally, Moon in Virgo enjoys feeling neat, clean, and tidy.

Sleeping is usually not a problem unless the mind is overstimulated or there is a lack of routine. Being an earth sign, Moon in Virgo needs to have all his meals and sleeping patterns set in a rhythm that is instilled into his body and inspires a sense of security.

What Moon in Virgo Needs to Feel Safe and Secure

Moon in Virgo is a creature of habit, and he or she likes to feel that there is continuity and order in life, a pattern that dictates events and responses. Virgo is associated with efficiency and precision, and the smallest alterations to plans can upset the balance of Moon in Virgo. He basically likes to know where he stands, what the plan is, and doesn't respond well to sudden changes in the itinerary.

Virgo has a highly developed mind, and his sense of well-being comes from being able to understand the world. He is a great observer and constantly asks questions and soaks up information. In fact, the mind is so keen he doesn't miss a trick and can pick up the smallest details at a very young age. In order to feel on top of things, Moon in Virgo needs plenty of mental stimulation and an opportunity to organize his world. He loves to choose between one thing and another, weighing the merits of each option carefully before coming to a decision.

How Moon in Virgo Expresses Feelings

The Moon in Virgo child is a gentle and compliant soul, generally loving and giving unless pushed too far, when he or she can become petulant and complaining. He tends to express the caring side of his nature by actually doing something for others. The Virgoan desire to be of service and to give to others enables him to establish a connection with people from an early age.

Moon in Virgo can seem a little shy, and it is this modesty that prevents him or her from grabbing the limelight. He is not one to take the star position, to show off, or assume leadership in games. Yet this Moon sign possesses a quiet inner strength and confidence that comes from a really good grasp of the workings of the world and an interest in people and their environment. His mind is so alert and absorbed that he does not need to be the center of attention. He is quite happy to stand back and watch.

How Moon in Virgo Reacts to the Environment

Even as a child, this Moon sign has exceptionally high standards for both himself and others. He can turn really despondent if his drawing isn't the absolute best, and, of course, if you have not put the required number of birthday candles on his cake, then the whole thing will be regarded as a disaster. This does not mean, however, that Moon in Virgo is a tyrant, because he does not tend to put himself first. He knows the value of sharing and giving. It is just that he can turn somewhat critical when people and events fail to live up to his expectations.

It is important to help the child with the Moon in Virgo deal with this desire for perfection, because otherwise, in later life, it can be a bugbear leading to huge dissatisfaction. Pointing out the beauty of the flaw or the lesson learned by the mistake can help Moon in Virgo to accept that it is allowable to be less than perfect sometimes.

Moon in Virgo is born to compare and contrast, so measuring success is important to children of this sign. They like to see themselves improve in a given skill, and their innate patience gives them plenty of sticking power.

Their sense of discrimination is very strong, so they will not necessarily take to certain people or situations. It is difficult to hoodwink them because they are never naive. They were born with the blinders off, and they will not pretend everything is up to scratch if they don't believe it is.

Moon in Libra

MOON IN LIBRA IS A CHARMER, A PLEASER, AND STEPS RIGHT into his natural place as an easy child. He has the most heart-warming smile imaginable and seems to know just when to respond. In fact, this child is cued into his environment and predisposed never to rock the boat. This, of course, produces the harmonious atmosphere around him that makes Libra so well liked.

How Moon in Libra Feels About Mother

In some instances Moon in Libra can be a "designer baby." That is, he or she is packaged and prepared for public consumption to look as sweet as possible. This, coupled with his equable nature, is usually a surefire winner, and apt to draw appreciation from others. Straight from the cradle, Moon in Libra realizes that appearances matter, and that in order to get approval one has to put one's best foot forward.

The mother of the child with the Moon in Libra usually sets great store by the look of things. Being beautiful, polite, and nicely behaved produces the right kind of attention from mother, and thus Moon in Libra figures that the world will respond accordingly. And, because we attract what we put out, very soon Moon in Libra sets himself up for an environment that looks good, but where a lot of the things that might upset the apple cart are swept under the carpet.

The mother of the child with the Moon in Libra is perceived by him or her as performing some kind of balancing act and distributing her favors accordingly. To this child, his mother's love is rather like a set of traffic lights, given out in supposedly fair and equal amounts but sometimes leaving him on red against his own personal wishes. In other words, the mother of the Moon in Libra child can seem rather cerebral. She lives in her mind, balancing everything to add up and look good. And the Moon in Libra child learns that fitting in equals peacefulness.

The Body: Feeding and Sleeping Patterns

The Moon in Libra baby will rarely make a fuss. He or she is noticeably content and good-natured, complying with the rules and regulations. However, because appearances are so important to this sign, he feels highly uncomfortable when wet or dirty—it is the ultimate indignity for this child. Changes to the schedule do not upset him too much because he is tuned into the idea of accommodating other people. If you are happy, he is happy—it is as simple as that. Moon in Libra also possesses an innate understanding of the laws of negotiation and fairness. So, he is always willing to play the game of "you can do that later if you do this now." He is not one for calling the shots at mealtimes and bedtimes, as he thrives on a harmonious atmosphere.

What Moon in Libra Needs to Feel Safe and Secure

The single most important ingredient for Moon in Libra's well-being is the approval of others. Without it he is miserable and lost, lacking that vital mirror in which he can measure his own self-worth. Through the admiring eyes of another, Moon in Libra feels that all is well in his world, so it is essential that he receives plenty of positive feedback from those close to him.

Libra is a people sign rather than a loner, so little Libra needs to have a full social life and the experience of relating to many different kinds of people. Libra is not naturally competitive and tends to withdraw from battle, but loves to talk to and play with others. Opportunities to mix with other children and adults build up the social skills that give Moon in Libra confidence in himself.

How Moon in Libra Expresses Feelings

Libra is a sign associated with poise and refinement. At times, people with the Moon in Libra can view the world of emotion as potentially messy, so they find it hard to immerse themselves fully in what they feel. Shouting and screaming is not their style—they are known for their reasonableness. Later in life they tend to express opinions rather than feelings and find it particularly difficult to recognize anger in themselves, although they are quick to spot it in others and experience a subsequent disturbance that rocks their sense of balance.

As a child, Moon in Libra is unfailingly polite and affable. His desire to please others makes him appear to be happy and content even when something is bothering him. As a parent, it is as well to recognize that much may be teeming beneath the smooth, unruffled surface that Moon in Libra presents to the world. This child needs to be actively encouraged to express his true inner nature, his will, his tears, his anger, his "unacceptable" sides. Accepting them as part of life when young will help the adult Moon in Libra to be authentic and real.

How Moon in Libra Reacts to the Environment

The key word for Moon in Libra is *adaptability*. This Moon sign will gauge what is expected of him and how he can best fit in, and then adapt his behavior accordingly. This is a great gift, ensuring popularity and a smooth path through choppy waters. The charming manner, diplomacy, and natural way of handling people really stands Moon in Libra in good stead throughout his or her life. However, responding and reacting, rather than acting, can become Moon in Libra's Achilles' heel if he never gets to be the one in the driver's seat.

Moon in Scorpio

SCORPIO IS A DEEP AND MYSTERIOUS SIGN, AND, WHEN IT IS the lens through which the feelings are experienced, it funnels a tremendous amount of power and intensity into the emotions. Such high-voltage feeling is never easy to handle and express, but for a child it can be even more unwieldy.

The Moon in Scorpio infant is sitting on the hot seat of emotion and usually learns early on that it is best to keep quiet about it if you want an easy ride. However, if his or her feelings can be expressed rather than repressed as a child, then the adult Moon in Scorpio will not be left with a legacy of bottled-up emotion. A great deal of understanding is needed in order for Moon in Scorpio to appreciate the richness of his emotional life and to value his depth instead of hiding it.

How Moon in Scorpio Feels About Mother

When the Moon is in the powerful sign of Scorpio, there is a definite theme of complexity about the mother. Usually she feels things very deeply, but for some reason she may have prevented herself from expressing her inner feelings. The child with the Moon in Scorpio, however, sniffs out the high level of emotion in the atmosphere around the mother, even thought it may be unspoken. Moon in Scorpio becomes attuned to looking below the surface and discovering things that may not always match up with what he or she is told or sees happening.

There is no point in trying to gloss over the reality of any situation with a child born with the Moon in Scorpio because he or she will have picked up the undercurrents and the truth. Scorpio is frequently associated with crisis and transformation, and, although not all Moon in Scorpio children come face to face with trauma in their early years, there is usually a penetrating perception of human nature that is gleaned during childhood. The child with the Moon in Scorpio rarely feels indifference toward his or her mother. Many emotions, including love, hate, envy, and fear, are triggered by this relationship—the raw stuff of feelings that meld together to produce the rich mix that characterizes the Moon in Scorpio.

The Body: Feeding and Sleeping Patterns

The Moon in Scorpio child possesses excellent recuperative powers, fighting back from illness with a vibrant will. Any depletion of energy is usually a result of unexpressed feelings. Bottling things up takes a huge amount of energy and exerts a heavy toll on the available resources, so a reduction in zest is a sign that something is troubling him.

Moderation does not come easily to Scorpio, and those with the Moon in this sign tend to have very strong dislikes and likes when it comes to food and a tendency to eat the preferred things to excess! A Moon in Scorpio child can really pit himself against you in a battle of wills when it comes to bedtime, and it is strange that this formidable strength can crumble in the night when alone in the dark—Moon in Scorpio can be prone to nightmares and a fear of things that go bump in the night.

What Moon in Scorpio Needs to Feel Safe and Secure

The Moon in Scorpio child needs to be able to trust people and to learn how to open up and express his or her feelings. If the early environment feeds his ability to play emotional games, then he will develop an incredibly strong need to control his emotions in order to feel safe. Scorpio is known for secretiveness, and this can be directly linked to a fear of his own vulnerability. Once the Moon in Scorpio child has put the lid on his feelings, it can take a lifetime to pry it off again, even in the face of immense turmoil.

This Moon placement needs to know that he is loved for both the "good" and "bad" aspects of his personality and that his emotions are a valuable part of him. The more he feels accepted by his family, the more he can accept himself and feel secure within himself.

How Moon in Scorpio Expresses Feelings

As the parent of a Moon in Scorpio child, you will be on the receiving end of either a hurricane or a balmy day—this is when his or her feelings are flowing. The trouble really starts when he refuses to let you know what is wrong and starts to manipulate you into playing guessing games.

The intensity of his feelings is such that Moon in Scorpio finds it hard to believe that others will still love him if they know what is going on in the deepest recesses of his mind. The destructiveness of his tantrums threaten to overwhelm him, and his biggest fear is that he will wipe out the love of those close to him. It is a real gift to allow Moon in Scorpio to experience his own rage and hate and then to show love, and far healthier than teaching him to bottle it all up where it turns poisonous inside him.

How Moon in Scorpio Reacts to the Environment

Scorpio puts on a brave face, even a frozen masklike one, in order not to show fear or surprise. It is up to the parent to try to read between the event and the reaction to discover what the Moon in Scorpio child truly feels, and then encourage him or her to talk about it. It is wonderful to see Moon in Scorpio acting spontaneously and being totally in touch with whatever he feels at a given moment, rather than controlling himself.

The Moon in Scorpio child often feels on the outside of social situations, yet finds it hard to say why he isn't comfortable. This sensitive Moon sign needs time alone, because even when young he truly values his privacy. It builds a kind of inner strength in Moon in Scorpio and helps him to discover himself.

Moon in Sagittarius

The Moon in Sagittarius child is generally happy-go-lucky and adventurous—which means into everything. He is naturally buoyant and exuberant, and his fiery spirit is active and energetic. *Vibrant* is also a word associated with Sagittarius, and since the Moon is the sign that comes into play when the individual is at home, he is at his most dynamic within his family and home. Keeping everyone amused but finding it hard to stand still, Moon in Sagittarius can be exhausting company if he or she is not fully occupied.

How Moon in Sagittarius Feels About Mother

The child with a Sagittarius Moon usually picks up that mother is a very active woman. Perhaps it is in order to keep up with her that the infant Moon in Sagittarius charges around so much. He senses that his mother responds well to someone who is a doer, and he notices that she is always encouraging him to try things, challenging him to stretch himself.

Having the Moon in Sagittarius usually means that when the child falls over, the mother encourages him or her to laugh instead of cry. It is amazing that this behavior pattern becomes so ingrained that even when an adult Moon in Sagittarius is desperately unhappy, he or she will often joke about it. Looking on the bright side is something that is sensed initially in the mother, and absorbed within the child. The mother is philosophical about setbacks, saying that everything eventually turns out for the best. So this child receives the message not to mind about whatever he hasn't managed today—because there is always another day to look forward to with expectation and optimism. All this adds up to a very positive start in life, and it's no wonder that the Moon in Sagittarius child is bursting with confidence.

The Body: Feeding and Sleeping Patterns

Sagittarius is the sign of excess and extremes, and Moon in Sagittarius often bites off more than he can chew both symbolically and literally. He can really exhaust himself because he has no idea of when to stop, of when he is getting tired or has taken on too much. Feeding is a different matter because, although he has a large appetite, his eyes are much bigger than his stomach. Wasting time, food, and energy are things he has no qualms about.

Moon in Sagittarius is so active and into the rough-and-tumble of life that it seems he can bounce about like rubber. Having an adventurous spirit and little concept of fear, he can be somewhat accident-prone. He really needs to slow down and learn a sense of limitation in the physical world, but it can be difficult for him to take advice, and so often he learns the hard way, with bumps and bruises to prove it.

The child with the Moon in Sagittarius will never admit to being tired even when he is dead on his feet. He can seem like a light bulb, with energy blazing brightly, and then it is as if he has suddenly been switched off. He doesn't seem to wind down or enter a sleepy state; he just goes out completely.

What Moon in Sagittarius Needs to Feel Safe and Secure

Moon in Sagittarius lives in a very different world than his earthy cousins. Instead of needing a high level of constancy and stability in his life, he needs challenge and adventure. Testing himself in this way is what builds up his own level of security. He is uncomfortable with too much order, structure, and sameness. His spirit is crushed by too much routine. He also feels bogged down when people are very serious. For him, fun and laughter make the world go around. The child with the Moon in Sagittarius responds readily to encouragement, much more carrot than stick. Yet he also needs to push against something, so he always needs to know exactly what the limit is.

How Moon in Sagittarius Expresses Feelings

Moon in Sagittarius rarely has a problem expressing his or her feelings. He does it loudly, playfully, and with energy. He is never one to sulk or bear grudges and tends to be up front with his emotions. As a baby, he will scream the house down when he needs feeding or changing—he is impatient and voluble about it. Yet, pass him around at a dinner party, or take him to the shopping mall, and he will surprise you with his affability and good nature. As long as there is stimulation he or she is happy.

How Moon in Sagittarius Reacts to the Environment

The Moon in Sagittarius child will wade right into the center of the action. He or she is sporty and competitive and loves to be in the thick of things, never on the sidelines. He is restless by nature and possesses a short attention span, so sitting still is never his idea of a good time. He is naturally sociable and friendly and can seem grown up for his age because of his confidence. In fact, this Moon sign remains very much in touch with being a child forever because, even as an adult, he or she adopts a playful attitude toward life.

Sagittarius is a generous sign. Those with the Moon placed here want to share life with others and to give, and what they can give others is their sense of fun and inspiration. There is a generosity of spirit here that is evident even when very young. Where Moon in Sagittarius has to be careful is in promising more than he can deliver, and not applying himself to the things that he considers boring. It can be difficult for him to accept that not all of life is fun and uplifting—that there are some humdrum aspects that have to be attended to, no matter how dreary they are.

Moon in Capricorn

IT WOULD APPEAR THAT THE CHILD WITH THE MOON IN CAPRIcorn is born with a sense of responsibility. As a practical, realistic earth sign, Capricorn exudes maturity and is not really comfortable or in his or her element as a child. It seems that he or she wants to get on, to learn more, and grow up as quickly as possible. Looking into his or her eyes, you can glimpse a little old man or woman, and this child does seem to be all-knowing, biding his time until he can speak.

How Moon in Capricorn Feels About Mother

When a child has the Moon in Capricorn, he often feels that the relationship he has with his mother constitutes an important lesson in life. Sometimes the birth itself was prolonged or difficult, and the baby senses that life is not "easy." The mother is very busy—Capricorn is associated with the puritan work ethic—and never seems to stop long enough to relax with her child. For whatever reason, the little Moon in Capricorn baby gets the message that it is important to be self-sufficient and independent.

As a reminder of life in the womb, babyhood can seem a rather floating time when life revolves around just being rather than doing. This is not easy for Moon in Capricorn—a sign that comes into its own once life starts to offer some kind of purpose. So Moon in Capricorn has to wait for life to ripen before he feels at one with himself. In the meantime, he likes to have the sense of order and routine that is common to most people born with the Moon in this sign.

The Body: Feeding and Sleeping Patterns

As an earth sign, Moon in Capricorn is naturally attuned to the body and its own internal clock. He is happy to be in the rhythm of things when life and his body are synchronized like clockwork. This moon sign actually enjoys predictability, so serving up his old favorites is never going to bore him. He is not likely to waste his energy or rush about like the fiery Moon signs of Aries, Leo, and Sagittarius. He is careful of his body, more fearful of injury than other toddlers. This is because Moon in Capricorn is born knowing his own limitations and doesn't need to pit himself against objects to know his own strength.

Time is important to this child, so there is an innate respect of bedtime or any other time. The ritual and pattern of life that can cause resentment and rebellion in other Moon signs offers comfort and security for Moon in Capricorn. This Moon sign also appreciates graduated bedtimes for different ages—it goes with his or her natural sense of progression.

The teeth and bones are the weak spots in the body for Moon in Capricorn. Generally, though, this child is remarkably resilient to infection.

What Moon in Capricorn Needs to Feel Safe and Secure

More than anything, Moon in Capricorn needs a routine to his or her life. This underpins everything for him and is something he always falls back on as an adult. Capricorn is a cautious sign and can be fearful of the unknown. Having a sense of pattern and familiarity in his domestic routine gives him something to hold on to when the going gets tough.

This Moon sign also has a natural respect for authority and doesn't mind being told what to do in the slightest—it helps him to know where he stands. In fact, even as an adult, Moon in Capricorn will always try to work out the ground rules in any situation because it gives him a framework and makes him feel secure.

Encouragement is important if the child with the Moon in Capricorn is to realize his own capabilities. He needs recognition from adults that he has achieved something in his own right, because little Moon in Capricorn loves to prove he is capable.

How Moon in Capricorn Expresses Feelings

Because Moon in Capricorn tries so hard to be grown-up, he can find it difficult to express his childlike feelings. He will hold back the tears, pretend he isn't hurt, and somehow thinks he will be a better person if he is strong. Moon in Capricorn has a reserve, a barrier that seems to erect itself between the feelings and their expression. He has remarkable self-control and needs help in allowing his feelings out. In the loyalty stakes, however, he is second to none and will always close ranks around the family.

How Moon in Capricorn Reacts to the Environment

The first thing Moon in Capricorn tries to do in any situation is understand how it works and what is expected of him. Moon in Capricorn is inherently conventional rather than a rule breaker, so he needs to know the status quo and act accordingly. He will not make waves or draw attention to himself, but instead is quietly present and correct. Nevertheless, Moon in Capricorn is not a pushover, or a mindless follower. He can be very strong-minded and a natural leader. When he knows his ground he can be rather bossy with others, making them toe the line.

He is serious as a child and dislikes any games that might make him look silly. He won't join in anything unless he can really see the point of it, and so he can seem rather standoffish. In fact, he is both sensitive and sensible and safeguards himself rather than following the crowd. As a child, Moon in Capricorn needs to be encouraged to let go, relax, have fun, make a mess, and not worry what other people think or what the outcome might be. In other words, he needs to know it is perfectly all right to be a child and not an adult.

Moon in Aquarius

THE CHILD BORN WITH THE MOON IN AQUARIUS IS A FREE spirit. He or she often behaves in quite an unconventional way in the early years, and continues to surprise people with a refreshing way of relating to others in later years. Aquarius is the sign of independence and friendship, and those born with the Moon in this sign usually love the company of other people, yet a part of them will always run free.

How Moon in Aquarius Feels About Mother

When the Moon, the planet associated with the mother, is in the sign of Aquarius, there is something quite individual about the relationship between the child and the mother. At their best, child and mother are bonded together in friendship and support, yet often the relationship is so characterized by friendship that close bonding is lacking in the early years.

In other words, once the child has reached an age where he or she can relate to others from a less emotionally needy perspective, the mother comes into her own and is able to relate to her child more easily. Up until this point, the mother many be pursuing her own interests and fighting free of being labeled as "just a mother." She is able to switch on and off from her role.

Aquarius is also the sign of disruption, and the early years may be characterized by changes on the home front—moving house, changes in circumstances and lifestyle—and the infant will pick up the feeling that life is liable to alter at any moment. Aquarius is an air sign and therefore primarily connected to the head rather than the heart. This enables the child to be detached from his or her feelings, and experience excitement rather than panic at the idea of change. The mother seems to take life's shifts in her stride, and so the child senses that one does not necessarily need to cling to the past. Through the model of the mother, the child grows up with an open outlook on life.

The Body: Feeding and Sleeping Patterns

The Moon in Aquarius suggests that the child is not really in touch with his or her body, because he or she is primarily a thinker. Therefore food is not really important to him because he has other things to think about. Nevertheless, problems can result from being out of tune with one's body, especially food-related problems, so it is essential that the child with Moon in Aquarius develops a respect for his natural appetites and the rhythms of his body.

Because Moon in Aquarius is apt to disconnect from any feelings of pain, this child can be a daredevil. He simply doesn't perceive himself as living within the confines of a body, and his imagination can run riot, encouraging him to take risks. He can be a restless, fitful sleeper, yet rest is just what he needs to relax his overstimulated mind. The Moon in Aquarius baby can be a dream for mothers whose lifestyle makes it difficult to stick to a routine, because the baby will hardly notice if the feeding time alters. He or she is born with a built-in predisposition to expect the unexpected and find it perfectly normal.

What Moon in Aquarius Needs to Feel Safe and Secure

Moon in Aquarius does not require a closeted sense of safety and security in life in order to feel psychologically complete. He or she thrives on excitement and needs a certain amount of independence and freedom to experiment. A Moon in Aquarius child needs to have a lot of opportunity to meet other children and to join teams, clubs, and groups in order to satisfy his or her craving for people. He also needs encouragement in developing his independent streak, by staying away from home and making strong ties outside his immediate family.

This child likes to have plenty of interests and may rebel against being limited to strictly family activities. The more he is confined, the more he tries to break away from the restriction, and Moon in Aquarius can be rebellious if he feels smothered. Of course, the child will still require the security of his family, but they will have to be very understanding of his need for plenty of personal space and room to grow into himself.

How Moon in Aquarius Expresses Feelings

A child with the Moon in Aquarius can seem to be the most "reasonable" member of the family. He or she doesn't appear to be ruffled by anything. But don't be fooled, because the Moon in Aquarius way of dealing with difficulties is often just to ignore them, separate from them, and detach from them rather than confront them. Therefore, the veneer of calmness that this child shows is deceptive.

In fact, detaching himself in this way can set a pattern for life that makes the world of emotions dangerous territory for the child with the Moon in Aquarius. Later in life he can feel flooded by feelings, yet still appear to have almost coldly cut himself off from his emotions. It is therefore extremely important during childhood to empathize with Moon in Aquarius, to talk things through and to gently encourage him to acknowledge whatever he is experiencing, and to express his tears and his happiness—the feelings rather than the thoughts.

How Moon in Aquarius Reacts to the Environment

Moon in Aquarius is able to wade straight into any social situation, to talk to people and make contract with them. He or she often feels awkward when expected to behave in a certain way and has an uncanny knack of surprising you with wayward behavior just at the wrong time. This is because Moon in Aquarius refuses to conform to people's expectations and almost enjoys throwing a wrench into the works just to create some excitement.

Moon in Pisces

PISCES IS THE TWELFTH SIGN OF THE ZODIAC AND ASTROLOGIcally is supposed to have accumulated the wisdom of the eleven preceding signs. Therefore, Pisces is a conglomeration of all experience and can reflect everything and anything. The Moon placed in Pisces denotes an ability to mirror other people, to merge with the surroundings rather than impose one's own feelings on others.

How Moon in Pisces Feels About Mother

Because the Moon in Pisces is so receptive to other people's feelings, the child with this placement can absorb the emotional life of his or her mother like a sponge. At best, this can create the most terrific attunement and feeling of oneness, yet if the mother is going through a difficult time, the baby will sense this and will display the same emotional imbalance.

It is very hard for the child with the Moon in Pisces to

separate himself from his mother, and it takes a long time. Even when this has been achieved, Moon in Pisces will usually try to re-create the same symbiotic relationship with another person, because he or she feels uncomfortable if not bonded to someone by a very close emotional connection.

Having the Moon in Pisces suggests that the mother has an abundance of feeling, and in some form or other has also made some kind of personal sacrifice for the family, or through being a mother. Pisces is the sign of adjustment to others, of giving and fitting in, and therefore the mother is seen as someone who may have put her own needs to one side or had to come to terms with an emotional trauma in her own life.

The Body: Feeding and Sleeping Patterns

Because Moon in Pisces is such a chameleon, the child will usually play back whatever is going on in his or her environment. Any unsettled undercurrents will produce digestive and sleeping problems. This is the most sensitive Moon placement, and therefore any illness is usually emotionally based. Whenever a stomachache or earache appears, it is usually a sign that all is not well emotionally. The person's system has gotten overloaded and just cannot take in any more.

With the Moon in the sign of the fish, it is also possible for someone with this placing to swim through life without causing a ripple, let alone make waves for other people.

The Moon in Pisces child lives in the world of emotions and senses, and later in life can have a problem with overindulgence. So a good grounding in the early years will teach respect for the health and value of the body.

What Moon in Pisces Needs to Feel Safe and Secure

The Moon in Pisces is a soft, dreamy placement, and this child needs room simply to "be," to get lost in an imaginary, fantasy realm and give time to his or her inner world. There is often tremendous creativity with this Moon sign, and the child can make sense of what is going on by drawing, writing, dressing up, and acting. The division between reality and imagination is often blurred.

This child really suffers without a close emotional bonding with his or her mother. If he doesn't feel truly accepted by her, then he will search for the perfect fit with someone else throughout his life. Therefore, this child needs constant reassurance that an emotional openness exists between himself and his family. He also needs to know that he is not responsible for the emotional well-being of other people. Moon in Pisces easily feels guilty and, if there are tensions around, can tend to think they are all his or her fault.

How Moon in Pisces Expresses Feelings

Because Moon in Pisces is so sensitive and apt to pick up what other people feel, it is vital that, in the early years, attention is drawn to his or her own needs and feelings. He needs encouragement to express what he feels inside rather than what he senses in the atmosphere around him.

The child with Moon in Pisces will express his feelings according to the way he observes others around him. He dislikes being "out of synch" with the rest of his family. As a parent to a child with the Moon in Pisces, it is more important to encourage him to think of himself rather than other people because he is a natural giver and sharer. This child can make you feel wonderful simply by picking you a daisy when you feel low, and his natural compassion uplifts other people.

How Moon in Pisces Reacts to the Environment

The child with the Moon in Pisces will never rush in where angels fear to tread. Instead, he will silently assess every person and new situation before committing himself. He is highly intuitive and is able to judge without asking questions—he just seems to know what is going on. Because of this there is no point in trying to pretend things are not as they seem, because he or she senses what is not being said.

Moon in Pisces needs to develop confidence in his or her own abilities and talents. He is inclined to underestimate his own capabilities, standing back and letting others take center stage simply because they are more spontaneous or sure of themselves. This child needs to trust in himself and other people, and to allow mistakes to happen without any feeling of regret. He needs support and compassion for his own sensitivity, because otherwise it can undermine the joy in his life.

SECTION II

Sun Signs

Sun in Aries Child

21 March–20 April

THE RAM

Qualities to Look for and Nurture in Your Aries Child

Energy, drive, and assertion

The Sun in Aries child is alive with energy that needs channeling into constructive activity. As soon as he can stand on his own two feet, he is constantly on the go. This is a child in a hurry, demanding to explore the world on his or her own terms. Aries needs a goal or he is lost, and a frequent cry from an Aries child who has been made to sit still for even five minutes is that he is bored.

Independence, the will to achieve

Aries is also bursting with a built-in independence and impatience to do things for himself. Learning the hard way is much more rewarding for this child than allowing a parent to show him or her how to do it. Because of his low threshold of boredom, Aries dislikes practicing to get better at something. The constant need to prove and test the self is something that is a vital ingredient of the Arien personality. Parents can encourage the child's willpower so he can grow up with the life energy he was born to radiate. Trying to crush or dampen the Aries willpower often causes an aggressive reaction—the key is to channel this drive constructively.

Honesty and directness

This sign hates pretence, and your Arien child will dare to come out with the truth even when it hurts. The wonderful thing about Aries is that you know exactly where you are with him or her; you don't have to guess, interpret, or imagine. It is this directness, evident in a young Aries child, that enables the Arien adult to cut through obstacles with such apparent ease.

A strong sense of self

From the age of two or three, Aries will exhibit the "me first" outlook that underlines his or her character. Yet he is a healthily selfish person. Even the word *selfish* is charged with negative connotations, yet the ability to value oneself and look after oneself is vital. Unless you truly care for yourself, how can you care for another? An Aries child has a strong sense of himself—what he wants to do, what he prefers, what he would like—and ideally this is to be nurtured in childhood, not stamped on. If the integrity of the self is protected in the early years, Aries will feel fine about choosing to put another first in later life. Overbearingness, bossiness, and an autocratic attitude in an Arien adult are caused by a fiery spirit that was devalued in the early years.

Aries Boys

This is a real boys-will-be-boys sign. Aries is a ram by name and a Rambo by nature. Having kicked off to a good start inside the womb, boy rams carry on in a state of constant movement and manage to keep their parents on the go at the same time. Activity is the name of the game. Aries boys often do things impulsively, without thinking of the consequences, which results in quite a few bumps and bangs. They recover quickly, however—Aries never wants to waste time!

Aries boys are always on the lookout for a challenge. They love to have a try at something that tests their level of fear, and they set great store by their own bravery. Courage is rarely lacking in this sign, but compassion for their own failings may be. Aries boys need to see that they are not infallible, and that choosing not to be a daredevil does not spell weakness. They need to know that the real achievement is in knowing when to push oneself and when to let go.

This sign is a natural leader, and in childhood, an Aries boy is an initiator. He is full of bounce and enthusiasm, eager to live life to the fullest. His rambunctious attitude can appear to be a little overpowering and demanding. Yet his motivation and high energy are the raw materials he is made of that translate, in his adult life, into effectiveness and the will to achieve.

Aries Girls

The qualities associated with Aries are traditionally seen as masculine—assertion, courage, and competitiveness—so an Aries daughter is no shrinking violet. Her strength of character needs to find expression and acceptance in the world in order for her to be true to herself; otherwise, she is forced to develop a stifling mask in order to please and conform. Acceptance begins at home, where it is important for her parents to recognize and appreciate her spiritedness.

The Aries drive pushes its daughters on, carried along by a tremendously potent life force, enthusiasm, and a desire to prove something. The Aries girl looks for constant stimulation from other people and from the world around her, and if it's missing, she can kick up quite a fuss to stir up some action. She may not be the quiet, "good little girl" type; her spunk always shines through, and she will challenge you to live your life as fully as she does.

An Aries girl can seem older than she really is, because she is eager to grow up and get on. She will leave behind the infantile dependent stages of childhood as quickly as she can in order to get on with the main business of her life, which revolves around her finding her independence and, ultimately, herself. Just because she has thrown away her security blanket, it doesn't necessarily follow that she is mature. Ariens often want to run before they can walk. It's as well to remember that Aries girls need as much support as the shyer signs, and perhaps even more than them.

Aries at School

Ariens have very quick minds—learning almost at the speed of light—yet the downside is they can forget it all just as quickly. In seconds the rams have "got it" and impatiently tap their feet while the slower minds catch up. The task is to keep them interested in what they are doing, because they have an exceedingly low threshold for boredom. Ariens never want to waste time on subjects that have lost their appeal, so learning the French vocabulary list for the umpteenth time is not high on their agenda of exciting things to do.

Ariens can also have a problem with the discipline of school, its order and routine. They are independent creatures and have no desire to follow the flock. These are rams, not sheep, and they want to be out there in front. It's not easy for Aries to be told what to do and how to do it. It all depends on the delivery. So an Aries child can clash with the kind of teacher who expects pupils to bow automatically to a greater authority. But he or she will run across hot coals for the teacher who inspires.

Being such a competitive creature, Aries loves the chance to prove him- or herself. If it's not on the sports field, then it's in the classroom, where Aries can be a trail blazer. Yet, Aries can jump to conclusions, often adding 2 and 2 and coming up with 5. He speaks before he has thought something through or misreads the question. He needs to slow down, to apply himself, above all to concentrate so that he can underpin his brightness with some solid learning.

Aries at Play

Ariens are exuberant, playful children, brimming with zest and high spirits. This sign really needs to blow off steam, run around, and express a seemingly inexhaustible supply of energy. The more boisterous the game, the better. It is hard for Ariens to stay focused on a game of Monopoly (unless they are winning, of course!). They get itchy feet sitting still for long periods and impatient with others who are slower than them. Ariens are great initiators, but tend to leave a trail of unfinished business behind them, such as half-built sand castles and model airplanes.

They prefer games that are fast-moving and highly competitive. Ariens love to be the leader of other children. Even at the age of eight, they possess the natural conviction that their ideas are the best, and others are often more than happy to follow suit. They attract playmates of like mind, spurning the quieter, more emotional types as "boring." Aries needs to learn to value sensitivity in others, and to be encouraged to spend time peacefully. Even Aries needs to recharge the batteries sometimes.

Aries Child with Aries Parent

As with any combination of the same Sun sign, there is potential for great rapport but also a possibility of bumping up against the other person. It depends to a large extent how in tune the parents are with themselves and whether they can allow the Aries child to express the full aliveness of the Aries energy without feeling undermined or threatened by it. Both parent and child are hot and fiery, so it can be an explosive combination and one that can turn into a battle of wills. Aries needs to win, and two Ariens in the same house can turn the home into a battleground at times.

However, although these two fire signs can ignite quickly, they do not bear grudges and have an intrinsically good understanding of each other. Honesty is usually an important component, as Aries is known for directness, so there is no confusion—each Arien knows where he or she stands.

The Aries mother is an achiever and wants her child to achieve—fortunately, little Aries is on the same wavelength and usually out in front in the egg-and-spoon race. Mother wants him or her to be a winner in life and will do everything in her power to help to make this happen. Call her pushy, but she will encourage little Aries to stand forward and to be independent.

Yet a balance will need to be found from someone else in order for Aries to learn about the quieter, containing side of life. An Aries mother often delegates the everyday practical details of life to someone else. Her philosophy may be that life is too short to do your own ironing, let alone stuff a mushroom. So unless the Aries child is able to rest up with a quieter member of the family, he or she may come to believe that life must always be lived in the fast lane.

The Aries father is in tune with his child's need for activity and enjoys doing things with him or her. Most importantly, an Aries father understands the world of the Aries child, which is one of grand visions and dragons to slay. He is likely to encourage the Aires energy to express itself as it should—with the Aries child's becoming his or her own hero or heroine. He knows the thrill of challenge and is not afraid to allow his Aries child to test and prove himself. The more boisterous the game, the better, as far as he is concerned. Rough-and-tumble, love and war—the Aries father understands it all.

Aries Child with Taurus Parent

Sooner rather than later in this relationship, Aries will demand his own way and run up against the immovable object of his Taurean parent. Taurus, the sign of the bull, is the most stubborn member of the zodiac, and Aries can exhaust himself trying to push against a bull who is digging in his heels. A roaring ram and a bellowing bull caught face to face is a sight to behold (and hear!). However, an Arien does not have the tenacity to remain stuck in conflict for long. What seemed like a matter of life or death five minutes earlier can be simply discarded when something new catches his or her interest.

The key to this combination is not to oppose each other but to work together—Taurus can plan something and Aries will do it! Unfortunately, Aries usually has his or her own ideas, too, and quickly goes off if something more interesting comes along—very frustrating for Taurus, who likes to see things finished. It will test the patience of Taurus to the limit, yet Taurus is a master at biding time. He knows that if he waits, he will get what he wants in the end—so he lets Aries wear himself out before bringing him back to reality.

"Hurry up," cries the Arien child; "Slow down," calls the Taurean mother. This is a relationship of quite different energies. The Aries child is volatile and spontaneous; the Taurean mother is inherently practical and constant. Yet they need each other, these two. The Aries child is held and contained by the security of the Taurean mother, and the Taurean mother is forced out of her habitual world to react to the demands of her Arien child. Both learn a lot from their differences.

Ultimately, an Aries child feels safe with a Taurean father. The Aries world never stops turning, but he or she knows his bull father is the axis in the middle, always a still point for him. Although the Arien child may believe that rules are made to be broken, he nevertheless needs the security of having the limits laid out for him. Taurus is a predominantly sensible sign, and Aries is a hothead, impulsively giving things a try. This is a dance of quick-quick, slow. Taurus and Aries will have to make some adjustments to each other's pace, yet as long as these two respect each other, they can live and let live.

Aries Child with Gemini Parent

The fieriness of Aries and the airiness of Gemini combine to make a relationship based around action and ideas. These two are a go-getting combination, but also at times full of hot air. If you are on the outside of this relationship, you will be enthralled by the exchange of ideas and enthusiasm, but the things that are talked about do not necessarily come to fruition. The reason is that neither Aries nor Gemini are stayers. They are fired up with plans, or may start something, but are both quickly distracted from what they have planned. This, of course, does not bother these two, who share an interest in the movement of life rather than its steadiness.

The Geminian mother is delighted by the quick responses of her Aries child. She will love the immediacy with which Aries plunges into everything and enjoy being kept constantly on her toes. Both Aries and Gemini detest boredom, but they are bored by different things. The Aries child is dampened by inertia and routine; the Gemini mother feels trapped by lack of mental stimulation. Aries needs to be busy in the body and Gemini busy in the mind. Bridging the gap here can be very valuable, as the Aries child can be stimulated to learn through action.

One thing that can be said about this combination is that they truly do enjoy each other's company, and in many respects bring out the best in each other. A Gemini mother can be a little distracted and scattered until her Aries child demands her undivided attention. An Aries child also appreciates the versatility of his or her Gemini mother—it seems that she can turn her hand to anything and knows about everything.

The Gemini father is naturally refined. He likes to talk things through reasonably rather than scream and shout—but a small Aries can throw logic out of the window with his driving desire to get his own way. The Geminian father, however, is usually one step ahead mentally and can turn verbal tricks that deflect Aries from his path. As an air sign,

Gemini can easily alter his mode of relating to people, and so he can switch levels according to whom he is with. An Aries child loves to be treated as an adult, or as an independent person at the very least. And inside every Gemini father is a Peter Pan, a little boy who never grew up. He is not at all hung up on his role as "parent," so he can offer his child the gift of freedom.

Aries Child with Cancer Parent

This is a combination of very different energies. The Aries child is bursting with a zest for life that the Cancerian parent finds rather wearing. Cancer energy tends to ebb and flow, which is in keeping with the watery nature of the sign. Sometimes Cancer likes to retreat into its shell, but then emerges to take the world by storm. When the energy tide is in, the Cancerian parent needs time to be quiet and peaceful, but the demanding nature of Aries can push him or her into a frazzled state. However, when the Cancerian energy is flowing outward, the parent will share the Arien enthusiasm and sparkle.

Cancer is a highly sensitive sign. For an Arien to be brought up by a Cancerian parent means that he or she will learn pretty quickly to consider the feelings of others. He will appreciate the close connection with his home and family that provides such a contrast to his desire for independence. Aries needs to learn how important it is to have solid foundations from which to launch forth; otherwise, in later life he gets caught up in constantly getting ahead because he has nothing to fall back on.

The Cancerian mother is a natural mother; she is supportive, protective, and attuned to the needs of her child. Therefore, she will adjust to her little Aries rather than lay down a law that demands that her Aries child curbs his or her energy. She must watch a tendency to be overprotective because Aries needs to test himself. If she tries to mollycoddle Aries, he will miss out on a vital stage of self-discovery. It can be very hard to stand back and let him try out his wall-climbing prowess when her instinct is to keep her child safe, but Aries needs to have a challenge.

Aries is an adventurous, sporty, outdoor type, while Daddy Cancer rules the roost. An Aries child wants to be out doing things from the word *go.* "What are we *doing* today?" is the oft-repeated Aries question. Cancer is happy just to be rather than do, but with a small Aries around it is not easy to putter. Little Aries wants to prove himself to be strong. This child will bite his lip rather than cry and pretend he hasn't hurt himself, but the Cancer father won't let him get away with it. It makes this child furious to have his vulnerability found out, yet a Cancerian father can help him to accept his own softness and therefore be more open to appreciating it in others.

Aries Child with Leo Parent

The relationship between an Aries child and a Leo parent will dominate any household. These two are world beaters, but in a small space may vie for the top position. So if other family members belong to the quieter water or earth signs, they will be treated to ringside seats at a jousting match. Usually, nobody gets hurt; it is merely a display, a spectacular show of bravado that is both entertaining and exhilarating to behold. Aries and Leo fire each other up into greater and greater states of enthusiasm, but basically they understand how far they can go with each other.

A Leo mother is the queen bee of the family, and Aries can be an upstart. He is always pushing his luck, but ultimately he must bow to the majesty of his Leonine mother. The Aries child learns that in order to get what he wants, he must respect her. For her part, the Leo mother is enormously proud of the vitality and boldness of her Aries child. She secretly thrills to the unquenchable Arien vigor, but she maintains her position by steering the child into the position of a worker bee. In other words, she finds him lots of things to conquer. He is constantly engaged in chasing the end of the rainbow, and the Leo mother poses him the challenge of bringing back the gold.

A Leo mother is warm and affectionate; she radiates the fire that makes Aries feel comfortable. These two are direct with each other and therefore build up a good understanding uncomplicated by resentments and hidden agendas. The Leo mother knows how it feels to be consumed by frustration when things don't work out, so an Arien tantrum doesn't rock her equilibrium one bit. In fact, she might even encourage it because, to her, expression is always preferable to repression.

An Aries child is full of daring and courage. He or she is the first to walk, the first to talk to strangers, the first to jump into the water. Yet his self-confidence might not be all that it appears, which is why he is always trying to prove he can do something. A Leo father knows just how vulnerable fiery pride can be to taking a knock, so although he encourages his Aries child to compete, he gently keeps his paws open ready to catch him when he falls.

It takes the generous spirit of the Leo father to help an Arien child believe in himself regardless of what he achieves. This is the valuable gift that a Leo father has to give. His love is so powerful that he convinces Aries he is special enough to win his unending admiration and attention. This means that in later life Aries knows he is worth something, and all the striving and reward in the world is just icing on the cake.

Aries Child with Virgo Parent

Aries and Virgo need to work at understanding and appreciating each other. Where Aries is full of verve and get-up-and-go, Virgo deliberates, analyzes, and values practicality. Two such different people have a hard time trying to see each other's point of view. However, as parent and child, they are in a position where contact must be made and some middle ground found between them. In fact, they have plenty to offer each other even though they will never think alike.

Both Aries and Virgo are great achievers, but they want to achieve for different reasons. Aries wants to win, to beat his rivals, be better than the rest. Virgo values excellence, perfection, and precision for its own sake. So the Aries child is triumphant when he or she wins the best painting award, while the Virgo parent revels in the quality of the painting itself.

The Virgo mother's organized world falls apart when little Aries arrives—bellowing with gusto, demanding attention, and generally speeding up the pace of life. All the textbook research she did before the baby's birth is little use in the face of an Aries infant who will not fit into anyone else's timetable. Aries actually refuses to be organized and to behave to order, however much Virgo tries to sort out the pattern of life into a fixed routine. This makes tough going for the Virgo mother, who sees herself as efficient and generally on top of things. The only way forward is for her to give a little, bend the rules, and be more spontaneous.

This child simply can't be bothered with "boring details" such as picking up toys and putting them away. He can only focus on what is catching his attention in the present—once the game is over, then Aries' enthusiasm passes quickly on to the next thing. Fortunately, his excitement can be sparked by presenting any mundane task as some sort of heroic challenge. Aries needs a goal. He gets no pleasure out of doing something just for the sake of it. Where would Virgos be without their excellent powers of analysis? So with a little deduction, a Virgo mother can work out exactly what makes her Arien offspring tick. Just don't expect him to be a lamb—he's a ram!

Having an Aries child around makes most fathers feel more alive. Aries will not allow others to stand on the sidelines; they must get involved with what Aries is doing, respond to what Aries is feeling. So the Virgo father finds himself being asked to make snap decisions, and it forces him out of his ordered world. In turn, Aries feels really safe with a Virgo father. Of course, Aries will have outbursts against the Virgoan sensible approach to life, but in the long run, he feels secure and he knows where he stands. A Virgo father offers an important foundation for Aries. Aries is taught the value of taking his time to accomplish the best rather than impatiently attempting to run before he can walk.

Aries Child with Libra Parent

Here we have two sides of the same coin in the opposite signs of Aries and Libra. What we are talking about is the meeting of individuality and cooperation, willfulness and harmony. Sounds pretty tricky? It is! Yet, this is the same coin; Aries and Libra have a great deal in common and are a necessary balance to each other. For all his fire and brimstone, Aries needs the calmness and coolness of Libra. Soothing words heal fevered brows, and an Aries child loves being in the gentle breeze provided by a Libran mother's equable company. Opposites attract, and the Aries/Libra mix is a source of fascination and stimulation for both parties.

Arien children usually take their families by storm. So it can shatter the peace of a Libran-run household to accommodate this robust little ram with a healthy pair of lungs. An Aries baby will certainly alter the balance of his Libran mother's scales, sending them rocking back and forth from one moment to the next. As fast as Libra tries to restore harmony, Aries will upset the apple cart or the apple juice all over the place.

A roaring ram is a noisy and obtrusive phenomenon, and unlike Libra, Aries doesn't care at all what other people think of him. He will scream in the street, shout at you in front of Grandma, and generally run riot through the supermarket if he doesn't get his own way. It's a good thing that Librans are equipped with more charm and reasoning power than any other sign in the zodiac because it takes a lot to smooth over the destruction caused by a small Aries on the warpath.

As Little Aries develops a mind of his own, a Libran father becomes increasingly intrigued by the confidence of this child in knowing his own mind. Aries is always so sure of what he wants and so direct about it. Yet making choices and decisions can be a painfully slow process for Libra, who always has to weigh all the alternatives first. Admiring his Arien child's forthrightness, but also feeling a bit uncomfortable with it, a Libran father may try to avoid direct confrontation. Libra sits behind his scales of justice, always trying to see fair play, but the Arien cry is that all is fair in love and war, and he is never afraid of a battle. In the face of little Aries' demands, his sheer need to have his own requirements met, a Libran father is forced off the fence he usually sits on. He has to make a stand, and he can teach Aries that there are always two sides to every story.

Aries Child with Scorpio Parent

This is a meeting of powerful strength and possible combustion. Not surprisingly, this relationship can closet two iron wills together in such a way that there is an inevitable clash—the clash of the Titans, no matter that one is considerably smaller than the other. There is enough energy and fire in a baby Aries to more than match the mighty Scorpionic willpower. Consequently, there are times, especially when Aries is big enough to stand on his own two feet, when he and his Scorpio parent stalk around each other like two gladiators.

Issues seem to revolve around what each will and will not do for the other. It seems strange to be talking like this about a parent–child relationship, but the nitty-gritty of it is that even if they love each other more than life itself, the bottom line is always about winning some kind of power struggle. The Scorpio parent knows that love conquers all eventually, even though the Aries child may be quite keen initially on putting his foot down—well, banging it up and down, actually!

Ultimately, Aries and Scorpio develop a tremendous respect for each other. They blow hot and cold, but they always come back for more. Aries will always push his luck, while Scorpio characteristically holds back. Aries will look at what is going on outside the window; Scorpio will be concerned with what is happening inside one's feelings. This mother and child bring together the outer and inner worlds, so as a pair they can enjoy a kind of double vision that is beneficial to both of them.

Scorpio is a controlled sign—although the female Scorpio is highly sensitive and emotionally vulnerable, she is a past mistress at keeping her feelings on ice. But Aries finds it impossible to sit on anything, to hide anything. Coming face to face with the spontaneity of her Aries child challenges a Scorpio mother to be more immediate with her own feelings. So the child can act as a catalyst for change in the mother. Discovering it is not the end of the world to own up to feeling bored, hungry, or tired can be quite a releasing experience for a Scorpio!

A Scorpio father can admire the spiritedness of Aries and is secretly glad that his offspring will not be walked over by anyone. Father and child will most probably engage in a few skirmishes. Scorpio is a powerful force, so Aries may win the battle but never the war, because ultimately a Scorpio father has an unquenchable inner strength. He can teach Aries when to hold back, to contain and hold himself in reserve, and these are valuable lessons for Aries, who often spends everything he's got. But Aries is not all about battle and angst. This child is brimming with a desire to live life as fully as possible, to make the most of every moment, and within this is a purity that is uplifting for everyone who encounters Aries.

Aries Child with Sagittarius Parent

It could be said that these two get on like a house on fire. Both Aries and Sagittarius belong to the element of fire, and so they understand their mutual need to blaze through life. Sagittarian parents adore the enthusiasm and spontaneity that is so often present in childhood before it is tempered by adult life.

Therefore, the archer parent will encourage his or her small ram to let off as much steam as he can wherever and whenever possible. This may sound rather irresponsible, but Sagittarians know what they are doing. They have an immense wisdom that allows people to be themselves so they can achieve their own vision in later life. By following the law of reverse psychology and actually allowing little Aries to express the full voltage or his or her energy, that energy becomes less wayward and more purposeful. Instead of tugging to be let off the leash, little Aries walks companionably to heel.

What the Sagittarius mother particularly has to offer her Aries child is her breezy sense of humor. For Aries, life is full of potential tests and challenges, and it can be a serious business constantly proving yourself. A Sagittarian mother will laugh when things go wrong or don't quite make the grade, and this can be a real relief for Aries, who is never quite sure if it is all right to fail. The Sagittarian philosophy of life is that you aim your arrows at your goal, and if they miss, you just ride on to the next one. There is always another opportunity around the corner, so there is no need to get tense about winning and losing.

There is usually nothing hidden below the surface in the relationship between an Aries child and a Sagittarian mother. They feel free to tell each other exactly how they feel without pulling any punches, which is enough to turn any Libran eavesdropper pale with anxiety. However, Aries and Sagittarius thrive on openness and honesty, and they are both quick to forgive and forget what was said in the heat of the moment.

A Sagittarian father encourages his Arien child to be independent and take risks in order to learn something. Nothing ventured, nothing gained is his attitude, and little Aries is more than happy to try his or her hand. Because his father doesn't concern himself with holding him back, the child eventually learns to recognize his own limits. Aries is able to become more controlled and disciplined from the inside rather than being constantly told what he cannot do. Sagittarius recognizes that sometimes walking a little on the wild side is preferable to not walking at all, and only by falling over a few times yourself can you progress.

Aries Child with Capricorn Parent

In the red corner we have little Aries, stamping his feet and raring to go, and in the blue corner is his Capricorn parent, who is checking the rules and sorting out the arrangements. Small wonder that those two drive each other to distraction at times, because one is so hotheaded and the other so proper. Aries can be associates with the word *yes,* and Capricorn with the word *no,* so you can imagine the struggle that can take place when these two signs lock horns. And lock horns they do, the ram and the goat jostling each other and getting caught up in a stalemate where neither wins. They are both strong-minded and determined to have their own way, but when it comes to digging in hooves, Capricorn is the victor. Capricorn will not budge for anyone.

From babyhood, no matter how loudly Aries yells for what he wants—and he always wants it *now*—his Capricorn mother will not waver in her steadfast adherence to knowing what's best. No other sign can sit through the Arien display of kicking feet, flailing arms, and wild screaming with such dignified aplomb before calmly announcing that the toddler's bedtime is eight o'clock and not a minute later. A Capricorn mother can issue words as if they have been written as law for centuries, and not even an Aries would dare to transgress these rules.

The fact is that a Capricorn mother is the original Girl Scout, always prepared, but probably even she would not be able to prepare herself for every Arien eventuality. The ram is a bundle of energy, into everything and anything and forcing his Capricorn mother out of the confines of her organized world.

Despite their different outlooks on life, an Aries child and a Capricorn father do have things in common. They both need to be constantly occupied and to prove that they are good at what they do. A Capricorn father encourages his Aries child to go out in the world and reach for the top. He teaches little Aries right from the start to take pride in standing on his or her own two feet. Pretty soon Aries is up and running and doing what he or she loves best, which is winning.

Aries Child with Aquarius Parent

It can be hard for an Aquarian parent to understand the fieriness of a little ram. Why does he or she get so worked up about things? Aries is a fire sign, and therefore impulsive, spontaneous, and hot by nature. In contrast, Aquarius as a cool-thinking air sign will never allow events or feelings to overtake him, because his rational perception of life offers a perspective on everything.

So, having an Arien child will warm up the Aquarian, who will be drawn into the exciting, active Arien world when his or her usual inclination might be to stand back. Aquarius has a real gift to impart here, too. He can encourage Aries to think first before acting, to make choices before rushing into the fray. So Aries can become used to balancing mind and action, head and heart.

Aquarian mothers are all for "live and let live." They are not about to push their children into certain behavior just to conform, because they have little time for keeping up social appearances. This is not to say that all Aquarian mothers encourage their children to drop out of nursery school in order to watch the grass grow. On the other hand, they will not favor their child's learning ballet, or Nintendo, for that matter, just because everyone else is. Her message as a mother is to be original and to be true to yourself in order to be free. Aries enjoys being around these ideas; growing up in this atmosphere enables him or her to be independent, which is one of the chief aims of this sign.

The relationship between these two is primarily one of incredible stimulation. They spark off each other. Aquarius is a sign that sometimes feels trapped by motherhood, but an Arien child is not the clingy type, so this gives the Aquarian mother more room to breathe. And Aries is happy as long as he is able to do what he wants. This is where he is in for a shock, because although Aquarius is so free-spirited, this is a fixed sign—determined, sometimes stubborn. So Aries will not always be able to get his own way, despite the unconventionality and open-mindedness of his mother.

The wonderful thing about Aquarian fathers is that they are brilliant at explaining the reasons why, so Aries is never left without something to think about. His mind will be challenged by his father, and Aries thrives on challenges, goals, and achievements. An Aquarius father can be quite laid back, so he won't enter the fray with Aries and constantly rub up against him. Instead, his cool detachment offers little Aries a new perspective. And he can introduce his child to the excitement of the mind.

Aries Child with Pisces Parent

Pisces is the most gentle sign and Aries the fieriest, but the soothing influence of the fish on the ram can truly soften the blow. As a youngster, Aries is hell-bent on proving he can do whatever he sets out to tackle. He is flexing his muscles and getting the measure of his own strength. This is a necessary stage in the growth of Aries, but if taken into adulthood, it can be a little wearing on others. Yet a Piscean mother will continually point out to her Arien child that there are other ways of going about things. Throwing your weight around and demanding people pay attention to you is not the only option. It's not easy to turn a ram into a lamb, but Pisces can make it happen—sometimes!

Adventure and action dominate the Arien world. This child is fired with enthusiasm, can't wait to give things a try. His or her Piscean parent belongs to a quieter world of feelings and sensitivity to others. Because Pisces has such a talent for tuning into others, he or she knows what lies underneath the Arien bravado. Other people may mistake the assertiveness of Aries for brash selfishness and never realize the fear of being vulnerable that lies behind it. But a Pisces will always appreciate the inner person rather than the outer behavior.

As a mother, Pisces will always be there for Aries to give him love and understanding when his impulsiveness has misguided him. She knows that Aries has to learn through his own experience, and a ram with the bit between his teeth is not about to let go. She will not stand in his way or force him to change because Pisceans believe in accepting others as they are. Some of the more up-front signs might feel personally threatened by a small Arien displaying so much headstrong zeal, but not Pisces. A Piscean mother doesn't have to enter into a showdown with a ram to gain respect. She has other ways. Fish are able to maneuver around most obstacles without banging into them. She is not one to set him targets, or mind too much whether he wins or loses. Most importantly, she believes in him and helps him to believe in himself.

An Aries child with a Piscean father will learn the lesson of subtlety—something that is not the front-runner of the Arien repertoire. A Piscean father is gentle and loving, but sometimes seems rather elusive to the exuberant Aries. The child may feel that his or her father is sometimes a slippery fish—magical, but somehow difficult to get hold of, hard to catch. Pisces is the sign of the mystic, and without realizing it, Pisceans can appear to be rather unavailable to the ordinary human mind. So a Pisces father needs to work at really "being there" for his young Aries child, who needs the reality of flesh and blood, not absence or absentmindedness. For his part, a Pisces father may find himself enjoying himself in the here and now rather than the there and then!

Sun in Taurus Child

21 April–21 May

THE BULL

Qualities to Look for and Nurture in Your Taurus Child

A natural common sense, reliability, and practicality

AS AN EARTH SIGN, IT IS IMPORTANT FOR TAUREANS TO FEEL good about keeping their feet on the ground. Not wanting to live with their heads in the clouds, they quickly feel disoriented by sudden changes and lack of routine and structure. A Taurean child needs to discover his own capabilities in his own time and does not respond well to being pushed.

An inner calm security and ability to comfort and nourish oneself and others

Taureans like security around them and are then able to internalize it and give out a sense of tranquillity and peace to other people. Taurus is a rock and in later life often takes on the role of holding up and supporting other people. Taureans dislike getting caught up in emotional confrontations and crises and tend to stand firm. Their emotional strength comes from their ability to see continuity in life and to take pleasure in simple things.

The patience to stick to something and build relationships over a long period

Taureans are the builders of the zodiac. They persevere through difficulties and setbacks in order to achieve their goals, however long it takes. It is fascinating to observe the staying power of Taurean children and the constancy and loyalty that is characteristic of their way of relating to others.

Valuing and respecting the tangible, physical things in life

Taureans are essentially realists, living very much in the material world. What matters to them is what they can see and touch, not abstract ideas. In childhood it is essential that they develop a good relationship with their own bodies and are able to enjoy the physicality of the world around them.

Taurus Boys

Little boy bulls are fascinated by how things work. They want to take things apart just so they can understand how to put them together again. It's not easy standing back and letting your small Taurean son pull your vacuum cleaner apart, but you'll be amazed when he triumphantly rebuilds it and, what's more, has taken out the pieces that clogged up the system! As a practical earth sign, these boys like "hands-on" experience. They are never ones for reading a book when they could be making or building something instead, and they have the patience to see something through right to the end.

Taurus is one of the most affectionate signs of the zodiac,

and as well as giving out lots of hugs, the desire for body contact may appear as a playful bullishness in a male child. Taurus is unique in being able to express through touch as well as words; so if you are a parent of a Taurean boy, it is vital to make physical contact, even if it does not come naturally to you.

A Taurean boy looks so solid and robust that he might be mistaken for being a bit of a bruiser—well, he is a baby bull, after all. In fact he looks a lot tougher than he is, because that strong body contains a gentle soul. Taureans never fall prey to the emotional vulnerability of the water signs, as they cultivate a breathtaking sense and sensibility. Because of this they need less in the way of parental guidance, but require an enormous amount of loving security so they can put their emotional roots down in fertile soil.

Taurus Girls

Taurean girls share the same interest in the practical world as the boys and the same need to make physical contact with it. It is useless to tell your Taurean daughter "Don't touch" when she wants to put her fingers in your makeup or cake mix to feel what it's like; she is already practicing the sensuality that is her birthright in the adult world.

Little girl bulls are happy to putter around, exploring the world at their own pace and taking great pleasure from ordinary, everyday things. As a parent, you will be able to get away from the complexities of life when you are with her, and she will communicate to you the delight in simplicity. Taurus values the basics—good food, beauty in nature, and affection between people. A little girl bull wants to fill herself in childhood with these things; they form a kind of emotional ballast for her in later life.

Taurean girls have their own particular brand of femininity. They are not keen to be dressed up in ribbons and bows because they like to be comfortable above all else. *Fragility* is not a word that springs to mind when you look at a small Taurean girl, because she has a certain sturdiness that is characteristic of earth signs. She possesses a fullness, a richness that is a quality of her sensuality and earthiness. Taurus is also a charmer, so she knows just how to use her feminine wiles to get what she wants. She revels in touching and being touched, but it is not a clinginess, more a reassurance of your constancy. If she can touch you, she knows you are really there.

Taurus at School

Taureans are usually happy to conform to the routine of school. They are not great rule breakers or benders because they have a natural respect for authority and appreciate having a framework of dos and don'ts so they know where they stand. Schooldays can be some of the happiest of a Taurean's life because Taureans simply love to know that if it's Monday then such and such is happening. Sometimes in later life they carry on with a regimen that is similar to a school timetable because it removes uncertainty. Taureans really can take a tremendous amount of predictability without becoming bored.

Because Taurus is such a practical sign, these people are drawn to subjects that entail using common sense rather than imagination. They can master a Bunsen burner quicker than Shakespeare's imagery. It is a great mistake to assume, however, that this child is slower than average just because he or she takes a long time to get the hang of something. A Taurean will not interrupt class with half-baked answers and ideas, because he always makes sure that he has thought something through before he speaks. There is a deliberation about him. Mentally he needs to pace himself, to assimilate things at a comfortable speed. Once he has learned something, he files it away carefully, rather than chucking it carelessly into a mental cupboard where he cannot find it again.

Although Taurus is a sign that has a reputation for being self-indulgent, these people will not easily give up on something without a really good try. They may have a problem about getting stuck—for example, they are not able to make that leap out of the math problem—and so they need encouragement to find a way around a situation. Their minds tend to work in a literal way, so they do not see all sides of something. Taureans are able to turn in a regular standard of work; they are not erratic and revel in getting a really good grasp of a subject and displaying their competency. On the other hand, enjoying something is more important to them than dazzling others with their high achievement.

Taurus at Play

Taurus is a sign that tends not to differentiate between work and play because these people enjoy the practical things in life. As children, Taureans enjoy making and building things, working with their hands. Because this sign is ruled by Venus, the planet of beauty, Taurus is associated with creativity, and, in particular, young Taureans might enjoy painting and singing. Generally though, they like to be engaged in activities where they can learn how to do something, and in this respect building a doll's house can be just as much fun as mastering how to mow the lawn.

Young Taureans enjoy the company of other children and do not feel the need to be the center of attention all the time. They can be possessive about their toys, however, and fairly dictatorial about how a game should be played—the rules are the rules! They can be outdoor types, and, although they are not as competitive and exuberant as the fire signs, they enjoy physical activities.

Taurus Child with Aries Parent

If you are the Aries parent of a Taurus child, you are in for some surprises. Aries tends to measure strength of character by the amount of force that is immediately visible. As an Arien yourself, you are gutsy, independent, and full of drive; therefore, you might assume that your gentle, affectionate Taurean child is not made of the same mettle! Quite right, he is not as up front as you, but he is number one in the determination stakes, and if you ever push a bull too far, you come face to face with the famous Taurean stubbornness. Nothing, but nothing, will make a Taurean change his mind once it is made up.

It is best to allow your Taurean child to do things in his or her own time. Even if your collar has turned red with heat, it will still not encourage him to speed up the time it takes to tie his shoelaces. We are working on Taurean Time here, which I am sure you realize has a few more hours in the day than the average Arien clock.

Aries mothers tend to charge on ahead, but a Taurean child is enraptured by what he sees in the world around him. He or she is totally absorbed by watching a squirrel run up a tree or a snail making its silvery trail. He needs to make contact with the world around him on this level because he is an earth sign. Other children can live in their imaginations or in their minds, but the bull needs to touch and feel in order to make sense of life. As an Aries, you need to slow down if you are to comprehend what is important to Taurus.

The bull is so strong-minded that you might be caught unawares by his resoluteness. He is brimming with love and affection, but if you cross him he can turn to stone. Taurus is a fixed sign—that means his ideas are set in cement—and the more Aries tries to push, push, push, the more intractable Taurus becomes. It can be very frustrating! Aries mothers have no alternative but to stop and think before delivering some of their quick-fire suggestions that somehow translate as a red flag to the normally placid bull. Treat your Taurean gently, and you will be amazed to find cooperation follows. But if you insist on playing matador, you will find yourself stopped in your tracks by an immovable bull standing firmly in the way.

Arien fathers tend to keep their children on the move, and they usually have a constant agenda of things to do. Ariens hate inertia, and the bull enjoys relaxing, puttering, ambling. But a ram father with a bull child will be flabbergasted by the total dedication that Taurus can give to a particular task once he has made up his mind to do it. Ariens are quick starters, motivators of other people, and Taureans enjoy finishing things and accomplishing a goal. So an Aries father can fire his Taurean child with an idea and then just leave him or her to it—hours of peace and quiet will follow.

Taurus Child with Taurus Parent

Two bulls can usually stand firm and look each other in the eye with enormous respect and understanding. A Taurean parent will pace life exactly right for his or her Taurean child, and going at the right speed is very important for this sign. Rushing a Taurus through life is certain to give him indigestion; he needs time to assimilate and understand what is going on. Two bulls will usually jog along comfortably together—that is, unless one waves the red flag, in which case the other bull will charge!

The only danger with twin Sun signs is that there is similarity instead of stimulation. The Taurean parent reinforces his own patterns instead of challenging the child to try another way. Taureans love familiarity, so they can really settle into a routine with each other. Fine, but little Taurus is going to be in for a shock when he comes into contact with a trailblazing fire sign, or the mental high jinks of an air sign. He will be unprepared, and that is not an easy state for a Taurean.

Taureans know which side their bread is buttered and, while we're on the subject of food, a Taurean mother will know exactly how to nourish and nurture her little bull. Food is incredibly important to this sign, so at least mother and child are thinking along the same lines here. She makes all the practical things in life a priority. You won't find her with her head in a book and the beds unmade. She establishes a pattern of routine that feels comfortable, if a little predictable. Of course, a young Taurean revels in it all. So what if it's always sausages on Mondays—he likes them! Taureans will never be bored by what they know and love. They will always remember the things they enjoyed doing over and over again as children, and as adults they believe in the sanctity of ritual as a talisman against the uncertainties of life.

Taurean fathers take their role seriously, and chief among the qualities they know they have to offer is their dependability. Little Taurus hero-worships this kind of rocklike steadiness and is well-equipped to model himself on his father's behavior. It is touching to see a full-grown bull with his calf, proudly showing him the proper way to do things. Later on, when little Taurus grows into a young buck, they may lock horns and bellow at each other. Taurean daughters in particular may wish their fathers weren't so old-fashioned! But they are made of the same material, and coming from the same stock—the blue-blood bull line—they desire to uphold the family tradition.

Taurus Child with Gemini Parent

The mix of Taurean earth with Geminian air can produce a little turbulence in the atmosphere! A Taurus child likes to know what is happening, what is the order of play today, whereas Gemini likes to be flexible, adaptable, and open to whatever comes along. Gemini will find himself put on the spot many times in the course of a day by a Taurean who needs to know exactly what and when he is going to eat, and when he can go home, please.

Geminis place a lot of importance on the mind. Not that they consider Einstein's theory of relativity to be a good bedtime story, but they will be waiting with baited breath for baby's first words, because a Gemini relates primarily through communication. It seems strange then for Gemini to discover that actions speak louder than words in the Taurean world. If you can't taste it, touch it, smell it, hear it, or see it, then it doesn't exist. Taurus wants to explore the physical aspects of being, see how things work, pull them apart, and put them back together again. He is an earthy rather than an erudite child, and he must follow this path to be true to himself.

A Gemini mother thinks at the speed of light. She can whiz around the supermarket, shopping for a dinner party and for her aged next-door neighbor while carrying on a conversation with a friend and taking off her child's coat all at the same time, without batting an eyelid. It is hard for her to take into account the slower-turning wheels of her Taurean child's world. The little bull can find it difficult to catch the Gemini mother's attention for long enough to be understood. It seems as if the Gemini mother is a butterfly, constantly on the wing, hard to keep up with and impossible to get hold of much of the time.

Funny how the Taurean child can make a Gemini mother come down to earth. Before you know it, he is reminding her to fill up the gas tank in her car and telling her it's past his bedtime! Taurus is the sign of common sense, and even in childhood those bull hooves are planted firmly on the ground. Although living in the constantly moving world of a Gemini mother is not the most comfortable place for a little bull (it's like trying to set up home on a merry-go-round), Taurus is essentially calm and good-natured. It takes a lot to ruffle him. He finds the breeziness of a Gemini mother enjoyable, amusing, and stimulating, but don't forget supper at six!

It is not easy for a Gemini father to accept that his Taurean child is equally happy mucking about in the garden as on a trip to see the dinosaurs or the adventure park. He needs social interchange and new ideas, while the bull is content just to be. Taureans really are happy with the simple things in life—they don't need Disney to enthrall them when there is so much to interest them in the everyday things going on right under their noses. Taurus needs to find his feet in his own way, and he progresses cautiously. It's a great mistake for a Gemini father to think the bull is slow-witted just because he takes his time to count to ten—he is making sure, that's all.

Taurus Child with Cancer Parent

Taurean children placidly amble along, taking the rough with the smooth, and they are rarely thrown by anything that comes into their path. Because Taurus appears to be outwardly as strong as an ox, many people fail to see the gentle spirit underneath, but a Cancerian mother is specially tuned in to receive the messages that other people miss. She always knows when to give that extra bit of tender loving care. In particular, Taurean children need a great deal of physical contact to reassure them that they are loved. A hug is worth more than a thousand "I love yous" for this sign.

Taurus tends toward the conventional, so a crab parent will not be stretched to accommodate all the latest fads and fashions that change rapidly within the child's school. You won't find a bull child taking the fourth grade by storm with anything unusual in his appearance—at least, not until it has been firmly established as *de rigueur* by the rest of his classmates. Even then, Taurus is ruled by Venus and loathes anything that is ugly or distasteful.

Taurus is a collector, and Cancer is a hoarder, stashing away memories in physical form. The bull and the crab would keep everything if it were possible. If a bull is not amassing an ever-increasing stockpile of stamps or stickers, then he is saving his pocket money with a dedication that would impress your banker. From a young age, Taurus is fascinated by money and loves to count out what's in his piggy bank—a trait that develops into financial flair in adulthood.

A Cancerian mother and Taurean child understand each other very well on the level of the comfort zone. Cancer loves to nurture and look after others, and Taurus laps up all the emotional and physical nourishment he can get. A Cancerian mother makes her home and family the center of her being, providing the kind of fertile soil in which a Taurus can take root! In fact, the only drawback with this combination is that the rooting is so solid, it is incredibly difficult to wretch a Taurus away to grow in another place. When Taurus feels comfortable, he or she is not inclined to look for new pastures. Feeling so utterly content at home with mother, he can see no reason to go even to school. This is where it is important for the Cancer mother to let go of her child and encourage him or her to go out into the world and explore.

A crab father is a softie at heart, but he is protected by a hard outer shell that can make him appear tough on the outside. He often withdraws into this shell, and the Taurus child has to beckon him out of it. A Cancerian father can never resist the call of the bull to come and see what he is doing, and soon he has rolled his sleeves up and gotten his claws in too. A Taurus child and Cancer father adore each other, feel completely at ease together, and share an openness that doesn't even require words.

Taurus Child with Leo Parent

Having a lion as a parent means that you are pretty well obliged to shine at something. Leo parents love to bask in the glory of their children—this inspires fire and air sign children to even greater heights, but can make earth and water children a little anxious. A bull anxious? It sounds incongruous, I know, but the bull is simply not comfortable standing in the limelight. He likes to lounge around in the shade, away from the glaring heat of the spotlight that makes his blood too hot. And when a bull gets hot and bothered, he is likely to go on the rampage. So a Leo parent must understand that not all children are born to go on the stage, and that a Taurean child likes to graze at his own pace.

The other important difference between Leo and Taurus is that Leo likes everything to be special, and Taurus appreciates simplicity. It cuts no ice with a bull that mother has presented the most beautifully decorated castle cake complete with turrets and moat if it is lemon-flavored and not his favorite chocolate! Forget the showmanship as long as the cake's made of the vital ingredients. It's as well to remember that familiarity breeds content, not contempt, for Taurus.

Leo mothers and Taurus children are physical people, so they do give each other a lot of affection and attention, which breaks down the stubbornness that can set in between these determined souls. Touching is the language that soothes them both.

Leo fathers are loving and exuberant, but often seem rather high-flying to a down-to-earth bull. A Taurean is happy to get on with what is in front of him or her rather than looking ahead to see what the possibilities are. This is where a Leo father can really encourage a bull to make the most of himself. Leo will exaggerate his child's capabilities purely because he has confidence in himself and in others. He is of the "of course you can do it" school, while Taurus is naturally cautious and afraid to make a fool of himself.

It might seem almost irritating to a Leo that a Taurean will patiently apply himself to something, going over and overs it again until he has mastered it. But Taurus gets pleasure out of making small steps; he doesn't have to dazzle others with great leaps and bounds. A Leo's pride often stands in the way of being prepared to admit humbly that he will need to practice something before he will be any good at it. It can come as a shock to a Leo father that a small Taurean boy or girl will doggedly stick at something long after he would have thrown in the towel himself.

Taurus Child with Virgo Parent

Virgo sets great store by being sensible and having a good head on one's shoulders, so it is immensely gratifying for a Virgo parent to observe the steadiness of his or her Taurean child. The bull is naturally relaxed—he moves around at an even pace and takes things in his stride; Virgo could do with adopting this tranquil attitude at times—after all, it's only common sense!

Virgo and Taurus agree on all the basics in life. They have a familiar perspective and consider the same things to be important. As earth signs, both parent and child enjoy *doing* things together. Making things, building them, fixing them, sorting them out—they can get totally absorbed in the matter of life. They don't want to just talk about it, they want to do it.

The earthy vibration between a Virgo mother and a Taurus child settles into a harmonious tone of mutual understanding. They both admire practicality and like to take their time getting things just right. Of course, Virgo can be so finicky that nothing is ever completely perfect, but the famous patience of the bull means that the critical eye of his or her mother doesn't ruffle the child. A bull child knows all that fussing and worrying that emanates from his mother is really a sign that she loves and cares about him. Virgo is the original mother hen, forever clucking over her brood.

A Virgo mother is highly organized, and regards her role as mother as a full-time job that must be carried out to the letter. She will set certain standards, rules, and requirements and expect others to abide by them. The bull likes knowing exactly where he stands and what the bottom line is, but he can be quite self-indulgent—all you have to do is look at the cookie jar to find out exactly how much! Virgo is more keen on "what's good for you" and is not above counting every cookie beforehand to make sure you haven't eaten too many. Still, both being so sensible, they can work out a practical solution between them.

It is satisfying for a Taurus child to have a Virgo father who has the time and inclination to spend hours mending a broken toy or painting a bicycle. These two earthy types understand perfectly that there is pleasure in getting absorbed by something practical. Virgo also has an innate talent for teaching and absolutely loves to show other people how to do something properly. Fortunately, Taurus possesses the patience to go through the steps without rushing them or losing interest. In many ways the Taurus child and the Virgo father are a perfect match for each other.

Virgo fathers can be critical—it doesn't matter how much they love someone; no one escapes being given the once-over. Taurus is generally a little more easygoing. The bull will ask himself if something really does matter that much—he wants an easy life. But it is rare for the bull to enter into battle because Taurus has a natural respect for authority.

He will accept his Virgoan father's judgment, even if he privately thinks he is being overly fussy.

Taurus Child with Libra Parent

Librans tend to skip lightly through life trying not to get embroiled in messy issues—in their book, people should be nice to each other at all costs. So although Libra is the sign of justice and the law, when it comes to laying it down, they tend to oscillate. A Libran parent's scales are never in one place for long. This can be dangerous because the bull needs security.

He wants to know that what you say today is what you will still mean tomorrow, next month, and next year. So little Taurus is puzzled when the Libran parent, who was adamant about not allowing him to do something yesterday, has now reconsidered and given him the okay. Librans need to be nice. They can't bear the thought of being unfair, so of course they try to see all sides of the situation and be reasonable. The problem is, Taurus loves constancy more than anything. So he would prefer you to mean no from the bottom of your heart rather than see you flip-flop.

Libra and Taurus are both ruled by Venus, the planet of love and beauty. For Libran mothers, this translates as an innate gracefulness and appreciation of symmetry and style, but Taurus interprets the planet differently—this sign is not the delicately exquisite type. Magnificent, yes. This means that however much a Libran mother attempts to keep her Taurean child looking pristine and perfect, the bull will somehow manage to spoil the effect (in Libra's eyes, that is).

A Libran mother can appreciate most things by means of her eyesight, and she probably invented the line "Look but don't touch." However, the bull lives in a world where mud, butter, and dust are playthings to be smeared, tasted, and touched. In fact, Taurus can give new meaning to the phrase "hands-on experience," because he needs to make actual physical contact with all things before he can really understand them. This is difficult for a Libran mother to comprehend because air signs live in the world of words—tell them something and they comprehend it immediately. Still, Librans are famous for their ability to be able to adjust to others!

A Libran father tends to be rather cerebral, perhaps more interested in teaching little Taurus how to play chess rather than baseball. He does not share the Taurean desire to understand how things work, take them apart, and put them back together again. He is refined and considers handling the nuts and bolts of life to be rather an uncivilized way of spending his time. Nevertheless, a Taurean child brings a Libran father down to earth. Libra has to get involved with the physical world through this child, and it gives him an extra dimension in life.

With incredible charm, Libra knows just what to say to get others to acquiesce without creating a storm. Even an intransigent bull can be completely disarmed by the lightness of the Libran reasoning power. Brilliant Libran negotiating skills avoid the Taurean sulks by providing a little give and take, so the bull is won over by the fairness of the deal, and happiness reigns once more.

Taurus Child with Scorpio Parent

These two are opposites, but look closely at them and you will see they are really two halves of a whole, and that at times they behave similarly although they would never admit it. Taurus is sometimes so bull-headed and Scorpio so passionately determined to have his or her own way that they will accuse each other of being stubborn. In fact, they both are.

A Scorpio parent will challenge the bull to reach for greater self-discovery in everything he or she does. Scorpio believes that life holds a series of challenges that contain important lessons—even setbacks can be viewed as an opportunity to learn about oneself and refine one's perspective. The bull, though, is a more earthbound individual who takes life as he or she sees it. He doesn't want to delve into uncharted waters that might endanger his security. A Scorpio parent needs to respect the Taurean need for creature comforts and the desire to stay at a level that is safe.

A Scorpio mother is always psychologically attuned to her child. She looks deep into his or her soul and worries about the state of the inner psyche. When she is thinking about personal growth, she doesn't mean shoe sizes. What she has to watch is a tendency to invade her child. Taurus will pull up the drawbridge if this happens—he doesn't want to ponder about himself or life when his main priority is to enjoy himself. After all, Taurus is ruled by Venus, the planet of pleasure, and a far cry from Pluto, which is Scorpio's natural domain. If she can just let go, she will find a bridge exists between Taurus and Scorpio that is strong, enduring, and loving. There is room for them to walk along it together, but they must hold hands.

A Scorpio father can also seem rather a mystery to a bull child. It depends on whether he is a silent, still-waters-run-deep type or one who has learned to trust and be open. Once Scorpio has decided not to control himself so much, and therefore not to try and control others, he finds being a father is easier to handle.

A Taurean child needs a relationship that is founded on everyday things, the ordinary events that make the world go around. Taurus is not looking for a superhero father, just one who will play Monopoly (a favorite Taurean game—all that property to accumulate!). So if Scorpio can steal himself away from all the other games of life he plays, he can immerse himself in something simple. His Taurean child can show him that life need not be so complicated—and that is a real gift.

Taurus Child with Sagittarius Parent

The straightforward bull has his four feet planted firmly on the ground, and looking across at his Sagittarian parent, he notices that the horse has four feet as well. Good, they can play together, gamble, and frolic. But the trouble is that the horse has a rider—well, an archer to be exact—who is constantly directing the proceedings, aiming his arrows, and generally calling the shots!

To the bull it can seem as if the archer parent always has one eye on something else, and he is right. Sagittarians are constantly thinking about what tomorrow will bring, whereas the bull is wholly immersed in today. No doubt about it, a Taurean child is entranced by the excitement and energy generated by a Sagittarian, but it also makes him feel giddy. So the archer must slow down his pace. That means adjusting his speed from "fast forward" to "play."

A Taurean child needs the sort of order, pattern, and rhythm in life that is anathema to a spontaneous Sagittarian mother. She prefers not to get bogged down in the daily rituals of life, which is why she has a reputation for being somewhat slapdash, and Sagittarians are the first to admit that housework bores them. Why bother to sweep behind the television set if no one will notice? But little Taurus is practicing with his toy dustpan and likes to see a job well done. Taureans are thorough, and they don't get bored with repetition—"Do it again," they cry. It's really quite an eye-opener for an archer mother.

Sagittarian fathers are often sporty, outdoor types. They are constantly thrusting their children out of the house to get plenty of fresh air as if they are some rare kind of plant species in danger of dying from lack of oxygen. The bull isn't about to hang up his hooves from lack of anything, however, because he is naturally sturdy and robust. The archer will always be impressed by the amount of stamina present in a Taurean child, and he or she has a tremendous amount of staying power, too. Taurus won't whine or complain, and that endears him to an archer father, who is rather hale and hearty, with absolutely no time for malingerers.

The brand of humor that a Sagittarian father possesses can make a Taurean pout. Taurus can take himself rather seriously and certainly doesn't like the joke to be at his expense, but he will laugh until the bulls come home when father is playing the fool. A Sagittarian father can encourage young Taurus to take a risk sometimes, to let rip. It would seem that Sagittarius is more in touch with being a child than Taurus, particularly in the jokes department. But the bull has a thing or two to show his father—just watch him set his mind on something and see the result.

Taurus Child with Capricorn Parent

You could say this combination is a surefire winner, which is true, except that these two belong to the element of earth. Anyway, from the moment of birth, the proud goat knows he has produced one of his own kind, not some head-in-the-clouds air sign or over-the-top fiery type. He feels safe in the knowledge that his offspring possesses the same sense of loyalty, responsibility, and practicality as himself and that his feet are solidly planted on terra firma. From this springs mutual respect, which is the secret ingredient that makes this relationship so special.

Neither a Capricorn parent nor a Taurean child is particularly keen to rush things. They act as if they have all the time in the world, but the amazing thing is that they don't waste a second of it. The bull and the goat are always to be found engaged in some *useful* activity, such as polishing their shoes while watching television.

However, there is an important difference between Taurus and Capricorn that can threaten this cozy scene. Capricorn is a sign that believes in self-discipline, even self-denial, and Taurus is in the other corner—on the side of self-indulgence. Give a bull some sweets, and he won't be able to resist popping every one into his mouth. That will draw a frown across the face of the goat, who remembers being a child who saved up his sweet as a special reward for doing something.

A Capricorn mother is usually hard at work. In many senses she is a professional mother, and because she takes the job so seriously, she appears to be aiming for a seat on the board. She is chief organizer, which suits the bull, who rather enjoys having a set timetable handed out at the beginning of each day. He appreciates an ordered life; it makes him feel settled and contented.

However, Capricorn will blow the whistle when time is up regardless of how much fun the bull is having, and little Taurus wants to enjoy himself as much as possible. When he is involved in something, it is hard to tear him away. But a Capricorn mother is a strict timekeeper and not impressed by tears and tantrums. Not that she's an ogre, but she believes in the power of the word *no.* Taurus is not a rebellious type, and he might sulk a little, but sooner or later he will press his hand into hers, and she will feel the warmth seeping into her soul.

Capricorn is the sign associated with fatherhood. Just as its opposite sign, Cancer, is associated with mothering and nurturing, Capricorn possesses the balancing qualities of fathering and protecting. The goat guides his offspring with a firm hand, watching that they do not step out of line. He is not one to let them get away with anything because he is big on respect for the rules and for himself as a father. A baby bull fits into this kind of environment like a hand fits a glove. Taurus may be a bull, but he is no bucking bronco, so he finds it comforting and supportive to lean on the rigid backbone of his father.

Taurus Child with Aquarius Parent

This relationship contains a kind of reversal of the norm, but then, most Aquarian relationships usually do. The bull child is the cautious, careful one, and the water bearer parent has that wild and wacky tendency to surprise you. So let's not mince words; I have to tell you that surprises make Taureans anxious. They're just not his thing, even if it's an unplanned trip to the seashore. Taurus likes to look forward to something, to count down the days and work out what he is going to do—for that he has to know when he is going to do it.

It can make an Aquarian parent feel somewhat crestfallen when a brainstorm is met by a wet blanket, because this sign loves to keep things exciting and unpredictable. However, the bull child needs constancy, permanency, and security, so what's a water bearer to do? Luckily, Aquarians are born with an incredible amount of understanding for the vagaries of human nature, and they are probably the most tolerant sign in the zodiac. Because of this they are great at getting along with all sorts of people—even a down-to-earth bull. Aquarians can accept that not everyone is the same, and it even gives them a buzz trying to find a solution that will keep both sides happy.

An Aquarian mother leans toward the experimental, a Taurean child to the conventional. It can cause a few problems at sporting events, when little Taurus is in tears because you have embarrassed him by wearing *that* dress, while you thought you were knocking them dead with your version of the modern mother. Taurus is uncomfortable drawing attention to him- or herself, so that means keeping it low-key—even a dowdy mother is preferable to a outrageous one. When his friends come around, don't ask their opinion on drugs or safe sex, and don't serve up that macrobiotic food that's supposed to keep you so healthy but looks so weird. An Aquarian mother may feel restricted by her Taurean child and unable to express her true identity in the mothering role. Yet the gift she has to offer Taurus is to look further than his own nose, to consider other options and to stretch his mind.

Aquarian fathers can have that detached look about them. They are kindly people, but can be just out of reach. That is no good to a Taurus, who needs contact with someone who is 100 percent present, not abstractedly there in body and away somewhere else in mind. But it can be a relief for Aquarius to come back down to earth through this child.

Their relationship can be puzzling to Taurus, who expects his father to tell him the answers to what he wants to know. Things should be simple. But Aquarian fathers encourage individuality, so his answer to little Taurus will often be that he must work out his own solution. Having an Aquarian father prods the bull into action when he or she is inclined to take the easy way out. It may not feel so cozy, but it gets

Taurus to stand on his own two feet and encourages him to develop himself.

Taurus Child with Pisces Parent

It may be surprising, but a bull and a fish get along together very well. To begin with, being a parent can make a Pisces feel like a fish out of water, because so many daily duties dampen his or her soul. And Taurus is very insistent on having his practical needs met. But Pisceans see magic in everything, even the way little Taurus waves his rattle—perhaps he is a budding symphony conductor. Pisceans have the most fertile imaginations. By the time the bull has reached the age of maturity, Pisces has mentally visualized him as the President and Pavarotti—but not at the same time, of course.

For his part, little Taurus is enchanted by a Piscean parent, who can make up such wonderful stories and create something out of nothing. Because Taurus is ruled by the artistic planet Venus, he is open to the poetry that is evident in the life of Pisces, even though as a bull he prefers something a little more solid than poems—building blocks, perhaps. Anyway, these two possess a natural understanding and empathy and seem able to chug along together amiably even though they are quite different.

A Piscean mother with a Taurus child knows just how to soothe that troubled forelock with a kindly word. Taureans love to be pampered emotionally and physically. They lap up all the love that Pisces pours out, and as the givers of the zodiac, Pisces needs to be needed. A Pisces mother is quite different from a fishwife. Piscean mothers sacrifice themselves at the altar of motherhood. Not that this is really necessary with a Taurus. He is easy to please, which is one of the most heart-warming things about him. He is so straightforward that life takes on quite a different hue for a Piscean mother, who is used to swimming in complicated waters. She cannot become confused by this child because

Taurus has such a purity. Simple gestures and plain speaking make the Taurean world go around.

A Piscean father will find his gentle approach is just what is needed to coax the bull out of his or her reluctance. Pisces and Taurus can be compared to water finding a way around a rock in the middle of a stream. Water may look weak in comparison to such a solid object (and Taureans can be defiantly stubborn), but a Piscean father will always find an opening. In fact, Taurus can grow quite panicky when he is in one of his stuck-in-the-mud moods; he cannot imagine how to shift direction, and so he digs himself deeper and deeper into a hole. A Piscean father has the imagination and ability to encourage Taurus to accomplish the seemingly impossible. He soothes away the fear of the unknown and allows Taurus to feel secure in the face of challenge.

Sun in Gemini Child

22 May–21 June

THE TWINS

Qualities to Look for and Nurture in Your Gemini Child

A quick mind and ability to communicate

As an air sign, Gemini relates to the mind. Life revolves around thoughts, ideas, and the expression of them. In the early years, Gemini needs plenty of mental stimulation in order to stretch and exercise his or her naturally alert mind. This child is a born communicator, and his curiosity about everything around him means he is constantly asking questions and building up knowledge, which he then needs to communicate to other people.

The capacity to do several things at once

The versatility of Gemini shows itself in adulthood as a talent for handling many things simultaneously. Gemini is able to divide his or her attention and actually enjoys playing one thing off against another. It is symptomatic of the duality of this sign: One thing is never enough. In childhood, this restlessness is evident in the way little Gemini gets bored with a particular activity. His interest is often distracted. Although too much fragmentation can result in an inability to concentrate, it is important to appreciate that the butterfly mind also contains the gift of cross-pollination of ideas.

A natural sociability and interest in people

Gemini enjoys other people and even in the early years has a full calendar of people to see and places to go. This child simply doesn't like being on his own—he is always on the lookout for his twin. It is rare for Gemini to be shy, and he or she normally has enough self-confidence to be able to make friends easily and to get on with many different types of people.

A fresh, youthful approach to life

Gemini is the sign most associated with the qualities of being a child. Even though they radiate brightness and cleverness, Geminis always retain a naiveté. There is nothing jaundiced or cynical about Geminis; they look with wonderment at the world and the people and things in it. There is a vital part of them that never grows up and always remains a mischievous child, playing tricks on people and acting skittishly. This innocent inner child is an important ingredient of the adult Gemini personality.

Gemini Boys

Your Gemini son can be a delightful Peter Pan, mesmerizing you with his agility and brilliance. Yet, like Peter, he tests your patience by flying just out of reach and refusing to come down to earth. Gemini boys will turn tricks with an impishness that both delights and infuriates. They can run so fast and talk so quickly that they leave you behind, and Geminis love to have people chase after them.

Verbal skills come easily to him; he has an astounding ability to pick up what is happening around him and a well-tuned ear. In fact, he is a natural mimic and full of fun with it. Just listening to him provides hours of amusement as he practices his after-dinner speaking around the kitchen table. Geminis are masters at holding people's attention with their wit. This child can recount an everyday event in such a way that you are spellbound.

His interests are many and varied. It's soccer one day and the flute the next. He finds it difficult to stick to one thing and enjoys activities that involve other people. A sign of when he is nearing his boredom threshold is when he starts to fidget. Geminis simply cannot sit still if they are not interested in what they are doing. They seek constant mental stimulation, both from their surroundings and from you as a parent.

Gemini Girls

She is a pixie, enchanting you with her repertoire of stories and sayings. She is so entertaining that you might overlook the fact that her mind is so alert that she is always right on the button and doesn't miss a trick. It is always a Gemini who will notice what is happening right in front of their noses while other people are abstractedly dreaming. Your Gemini daughter is an information gatherer; she needs to know what you think about everything from the next-door neighbor to the reason why the sun disappears at night. Her curiosity about the world is endless.

Miss Gemini is a changeable child. Gemini is the sign of the twins, and you could be forgiven for thinking you had two of her because she can switch in the wink of an eye from being an angel to a devil, a quiet mouse to a stampeding elephant, or from an excitable kitten to a sourpuss. It's all part of the Gemini personality, and like a magician, she will keep you guessing.

She loves games that stretch her mind and all forms of movement. Gemini is the type of child who can ski downhill at the age of five. Her mental and physical agility and sense of coordination are superb, so she can master the intricacy of a computer or the plot of a story at the speed of light. Her mind is constantly ticking, wondering why, how, when, what for? If she doesn't have something to chew on mentally, she literally feels empty and starved. A Gemini daughter needs to be given plenty of food for thought.

Gemini at School

As Gemini is so mentally alive, the good news is that this child enjoys learning. The bad news, unfortunately, is that his or her mind often reacts to formalized education methods by skipping over them, not paying attention, and being distracted. The hardest thing for a Gemini is to stay focused for long periods, because his or her mind starts to wander on to something more interesting than the chemical formula for hydrogen. Because he makes connections between words with such ease, his mind jumps from one subject to another sometimes without his even realizing it.

It is often the case that Gemini won't develop an aptitude for any one particular subject over another—he or she is a jack of all trades, enjoying the variety. In many ways the curriculum at school suits him perfectly—he might be drawing maps, doing woodwork, learning French, and playing baseball all in a morning. Not many jobs offer such a diversity of interest. He loves the constant moving and changing.

Because Geminis appear to assimilate knowledge so readily, they can fool you into believing they are making better progress than is really the case. In fact, they tend to skim the surface, picking up a few bits here and there without really concentrating. Homework and exams are definitely not Gemini's favorite occupations; he often just can't see the point of them at all and hates the discipline of having to work on subjects he would rather avoid. Nevertheless, he often finds he can turn out answers without much effort because he always has something to say!

Gemini at Play

Any parent who has a Gemini child in the household must quickly realize that there are really two of them. That means two minds to keep stimulated, two pairs of hands to keep occupied, and if Gemini gets bored, then you are in for double trouble. This sign enjoys doing things with other people. He is not one to sit for hours on end amusing himself; he prefers company. Although Gemini is amazingly agile and therefore often good at sports, he or she is not hugely competitive, and playing the game is more important than winning.

Geminis are often good with their hands. They tend to lack patience, but enjoy creative activities that do not bog them down. With Geminis, it is all about deftness, movement, dexterity. Being an air sign, they love mental amusements, games that allow opportunities to outsmart their opponents, or that require a high degree of mental alertness. And they love communication in all its forms, of course—that includes television, films, and just plain talking!

Gemini Child with Aries Parent

Gemini adds fuel to Aries fire. In other words, Gemini stimulates Aries into action; not that Aries needs much stimulation, because the ram is rarely at rest, but having a Gemini child is not usually a peaceful occupation! For a start there are the constant questions—"What are you doing?," "Why are you doing it?" It makes Aries think; he is forced to justify his actions, and this goes against his basic nature because he is used to just getting on and doing things without having to explain himself.

Generally, though, these two signs feel at ease with each other. They are both restless by nature, although with Gemini the scattering is more of the mind than the body. The beauty of this combination is that they both understand the itchy feet syndrome and can take off in new directions together. The aspect of parenthood that an Aries dreads the most is the possibility of being limited and tied down to a mundane routine. Therefore, Aries is delighted to meet in the Gemini child the curiosity of a kindred spirit.

An Aries mother with a Gemini child is comparatively free to live her life as adventurously as before his or her arrival, because Gemini is an eminently transportable child. There is nothing Gemini loves more than being taken off to see people and places. He is like a bird flitting from tree to tree—as long as there is something interesting to look at and movement in the air, he is a happy child. Little Gemini won't be bored with an Aries mother because she is one of life's doers. She generates heat and energy around her; there is always something going on.

She usually runs a tight schedule, because there is not much leeway in the Aries timetable for distractions. A Gemini child is fascinated by his environment and cannot keep on the straight line of his goal-directed mother. He is bound to waver a bit and go off the track to look at whatever catches his fancy, so she will have to keep reeling him in.

Aries fathers are the spontaneous types—in a way they call Gemini's bluff. Gemini is forever throwing out lots of ideas and suggestions, and Aries will suddenly say, "So you want to go to the seashore today? Okay, come on, everyone in the car, let's go!" There is never a dull moment, with the spark produced by the combination of Aries and Gemini aiding and abetting them both into spreading their wings as much as possible.

Gemini Child with Taurus Parent

Water and oil are usually a difficult mix. Gemini is the water wanting to express ideas, and Taurus is the oil, more concerned with the practical matters of life. In terms of the purpose of life, Gemini wants to be involved in communication; he or she is a soul with something to say. And for

Taurus, the purpose of life is to sustain, preserve, and organize resources to the best of his or her ability.

As with any other people born under signs that are next door to each other on the astrological wheel, one often finds that there are points of similarity when the whole natal chart is examined. So, on closer inspection it is probable that the water and oil have a lot more in common than was at first suspected. Also, the sign of the bull and the sign of the twins are a necessary balance for each other. "It's all very well having all these ideas," cries the bull, "but will they really work?" Gemini replies, "There is always something new to learn, so let's be flexible." Within the parent–child relationship the energies of these two signs rub off on each other over the years, so they start to understand one another.

A Taurus mother places a great deal of value on practicality, common sense, and creature comforts. The wheels of her life generally spin at a set pace. For a Gemini child, she can seem like the immovable object, and she can certainly be stubborn when it comes to not changing her mind! Gemini can leap about, make a song and dance, and try every trick in the book to get her to make a detour from her routine, and she will just smile benignly and carry on as usual.

Her philosophy is "one thing at a time," and she finds the constant barrage of Geminian mental gymnastics rather uncomfortable. Gemini is always trying to ferret out information. He or she lives life on a need-to-know basis, which can be quite wearing for a Taurean mother, who tends to take things as they come without analyzing all the whys and wherefores. She is a rock around which he spins, dazzling her with his performance. She is uplifted by the free spiritedness of Gemini because it releases the silt at the bottom of her being. And little Gemini feels protected and looked after by a Taurean mother. He is held and contained, and he knows that after all his mental and physical wanderings, there is always a safe place to come back to.

The bull may look fierce, but as a father he is kindly and indulgent toward the children. It is only when Gemini starts running around hither and thither like a will-o'-the-wisp that he starts to take umbrage. Taurus can sit and concentrate for a long time, and it's hard for him to understand the Geminian butterfly mind, but he can encourage little Gemini to stick at something instead of flying off in another direction. Taurus has the gift of being able to give time and patience to other people, and this soothes the Gemini child. He realizes that if he stays around, he can learn something.

Gemini Child with Gemini Parent

A household with two sets of Gemini twins in it can seem a little crowded—there are four of them to start with, never mind the other members of the family! Gemini is ruled by the planet Mercury, and this mercurial energy enables people born under this sign to change tack in a split second. This duality manifests as a changeability that keeps other people guessing—the twins keep replacing each other. With a Gemini child and parent, at least they understand and accept this phenomenon as being perfectly normal.

Their minds are tuned into the same wavelength, creating an impressive double act. They twist and turn together in harmony like a pair of ice skaters, but they can also tie each other up in knots. Geminis have a nervy, restless quality, and internally they are like a kaleidoscope, constantly changing colors and patterns. It is hard for them to find a still place inside themselves.

A Gemini mother looks on the whole concept of parenthood as an exciting learning process. She is devoted to helping her child develop and to stretching the mental horizons of her little Gemini. Since Gemini is not too hot on domestic responsibilities, she can find the early nonverbal years rather wearing. She relates more easily to the mind than the body, which she considers to be just a container for the precious workings of the brain. However, she doesn't have to remain stuck in earth-mother mode for long, as her Gemini child is itching to communicate. A Gemini child tries to talk before he can walk, and words are a fascination to him.

Because Geminis are not comfortable with the emotional

side of life, they often rationalize everything. Emotion is not their natural domain—they don't want to get bogged down in feelings that threaten to overwhelm them. Their solution to problems is to talk about them—objectively, of course. Two Geminis together tend to encourage each other to live in their heads. A Gemini mother takes pride in the fact that her child can read a newspaper, and the quality of their relationship is mentally alive; they are forever talking animatedly, but feelings are not often part of the discussion. Little Gemini takes to this environment like a duck to water; it feels fine to him. Later on, though, he might have trouble relating to people who are more emotionally oriented.

A Gemini father uses parenthood as the perfect excuse to be a child again. There he is playing with the train set and the computer games. He is able to relate to children because he has never lost his boyish sparkle and ability to have fun. It is Peter Pan revisited. It is wonderful for little Gemini to experience this kindred soul, but at times there can be a confusion of roles. Sometimes the child really needs him to be a solid father figure, and Gemini likes to disappear from situations that threaten his freedom. He leaves other people to sort out all the boring things like bedtimes, but with his superb ability to communicate, he can dream up a pretty good bedtime story.

Gemini Child with Cancer Parent

The crab finds the Gemini character entices him or her toward the outer world. Normally, Cancer dances between the inner private depths of the sea and the brilliant light of the land. He chooses to go back and forth, in and out, as the mood takes him. But Gemini is a child of the world, totally entranced by what is going on out there. He or she skips along from one thing to another and has no need to fathom the emotional waters that Cancer finds so intriguing. Unless the full natal chart reveals that the Gemini child has some planets in Cancer, or that the Cancerian parent has some planets in Gemini (which is often the case with these next-door-neighbor Sun signs), they see life essentially from different perspectives.

Cancer is the sign associated with motherhood, and the qualities of nurturing, protecting, and caring for others spill out of those born under this sign. However, little Gemini feels quite suffocated unless he can remove himself and breathe some air—he is an air sign, after all. A Cancer mother has to allow Gemini space to discover himself all on his own, away from her watchful eye.

It can come as quite a shock to the Cancer mother that in fact Gemini has not dissolved into floods of tears in the Halloween fun house or while watching a horror film, but finds the macabre just "interesting." She had better put her cotton wool away, because this child does not want to be wrapped up in it. Gemini, in fact, is a spectator of life; he doesn't get emotionally involved in its contents unless he chooses. Cancer cannot help getting pulled into feelings because life tugs at the Cancerian heartstrings.

The big Daddy crab may look fierce, brandishing his pincers and trying to convince you that he is all hard shell, but underneath he is soft, fleshy, and sensitive. There are two sides to him, something that Gemini can relate to easily because inside this child is a pair of twins—sparkling in an amazing double act. Gemini constantly calls his Cancerian father out of his shell to look at this or that and tell him all about it. Even if at times the crab would undoubtedly prefer to withdraw from the hurly-burly, Gemini somehow manages to lure his father out. He cannot help but be drawn into the excitement of it all.

Gemini Child with Leo Parent

Gemini needs to know about everything, and Leo can give the impression of knowing everything, so this is a brilliant learning combination. A Leo parent takes pride in watching the bud of the Gemini child's mind unfold into a flower. It appeals to the Leonine sense of creativity, and Leo glows at the thought of producing anything as clever as a little Gemini, who is a masterpiece indeed.

Yet before the lion can sit back to savor the delights of basking in the reflected glory of little Gemini, his child has his own ideas. And this is the crux of the issue. Gemini will not just learn the Leo lines and meekly perform in the show, he wants to be up there ad-libbing, making it up as he goes along and expressing is own ideas—in other words, trying to upstage Leo, and no lion will ever put up with being relegated to second fiddle. Gemini will have to pay homage to the king of the jungle and eat a slice of humble pie, along with the other ten signs of the zodiac who are subjects in the Leo kingdom. In the Leo household, the lion reigns supreme, and Gemini had better believe it.

A Leo mother will feed knowledge to her Gemini child like a French chef. She will teach him about the best of everything, because Leo will not touch anything that is of poor quality. Gemini, though, is the type who will sometimes sneak out for a hamburger to balance the Leo *haute cuisine*—he is hungry to know about life at all levels. All the ordinary, mundane things that do not make the Leo grade are still a source of fascination to Gemini.

It is a learning process for both of them. The Leo mother will be brought into contact with things she would have naturally dismissed, and the Gemini child will be encouraged always to aim to be the best, to gather himself and his thoughts into making one glorious achievement instead of his usual round of attempts and abandonments. "Did you try your best?" she will ask him, and little Gemini will regale her with his story of how he was there in the classroom when suddenly, "You wouldn't believe what happened . . ."

The Leo father is usually generous to a fault with his time, his affection, and his money. He provides a sort of hothouse environment in which he expects his little seedlings to flourish. And Gemini is rarely a disappointment—his spiritedness never fails to draw attention. Leo, however, is a powerful authority figure, and he believes in bringing Gemini to heel. In fact, the Geminian mind can never be tamed by anyone.

He is born to play freely in the mind, to experiment with different ideas, and explore many mental avenues. So, although he may pay royal lip service to his father's ways, he must pursue his own path, which may have a few surprising twists and turns in it, but it takes him in the direction of himself.

Gemini Child with Virgo Parent

Gemini and Virgo are signs that share Mercury as their ruler, so both are tuned into the mind as their primary reference point. However, as an earth sign, Virgo thinks more along straight and narrow lines, while Gemini skips around and takes detours. Traditionally, Gemini and Virgo are apt to rub each other the wrong way because Gemini is the errant child of the zodiac and Virgo the sensible parent, but they share a love of mental stimulation and always have something in common, besides, of course, a great deal to say to each other.

The difficulty with the Virgo–Gemini combination is that the Gemini child begins to feel judged by his or her critical Virgo parent and becomes nervous that nothing he does will ever be good enough. And although the incessant Gemini chatter can give the impression that he is bursting with confidence, he often lacks self-assurance. The reason he darts around has something to do with an inner worry that life will catch up with him if he stays in one place, so he won't be caught as a moving target. And Virgo can put Gemini on the run, ducking and diving to avoid being examined. Of course, Virgoans don't mean to make people uncomfortable under their microscope; it's just that they can't help noticing every detail and commenting on it.

The Virgo mother leaves no stone unturned in her effort to be perfect. She feels guilty if she suspects for one moment that her child is not receiving 100 percent of the best attention, education, and practical caring that she deems is his due. But a Gemini child does not share Virgo's judgmental attitude and immensely high standards. He is not born to sort through the minutiae of life; he simply looks at what he is interested in and does not care about the rest. It looks slapdash to Virgo, careless and wasteful to skip through life in this way. But the other side of it is that Virgo would love to let go of all the habitual worry and just be absorbed in the moment instead of planning for tomorrow. If she lets herself enter the Gemini world, the Virgo mother feels lighter and freer; she remembers what it is to play instead of work. And Gemini needs her earthiness, too. She has so much stability to offer this airy Gemini soul; she plants his feet firmly on the ground so he won't fly away with all his ideas and schemes.

When it comes to explaining how things work and why, the Virgo father achieves top marks. He can be relied on to offer an informed opinion on just about anything little Gemini wants to know about—and, quite honestly, a Gemini child can make you feel like a contestant on *Jeopardy.* But Gemini will probably take in only about 20 percent of the answer, because his mind isn't geared to the kind of detail that fascinates Virgo. He wants to know a little about everything, just a taste, not a full meal. And if a Virgo father is truly to understand and support his Gemini child, he may have to accept that his handwriting is beautiful, even if not all the *i*'s are dotted.

Gemini Child with Libra Parent

How wonderful that the scales have produced twins! They may not look as if they belong to the same family, but scales and twins have a lot in common. They are both air signs, so they both belong to the same astrological family that values the mind over anything else in life. So, of course, to Libran parents it seems entirely fair and reasonable that they should be blessed with a little bundle of air. But air is a highly changeable element and is not always crystal clear. When it is hot, it produces steam; when it is cold; it becomes misty and foggy. When turbulent, air turns into a howling gale, and when calm, into a balmy breeze. So even in their mutual airiness, Gemini and Libra can sometimes surprise and confuse each other.

Mirror, mirror on the wall, the Libran mother wants to be the fairest of them all. In her view, everything should be beautiful, pleasant, and harmonious, and little Gemini appears to be an easy child who helps her Libran scales to remain evenly balanced. The only extreme in this child is his or her insatiable curiosity about life, which sometimes impinges on her beautifully manicured world. Gemini is literally into everything, and cannot resist diving into whatever attracts his attention.

It can make Libra feel messy and overloaded to have this child with so many fingers in so many pies. There are always choices and options around for a Gemini, and Libra is congenitally indecisive. But a Libran mother is able to accommodate the needs of other people. Not in the sacrificial style of Pisces, but just because it makes her happy to make other people happy. She likes to give pleasure because then there are no arguments to upset her equilibrium. So she is able to indulge Gemini's many whims and passing fancies, and discuss anything from global warming to gingerbread men. Which is just as well, because the Gemini mind can flip from the universe to food in the wink of an eye.

A Libran father is entranced by the sparkle of Gemini. For him, looks are of primary importance, and he adores the radiance of this bright-eyed and bushy-tailed child. The only problem with such alertness and aliveness is that Libra finds it hard to relax in the face of it, and at heart he can be a bit of a lounge lizard. Gemini pushes him out of his inertia, makes him do something or at the very least think and talk about it.

Gemini Child with Scorpio Parent

Scorpio is a bottomless sea, while Gemini is a boat skimming along the surface. They are made of different energy, but they can still share life together. As long as that Scorpionic sea doesn't try to tug the boat down to the depths, and the Gemini boat doesn't make too many waves, they can coexist in harmony and respect each other.

Scorpio has to accept that a Gemini child is quite happy on the surface of life; there is so much to explore here that he has no wish to look beyond. Scorpio, though, as a deeply penetrating sign, is never content for long with the superficialities; the scorpion needs to know more, to feel more, to understand more. Maybe the ultimate understanding is that everyone is born to experience a different facet of life, and Scorpio must allow Gemini to be himself.

It is the Scorpio mother's special gift that she is able to divine exactly what is going on in her child's mind, and that is no mean feat, because where Gemini is concerned there are usually a hundred fragmented thoughts whirling around at once. This child is as changeable as the wind, and as fast. He is undoubtedly one of life's bright sparks, doing a brilliant impression of a happy little sunbeam, until the dark clouds form and he becomes a veritable thunderstorm. Just as his caring, sharing mother has gotten a grip on the pain of it all, the storm rolls away, and dazzling light shines through again. What was the matter? He can't remember a thing about it, but can you come and have a look at something with him? With Gemini the other twin is always waiting in the wings, ready to swap places. Which one is which is hard to tell because they melt into each other, and there is never one true identity for Gemini. Even in childhood, he plays with being so many characters, and the Scorpio mother must get the point—it is playful, and to Gemini life is a game—quite an eye-opener for this sensitive lady who holds such reverence for the inner meaning of life.

Little Gemini sees his or her father as a mystery man. Scorpio always plays his cards close to his chest, never revealing himself unless he chooses. And Gemini is itching to know who he really is, wanting to see what is on those cards. The amazing thing is that before you know it, Gemini has distracted his attention enough to take a peek. This child's sheer innocence and impishness has somehow permeated the Scorpio barrier so that the defenses come down. A remarkable feat, this, but then Gemini moves so quickly that he can often seem like a magician.

Before he knows it, the Scorpio father is chatting away quite openly like a Gemini himself. But lest he forget himself, Scorpio will firmly close the door again and ensure that his power and dignity remain intact—he knows how to freeze the flibbertigibbet energy of Gemini with a look. And sometimes Gemini needs to calm down and contain himself like his Scorpio father.

Gemini Child with Sagittarius Parent

Sagittarius has met his match here with the arrival of little Gemini, complete with enough mental energy to bedazzle the archer and put him off his stroke. When you put these two together, you get enthusiasm. Well, a Sagittarian parent is always the enthusiastic type, egging on his or her offspring to go one better. But with Gemini, you have a lot of fuel to add to the Sagittarian fire, and the result can be mind-blowing. Just watching these two together is enough to exhaust any earth or water sign, but Gemini and Sagittarius simply don't have the time to worry about sticks-in-the-mud and wet blankets anyway. Ever onward and upward, they revel in making plans to set the world on fire.

In his early years, Gemini will receive all the encouragement he needs from his Sagittarian mother. The archeress is a supremely optimistic lady whose farsightedness allows her to overlook any present-day faults in the hope of a better future. Sagittarius is the opposite number on the astrological wheel to Gemini. The twins can get bogged down in detail, sidetracked, backtracked, and distracted by every other track but the path that leads them into the future. Having an archer mother riding along beside him means that little Gemini can't meander his way along but is scooped up and shown what to aim for. It seems to concentrate his mind wonderfully! Sagittarians are tuned into the purpose of life and seem to be able to help Gemini pour his mental energy into something worthwhile.

It's no good trying to get hold of an archer mother and her Gemini child at home, so try phoning the sports club or local library instead. They are always out together doing things, finding out things, and socializing. By the time you collect together all their mother and children friends, you are well on the way to forming a small army.

Gemini and Sagittarius both need a lot of freedom and independence from the daily routine of family life. Together they can travel and explore to their hearts' content. Sagittarians have a very relaxed attitude toward child rearing—they basically treat children like small adults, dispensing with the oughts and shoulds and letting them get on with it. And Gemini really appreciates the opportunity to meet life without being smothered and overprotected.

Hale and *hearty* are words that are often used to describe male Sagittarians. They admire those who are prepared to go for it. Gemini may have plans, but he or she doesn't always want to put them into action. For Gemini, talking about it is virtually the same as doing it. The father archer can entice little Gemini out of his head and into the world, to make things real. Being a little short on staying power himself, Sagittarius also understands the Geminian need for constant movement, but he shows him how to aim at other targets instead of just changing for change's sake.

Gemini Child with Capricorn Parent

"Is there no end to this banter?" asks the goat, who often does not find it necessary to talk, especially when he is undertaking the serious business of climbing a mountain. A goat wouldn't dream of opening his mouth to comment on something so banal as potato peelings. They are simply not worthy of consideration, let alone discussion, but little Gemini on the other hand is fascinated—why are they different shapes? Why is the skin different from the potato? The Capricorn world is divided up into what is Important and what is Unimportant. Gemini's curiosity knows no bounds or relativity. To him, everything and everyone in the world is equally interesting—but only for a short time!

The nanny goat mother tends to keep a rigid schedule—well, that's the plan, anyway. Geminis are allergic to schedules, so there can be a bit of a contest over who will do what and when. It's amazing how quickly a small Gemini can "forget" what you told him, even though mentally he is as lively as a cricket. And even if Gemini says he will do something, with the best of intentions he can't help getting distracted in another direction just at the crucial moment; one way of putting it would be to say that priorities are not his thing.

It can seem to Gemini that his Capricorn mother comes from another planet, and quite literally she does! Her sign is ruled by Saturn, which is heavy on self-discipline, structure, and order. She has achieved everything that she has in life through application and perseverence. So to her, Gemini can appear to have a somewhat casual attitude to life—the planet Mercury (Gemini's ruler) is an altogether different kettle of fish. The Mercurial world is one that spins in a constant buzz of communication, where all the balls are in the air, and some never come down to earth. She will get used to the Geminian chatter in time—Capricorns come around to most things in the end, but they never rush. Little Gemini will learn to be a bit more precise about his *p*'s and *q*'s, never mind the other letters of the alphabet. Ultimately, Gemini benefits from contact with his level-headed energy. He will wriggle a bit and pull a few faces, but he'll be glad in the end that his mother showed him a little sense and sensibility to add to his repertoire of tricks.

Goats are cautious creatures, and father billy goats especially so. But Capricorns actually live out a reverse age process, appearing to be more serious when they are young and loosening up later in life. Having a child can be a major turning point to trigger more flexibility in a Capricorn. Gemini is a sign that is especially resonant with childlikeness, and the Capricorn father can suddenly realize what he has missed when he beholds the spontaneity and ease of expression in this child. It is as if Gemini can provide the oil to mobilize his stiff joints, and gradually he warms to the idea of being a father, which also allows him to experience the joy of being a child—perhaps for the first time in his life.

Gemini Child with Aquarius Parent

Gemini and Aquarius meet on the mind level and like each other immediately. They both feel comfortable fanned by the cool breeziness of each other, and together they can conduct question and answer sessions to their hearts' content. As a parent, Aquarius extols the philosophy of life's being too short for dishonesty, fear, and emotional entrapment. The water bearer will always encourage Gemini to look beyond what is in front of his or her nose, to think broadly, and to travel lightly through life.

To tune into the Aquarius wavelength, you have to be prepared to change frequencies. Sometimes Aquarians can appear to be out of reach, and, although this is the sign of friendship and is usually surrounded by people, Aquarians can often feel detached and somewhat lonely. Becoming a parent poses the issue of closeness and togetherness for Aquarians. They like to establish relationships on their own terms and won't fit into the role of husband, wife, father, or mother according to the gospel of "what other people expect." In fact, Aquarius will usually translate most family relationships into the bond of friendship, because this is what they understand.

So a small Gemini will begin to see his or her Aquarian parent primarily as a buddy, a like mind. And being an air sign himself, Gemini can appreciate this more than most. He trusts and responds easily to people who are thinkers and talkers, and the inventive originality of Aquarius delights him.

Aquarian mothers often operate a rather haphazard schedule within the home. In their book, rules are made to be broken, so they won't turn a hair if little Gemini refuses to eat his greens or go to bed before finishing his video game. More important things occupy the Aquarian mind than enforcing regulations and getting his or her child to conform. Gemini is not a natural rebel, but he loves to feel that life is made up as it goes along rather than being determined in advance by routine. Certainly, his Aquarian mother gives him plenty of scope for his kind of creativity, and this in turn feeds the Gemini mind, which is continually thirsting for stimulation and variety.

The Aquarian father, too, is a man identified with what he thinks rather than how he feels. That is fine in the Gemini scheme of things, because these people are not primarily tactile like the earth signs, or emotional like the water signs. Gemini needs to know how to relate to others socially and intellectually rather than emphatically. The water bearer father is distanced from the ebb and flow of emotional tides—he can communicate logic, rationality, and reason, and Gemini laps it all up, adding to the reservoir of knowledge and learning that is his unique resource.

Gemini Child with Pisces Parent

Geminis can sometimes feel they are drowning when they are forced to float in the water of emotions. Yet these waters are the natural habitat of Piscean fish, who suffocate when exposed to the air, which is the element of Gemini. We can see at a glance here that the internal dynamics of Gemini and Pisces are markedly different. However, before jumping to the inevitable conclusion of incompatibility, it is worth considering that what these signs may have to give is a valuable insight into what makes each other tick. As the twelfth and final sign of the zodiac, Pisces can feel compassion for all that has gone before on the astrological wheel of life. Fish are not the types to throw something away because it is not a perfect fit; they see value in all experience and levels of being. Gemini is essentially open-minded. Gemini may not wallow in feelings like Pisces, but he or she will attempt to understand other people, because Gemini appreciates the differences rather than the sameness of all things.

As a young child, Gemini crawls around bursting with

curiosity and wanting to find out what makes everything in the world work. And Gemini never gets tired of asking questions, which is why he remains essentially a child forever. At sixty, the mercurial matter in the Geminian brain is as lively and irrepressible as ever, bubbling over with information that other signs may consider inconsequential but that is of unending fascination to Gemini. Laying good foundations for this inquiring mind is so important. Mentally, Gemini needs to be stretched and exercised if he is to know himself, and his role in the universal play.

A Piscean mother is the sensitive type, who tends to imagine that all people are emotionally paper-thin and therefore vulnerable and in constant need of her protection. However, the air signs are the least likely to crumble in distress. They can explain most things away and just take a step back when it suits them. The Gemini child is therefore a revelation to a Piscean mother. He is chirpy and breezy and will not bamboozle his mother with demands for emotional attention. He is far more likely to cry to be put down than to be picked up—he has usually spotted something very interesting *over there.* So mama Pisces will have to practice a literal and psychological letting go because little Gemini really doesn't want to hang on to her apron strings.

Mentally, Gemini can be very demanding—especially for Pisceans, who are often content to accept things and drift along without questioning the whys and wherefores. A Piscean father will be hounded out of his reverie (because all Pisceans are dreamers on the quiet) and made to answer Gemini's twenty questions. With Gemini it is impossible not to take notice of what is going on around you, so you get used to looking at life in a different way. It's best to jot down a few mental notes, because you will probably get tested on your recall and opinions later!

Sun in Cancer Child

22 June–23 July

THE CRAB

Qualities to Look for and Nurture in Your Cancer Child

Instinctively recognizing how to look after other people

CANCER IS EMOTIONALLY ATTUNED TO THE NEEDS OF OTHERS. The sensitivity and caring nature of this sign enabled Cancerians to spot when other people need their help and understanding. Cancerians have a gentleness and kindness that enables them to reach out to others emotionally. As a sign, they need to be needed and thrive on having an outlet for their nurturing instincts. Friendships, family, pets, projects, and, in later life, business and outside interests as well as the home all receive the special attention that Cancer is capable of giving. The wider the net of people and things that require their protection and support, the more fulfilled they feel.

Commitment to home and family, attachment to roots

Basically, Cancer needs to feel a sense of belonging, and the more he feels he belongs, the more secure he will be. The crab needs to have familiar objects and people around him in order to be comfortable, as he or she tends to retreat in the face of too much that is unknown. There is a fine balance between his intrinsic attachment to his family (and particularly his mother) and an ability to put down roots successfully in later life. In the years he is growing up, a Cancerian can get totally absorbed in his family, which hinders his ability to meet the world on his own terms as an adult. On the other hand, he suffers terribly if the bonds of attachment are severed too soon, or he feels left out in the cold during childhood. Later in life, he will be driven to find the security he needs and will continually look for the missing bonding that is so vital for his well-being.

A perception of the subtleties of life, a vivid imagination and intuition

A Cancer child is able to relate to the inner world of imagination, feelings, and intuition more easily than rational, logical thought. In other words, he is subjective rather than objective, and he tends to base opinions and ideas around what he feels at the time. As a parent of a Cancerian child, it is important to help him to differentiate between thinking and feeling, so he will eventually learn to stand back from his own emotions. However, the fine quality of his or her ability to bypass logical thought and just "know" something is not to be underestimated. Encouraging Cancerians to listen to their inner voice helps them to value their insight.

The ability to move between introvert and extrovert modes of behavior

Crabs are amphibian creatures. They can exist on the land or in the water, and this ability is reflected in the children born under this sign as an ebbing and flowing, between wanting to be out there where it's happening and needing to be securely wrapped up in their own privacy. In childhood, a Cancerian can be helped to value both sides of his personality and to respect his own natural rhythm that dictates (although not in a logical way) whether he wants to be outside or inside his shell.

The sign of Cancer is ruled by the Moon, which is continually passing through phases of fullness, when it is seen brightly, and newness, when it seems to disappear. Cancerians are strongly in tune with the cycles of the Moon and can experience a change in their emotions that other people may interpret as moodiness. The tides of their inner life are constantly turning, and you can no more ask them to remain in one state than you could ask George Washington to tell a lie. So really, the message for a young Cancerian is that it is okay to feel differently at different times and to accept his or her sensitivity rather than fight it.

Cancer Boys

He will always be a gentle soul even though he can cover it up with the hardest of protective shells. Early childhood is vital in allowing this boy to come to terms with his own sensitivity. Ensuring that kindness, compassion, and helpfulness are valued in your family will enable him to express his feelings with ease, instead of having to hide behind a gruff exterior.

Cancerian boys are especially close to their mothers. Although you wouldn't want him to be permanently hooked up with you as a fifty-year-old Mama's boy, it is a wonderful preparation for his adult relationships with women to have such a solid foundation of closeness as a child. In fact, Cancerian boys really do enjoy family life and love their homes and all home comforts—so much so that your home can be overrun by his friends, who are always being invited around to his inner sanctum!

Cancerian boys are not hell-raisers unless they have

learned how to deny totally their own vulnerability, and hence their compassion for others. Cancer wants to protect, not stir up conflict, so he lacks that aggressive drive that is so dominant in the fire signs. Stepping out of the proving and conquering fray, he carries within himself a kind of wise peacefulness that knows the cruelty of pulling the wings off flies. This is not to say that he is permanently serene, because he can turn sulky and sullen with the best of them when the mood takes him, but he won't lash out, for fear of hurting you.

Cancer Girls

Cancerian girls take their mothers to heart in such a way that they are inspired to become mothers themselves at the earliest opportunity. Now, don't panic! Rather than becoming a mother at the age of twelve, a Cancerian girl will find a brother, sister, or friend who is in need of her tender loving care. She is able to reach out and protect people who are insecure or vulnerable and take them under her small wing even before she has learned to fly herself. These little girls are the ones who hold tea parties for their dolls and teddy bears, remember their birthdays, and tuck them into bed every night.

Cancerians are very sensitive to the atmosphere at home. They are attuned to the undercurrents and can hear unspoken words. So, if your Cancerian daughter gets a tummy ache when your mother-in-law visits, she is merely reacting to the tension that she senses between you. If you are not careful, you will end up being looked after by her, rather than the other way around. As a mother of a Cancerian daughter, it is so important that you encourage her to separate her own feelings from those of the people around her and to know her own mind.

She needs security and the reassurance that she is loved, encouragement to overcome her fears, and understanding when she feels vulnerable. She can easily feel overwhelmed because she responds emotionally rather than logically. Consequently, problems can seem huge and need to be scaled down to size. Your Cancerian daughter needs help in discovering that she can hang on to her unique gift of sensitivity and also choose to look life straight in the eye!

Cancer at School

Because Cancer is associated with the past, those born under this sign are often able to memorize things easily—a useful talent for those at school. They tend to absorb facts through osmosis rather than conscious learning, as they are very receptive to ideas that just sink in. What Cancerians often lack, however, is the confidence in themselves to present their knowledge to their best ability. For instance, in tests and exams they can become so nervous that it undermines their entire performance. They are not pushy by nature, so it never occurs to them to show off what they can do, and instead they dwell on what they imagine they cannot do. With Cancer, the key to accomplishment is belief in oneself.

Cancerian children can also be put off certain subjects very easily if they feel they do not have a rapport with that particular teacher. They take criticism to heart—it often makes them want to give up rather than try again. Less sensitive souls who are unaware of the acute vulnerability of Cancer can disparage them with a heavy-handed remark that stays with them for life.

This sign usually shows aptitude for the arts because Cancerians are more skilled at using their imagination and perception than linear thinking. Purist scientific ideas leave them cold unless they can be applied to something human. It is always the personal side of life that is of interest to Cancer. If a Cancerian child is to do his best at school, he must really find a niche for himself and feel that he belongs and fits in—school is seen as an extension of his family.

Cancer at Play

Playing house is a favorite Cancerian game. Cancerian children are already dreaming of the home they will have when they are grown up. Making imaginary camps and castles or playing with doll's houses gives them an ideal opportunity to play around with the ingredients of home and family life, and Cancer is able to invent stories and scenarios with ease.

Cancerians are usually popular with other signs, but they can appear shy and may even retreat from children who are especially outgoing. Cancer tends to take his cue from others, so he will try to follow suit with whatever is going on. However, Cancer can take a dislike to another child, or suddenly not want to go to a party, without being able to say exactly why. It all has to do with the mysterious level of inner security within these children that is in a constant state of fluctuation and can be altered by a word, an idea, a look. It is important not to force these sensitive crabs into being sociable when their inner rhythm is telling them to be quiet.

Cancer Child with Aries Parent

A Cancerian is a sensitive soul, always looking for cues from other people as to whether he or she is acceptable or not, whereas the Arien philosophy is that you just let them have it and win them over. Cancer is in awe of the Arien self-confidence. It appears to him that Aries never has a moment of self-doubt and that he is always ready to charge ahead, sure that he will get it right. In fact, Aries is full of bluff and bravado, never letting anyone see the trembling lip by jutting out an assertive jaw instead.

Having a Cancerian child is an enlightening experience for the ram. He realizes that he will have to try a different approach if he is to coax this creature out of his shell. Seeing an Arien display his energetic magnetism makes a Cancerian run for cover—especially if he is afraid he will be next in the firing line. Cancer clams up if he feels threatened; he will venture out only if he can really trust someone. And building trust takes time, something that Aries always feels short of. However, unless an Arien really slows down to consider the feelings and sensitivities of a Cancerian, he will never truly enter into the ultimate bonding process with which Cancer welds people together.

A Cancerian child will feel strongly protected by an Aries mother who fiercely defends her brood. Aries mothers love to take charge, and Cancer is happy to be taken under her wing. But there comes a point when Cancer must discover for himself what he is made of. This is when the Aries mother must stand back and allow her Cancerian child to perform his sideways dance—Cancer is a sign that will not approach things directly and often takes one step forward and then one step backward. If the mother ram can curb her desire to take over and just allow her child to do things in his or her own way—which is most certainly different from her own trailblazing approach to life—then she will ultimately enable her small Cancerian to get in touch with his or her own will. This is a very important process for Cancer and entails a struggle to find his own voice, his own thoughts and ideas, instead of trying to blend into the status quo or allowing other people to do it all for him.

Ram fathers want their offspring to exhibit independence and guts. Cancer can do a good impersonation of toughness when he shows off his impenetrable shell, but really he is using his armor to hide his incredibly soft skin. Therefore, ram fathers have to be particularly careful not to push their Cancerian children into a state of permanent defense, where they pretend to be just like their fiery Arien fathers in order to please them, and contain their sensitivity for fear of being frowned on. In fact, Cancer is no weakling; he has his own unique sparkle, is brilliant with people, and knows how to make things happen around him—he just doesn't have to put on his boxing gloves, unlike Aries, in order to feel alive.

Cancer Child with Taurus Parent

This is a highly sympatico combination. Who better to nurture the internal security of Cancer than Taurus, the builder of the zodiac? There is a certain coziness to their relationship—and Cancer thrives when being cosseted. Psychologically wrapped up against the slings and arrows of outrageous fortune, Cancer slowly learns how to come out of his or her shell.

It is important to remember, too, that Taurus is an earth sign—feet on good old terra firma—and that Cancer, as a water sign, responds emotionally to life. It is sometimes difficult for Taureans to understand that meeting all the practical needs in their capable way does not always equal inner contentment for the other signs. Sometimes it pays for a Taurean to look beyond what is directly in front of him or her, particularly with a Cancerian child. To truly understand a Cancerian, you have to be able to look right into his or her heart.

Taurus mothers are great organizers. They enjoy busying themselves with all the things that "have to get done" in a day. The world of Cancerians is much more formless. These people do not wake up with agendas, but wait to see how they feel, and how they feel can change many times in the course of one day. This ability to float along can sometimes take Cancer into areas he might not want to go. He needs to cultivate the ability to say no, and to get in touch with his own will and desires—his own purpose in life—rather than going along with other people.

For the bull mother, being true to herself is second nature. Life presents clear-cut options to her, and she knows which way she wants to go. She has an opportunity with a Cancerian child to stand back and enable him to do his own choosing. If she takes the lead, as she is apt to do, then she can bulldoze Cancer into following her own ways. It may feel comfortable for her, but it doesn't serve this child in the long run.

Cancer loves the solidity of his or her Taurean father. He

is a rock—dependable, reliable, and secure. In his presence, Cancer feels soothed and safe from the unpredictabilities of life. The Taurus father encourages self-confidence because he is not a worrier himself. He can help Cancer get rid of self-doubt by making sure that he has attended to the practicalities and kept his eyes on the path ahead. The Cancerian imagination is both a gift and a thorn, because although it allows the crabs to live life so richly, he or she is often beset by fears of what might happen if . . . The Taurean father just holds Cancer's claws firmly in his grasp and helps him or her to stay in the here and now.

Cancer Child with Gemini Parent

Sometimes it is hard for Gemini to sit outside the Cancerian shell and wait for the little creature to come out. "What are you thinking?" he asks impatiently. "Talk to me." Cancer operates through emotions rather than thoughts (which is how Gemini works), and therefore it is not always easy for him to say exactly how he feels. Things remain nameless and formless in the Cancerian psyche.

Gemini can help Cancer to get things out in the open by talking. Once there, though, it becomes clear that the twins and the crab may look at the same thing and perceive it in totally different ways. "I am afraid of the dark," says Cancer. "Oh, there is no need to be," replies rational Gemini. "The fact is, everything is exactly the same as it is in the light, only you just can't see it." "But I feel frightened," wails Cancer. Here is the meeting of the mind and the feelings. Gemini has everything invested in being objective and logical, and Cancer identifies with the emotions.

For the two to understand each other, a shift needs to take place. Gemini can really try to listen to how Cancer is feeling instead of rationalizing it all away. And Cancer can help to clarify the situation by talking it out with Gemini. In fact, the Gemini drive for expression can be a real gift for Cancer because it helps him to make sense of himself and to see things in perspective. It gives him a working tool to use, which can prevent him from disappearing into a mire of feeling.

The restlessness of the Gemini mother keeps her Cancerian child in a constant state of stimulation. There are always ideas, plans, and comings and goings in the Gemini household. Actually, the Gemini mother is not a real home bird. She needs to fly, and every so often she will go out for a couple of laps around the circuit to see what is happening. She wouldn't want to miss out and wouldn't want her child to miss out on anything either. And by tossing her child the odd worm from the big outside world, she encourages a curiosity about life in her crab that makes him excited about taking a peek at it from underneath his shell. It is impossible not to feel interested in life in the company of a Gemini, and, although he might feel he is being force-fed and needs peace and quiet in order to digest it all, the little Cancerian actually enjoys himself.

Having a Gemini father is rather an unknown quantity for the crab, and actually all the other signs find Gemini rather elusive. He hops, skips, and jumps around, no matter what his age, which can be rather disconcerting for the signs that get dizzy easily. And Cancer is definitely one of them. It can seem that the Gemini father is a magician, doing conjuring tricks that mesmerize and delight, but he will never tell his child how he does it. Gemini hasn't the patience to explain it all because he's too eager to get on with the next trick. The entertainment is enthralling, but there will be something missing unless Gemini allows Cancer in on the act. And Cancer is the helper of the zodiac; he loves to belong and to share. This child really needs to feel he has a special part to play in his Gemini father's life.

Cancer Child with Cancer Parent

One would think that two crabs together could exist in perfect harmony. And of course they do understand and empathize with each other's idiosyncratic ways; but the trouble is that both of them are tuned into the changeable lunar vibrations that send them scuttling back and forth between the sea and the land according to their own inner timing. In other words, both possess their own internal kaleidoscope of feelings that is in constant motion and making different pictures. They are not synchronized. But it doesn't really matter too much, because Cancer possesses an innate respect for the feelings of others.

So two crabs can allow each other their trembling anticipation for life, their sentimentality, their crabby moodiness, and their emotional generosity. They can wrap their claws around each other, clinging tightly in embrace—and when they turn prickly, those claws dig into each other. But basically, they see the world through the same eyes; they truly recognize each other as being of the same family within the zodiac. They are cut from the same cloth, but they are tailors of their own lives.

When a Cancerian woman makes that important switch from identifying with being a child to becoming a mother, she takes the step into pouring her nurturing energies into another person. Yet it is probably because Cancerians never lose that ability to tune into how it feels to be a child that they are able to offer such emotional support. With two Cancerians, the issue of how much they should bond and how much they should remain individuals comes into question. The traditional matriarchal Cancerian image is of her brood nestling closely to her, relying on her for guidance, love, and protection. A Cancerian child is looking for this absolute connection with the mother, but the problem can be that, once formed, that psychological umbilical cord cannot be cut. Too much merging together can be an invasion, and the Cancerian child cannot find out who he really is unless he is free to do so. The Cancerian mother needs to let to go herself and to help her child to let go as well—she knows instinctively how to "be there" for her child, but what she needs to learn is how to stand back.

The crab father can sometimes hide his feelings behind a rather bluff exterior, but his gentleness always finds a way of leaking out. Cancerian fathers usually put home and family first on their agenda. For all Cancerians, personal life is of paramount importance—whatever they achieve in the outside world can never provide them with the fulfillment they will gain from establishing a secure family life. And a Cancerian child really blossoms when he knows that he is cared for in this way. Later on, the boy crab in particular will need to knock shells with his Cancerian father. He needs to know his own strength rather than rely on paternal protectiveness. Then, safe in himself, the Cancerian child can venture out knowing that he won't be walked over by anyone else on the beach.

Cancer Child with Leo Parent

Leo is such a self-confident sign, loving to be in the limelight and given opportunities to show what he or she can do. In contrast, Cancer waits in the wings, often letting other people go first, and hoping that he or she can see how to do it. The astounding thing is that, of the two of them, Cancer is more in tune with what is expected of him, more able to read the signs and therefore deliver the goods. Leo does his own thing and is crestfallen if the applause is not deafening. The main difference between the two signs is that Leo gives out energy and Cancer receives it. This is the speaker and the listener.

For Leo, having a child who frequently takes two steps backward (or sideways, in Cancer's case) before taking one forward is rather confusing. But Cancer needs to do this in order to weigh the situation and feel ready for it. There is never any guarantee with Cancerians that when it comes to any big day in their lives, they will feel ready to shine. They react according to their internal emotional levels and cannot perform on cue, but with a little coaching from Leo they can learn to "act as if . . ."

A Leo mother is spontaneously warm, which makes little Cancer feel as if the sun has come out. She is able to create a radiance around her that encourages the crab out of his shell. Cancer always picks up the atmosphere around him, and the type of environment produced by Leo is conducive to feeling good. Cautiously, Cancer comes out to bask in her light. As a mother, the lioness is very protective of her offspring. She may roar ferociously at other people, but as far as she is concerned, her children are to be pampered. She lavishes her time and attention on them. Leo is also good at making other people feel special, and this is exactly what Cancer needs. Under her tutelage the crab begins to relax, play with life, and enjoy himself—but Cancer will always retain his sensitivity.

With a Leo father, a Cancerian child flourishes in terms of developing self-confidence, but a father lion needs to know when to allow the crab to retreat. The crab needs private time because, unlike the lion, he has no particular desire to be on show. Usually these two are very affectionate and loving together and bring out the best in each other, but Leo fathers are often hard to live up to. They have their own inimitable style—and that is the key to this relationship. Leo can help Cancer to know his own way rather than groping in the shadow of what has gone before.

Cancer Child with Virgo Parent

Cancerians and Virgos are both gentle people. They know what it is to worry and feel anxious. In fact, at times it can seem that worrying is a Virgo's *raison d'être.* Their minds are constantly calculating a million permutations of potential happenings. And they are also endlessly analyzing what has already happened and mentally compartmentalizing it all.

Cancer is not as focused on the minutiae of life as Virgo, but the crab can turn fretful, develop a case of nerves, and generally go into a decline if the atmosphere doesn't feel right. In Virgo's hands, Cancer receives the kind of attention that smoothes his path, even though he still insists on walking along it sideways—crabs just do that!

The wonderful thing about a Virgo mother as far as a Cancerian child is concerned is that she will always notice the subtle emotional changes in her little crab. Fire sign mothers will often push on regardless and trample over the feelings of the sensitive Cancerian, but not Virgo. Virgos can detect the slightest nuance, because they are born observers. So Cancerians always feel appreciated by Virgos, and therefore they are safe and secure.

The puritan work ethic is well understood by any Virgo mother, who will always feel guilty if she sits down for one minute. Virgo is the server of the zodiac, and if she is not careful, she spends her life running around after other people. Since Cancer is a sign that needs to be mothered in the traditional sense, the crab can become rather lazy, allowing mother Virgo to do it all for him or her. Virgo actually needs to learn when to stop giving, or Cancer will remain in a childlike state forever. Fortunately, Cancer enjoys helping others, so the best thing is to recruit him or her as an assistant right from the beginning!

Virgo fathers cannot help but turn their appraising eye on their brood. It just comes naturally to them. And under their beady eyes, the crab can sometimes squirm uncomfortably and feel exposed, because Virgo never misses a thing. But Virgo is not unkind; he doesn't mean to find fault, but will simply point out what he sees, thinking that you will be as interested in the observation as he is. Cancer, though, will interpret what is said through his own emotional lens. If there is a hint of criticism within ten sentences of praise, then that is all he will hear. He needs to be handled very gently, so the less the Virgo carps, the better. However, there is usually an enormous amount of trust between these two signs. Virgo and Cancer are primarily friends, so any little misunderstandings are healed quickly.

Cancer Child with Libra Parent

Libra and Cancer can both be rather indirect. With Libra, the scales go up and down, and the high degree of energy involved in trying to achieve some kind of balance can prevent Libra from moving forward in life. Wanting to see all sides of a situation can also impair action. A Libran would never want to be seen to rush into a difficult situation, so he or she hangs back from making decisions and choices. Cancer, too, is not known for his propensity to charge around, throwing his shell about. The crab approaches situations sideways because, in common with Libra, he dislikes confrontation.

All in all, this combination could spend a very long time beating about the bush and not really understanding each other. Caught in Libra's determination to play happy families, Cancer can inwardly withdraw, afraid that if he says how he really feels then he will get short shrift. You see, Libra will always put on a smiling face regardless, while a Moon child will react to all the lunar phases that flow through him.

A Libran mother places a great deal of importance on being fair. To her, life is a stock exchange, where you can offset one thing against another to reach a reasonable equation. In her reckoning, if she has taken you to the adventure park, then in return you should enjoy it. But Cancerian moods are unpredictable. The sun may be shining when you set off, but when you arrive the storm clouds have gathered, Cancer has clammed up, and wants to go home. In fact, this is a common problem with Cancer—whenever he feels uncomfortable, he has an instinctive urge to return home. It is almost a desire to go back to the womb, where all is unity and security. And in a Libran mother's book, these moods are highly unreasonable. She will have to use all her diplomatic skills to negotiate her way around them.

In the face of the full range of Cancerian feelings, a Libran father can feel oddly at a loss. He is awkward with outpourings, and sulks are even worse. He will try to gloss over it all, or alternatively think of something that will please little Cancer. And he's usually got something that pleases in his bag of tricks—it is the Libran speciality. In a sense, because this sign refuses to get drawn into emotional chaos, a Libran father offers a really good sounding board for his small Cancerian. He will stand on the sidelines saying, "Surely it can't be as bad as all that," and once his or her eyes are dried, the crab can see his point.

Cancer Child with Scorpio Parent

Cancer really brings out the full volume of Scorpio's compassion. As a water sign, the scorpion is comfortable in the realm of feelings, but his or her emotions can sometimes freeze over like an icy pond. The crab wears his heart on his claws, though, and seeing such a cry for tenderness, Scorpio melts. It is obvious that Cancer needs his love and support. In fact, the crab and the scorpion are both crustaceans who attempt to hide their vulnerability by developing a hard outer shell. Scorpio instantly recognizes one of his own kind, and so he can treat Cancer with the double vision that he requires and allow both the inner and outer sides of him to coexist comfortably.

When it comes to sentimentality and attachment to the past, a Scorpio parent will indulge Cancer's whims. He knows that he must never throw away that treasured security blanket, doll's tea set, or scratched fire engine. Cancer has a very strong emotional investment in the possessions that have been around him, and he needs to know that they are still there as a kind of talisman. In fact, Scorpio probably still has his childhood toys too, but they will be hidden away—Scorpio stores things. So both Cancer and Scorpio can get broody about the past and want to hang on to it, revisit it. They need continuity.

A Scorpio mother has a deep emotional connection to her Cancerian child. The psychic bond between them is very intense and exists throughout their relationship. These two water signs feel 100 percent comfortable in each other's company. It is one of those cases of not needing to ask questions but just knowing and understanding. Yet the Scorpio mother must work on being able to let go of her child and must be careful not to invade with too much of an "I'm the only one who understands you" attitude. Ultimately, the crab has to learn how to come out of his shell by himself. But the total acceptance of his feelings that this child receives from a Scorpio mother means that he values himself, and therefore doesn't need to hide.

Scorpio fathers are great at pretending that they are not water signs. By that, I mean that they cover up their feelings a lot. But inside a Scorpio father is an enormous amount of emotional wisdom and understanding of what makes others tick. So he knows that a tender heart is beating underneath the bravado of the crab shell, and he appreciates this. A Cancerian child will always be encouraged by a Scorpio father to realize his or her strength and to use his or her assets to their best advantage. Scorpio can somehow turn things around and transform problems into opportunities. This is a very valuable lesson for Cancer, who needs to have the courage to become the best version of himself that he can possibly be.

Cancer Child with Sagittarius Parent

Bright and breezy Sagittarius does not make a traditionally close buddy of the somewhat shy and sensitive Cancerian. Yet, there is a sort of vibrational spark when these two come together as parent and child. Sagittarius is able to draw Cancer out of his or her shell. Something about the warmth and openness of the archer encourages the crab to throw his usual caution to the wind and take the odd risk. He ends up surprising himself by discovering that things aren't so frightening after all. And even if the archer has miscalculated (as he frequently does) and the crab has come up short, Cancer soon learns that if you laugh about it, the pain goes away a lot more quickly. He is taking lessons in the Sagittarian philosophy of life.

There is no doubt about it, Sagittarius is not the most tactful person to be around. The sensitivities of the Cancerian will take a battering because Sagittarius can be really blunt. These people don't dress things up when they have something to tell you; they just let you have it honestly. Is this such a bad thing? At least Cancer knows exactly where he stands, and there is no veil of illusion. And Sagittarius is never malicious; he is just incapable of telling a little white lie. This parent will show Cancer how to stand up for himself and, hopefully, not to take everything that happens so personally.

The archer mother will not protect little Cancer from experiencing life in its full spectrum. She believes that developing a positive attitude is protection enough, and that Cancer can dive into his or her own shell when the going gets tough anyway. Treating him as if he can cope has the magical effect of making him believe in himself. Of course, there are bound to be times when the lunar mood has made Cancer a little crabby. He has to be aware of his off days when he would rather pull the drawbridge up than deal with other people. But, generally, the spontaneity of the archer mother enables him to receive a constant flow of opportunities for new experiences. And, unlike the other fire signs, she really doesn't mind whether he achieves what he sets out to do or not, because for her making an effort is what's important, not collecting accolades.

The archer father will have to pull in the reins if he is not to tread on the toes, or claws, of his gentle Cancerian child. Cancer does not share the Sagittarian predilection for outdoor activity (unless it takes place by the sea). This child really enjoys the familiar surroundings of home, and the old favorites delight rather than bore him. Cancer is also a creative soul, so his imagination fulfills his needs, and he is happy being rather than doing. It's a bit of a puzzle to the active archer, but these signs do have something in common. The crab half inhabits the sea and half the land, and the archer is half-horse, half-man. It seems that both are neither quite one thing or another, but a blend of introvert and extrovert, intellect and instinct.

Cancer Child with Capricorn Parent

The opposing forces of Cancer and Capricorn provide a magnetism that pushes toward and away from each other. Cancer the crab and Capricorn the goat symbolize the mother and father principles of the zodiac. Watery Cancer embodies all the emotional nurturing responses attributed to mothering, and earthy Capricorn is in tune with the more protective, disciplining fatherly qualities.

So, when a Cancerian child is born to a Capricorn mother, it can feel to the crab that his mother is primarily concerned with keeping him on the straight and narrow rather than offering him the milk of human kindness. This is a subjective viewpoint, of course, but then Cancer is always inclined to see things from his own point of view. In fact, the crab is not a million miles away from the truth. Capricorn mothers often find it hard to let down their emotional defenses even with their own offspring, but they are brilliant organizers, providers, and teachers.

Capricorn believes that being strong is the most useful attribute one can develop, so the goat mother is very interested in making her small crab's shell as watertight as possible so that no one can get inside it to hurt or harm him. Unfortunately, little Cancer can't get out either if his protective shell is too tight, and he can become stuck inside it, safe but lonely and misunderstood. To really feel comfortable with himself, he needs to be able to acknowledge and express his sensitivity.

Capricorns are born to test their own resilience, and Cancerians are born to be in touch with the emotional side of life. Strangely, it is the Capricorn mother who particularly wants her child to pass the endurance test. Capricorn fathers are better at allowing others to be vulnerable. Nevertheless, if a Cancerian child receives the message that he must toughen up because it is unacceptable to be emotional, then the resulting damage can make him feel out of synch with himself forever.

Goat fathers are keen on having their children fit nicely into society. They are big on "finding your niche" in life because, once found, it can then be improved upon. With a Cancerian child, a Capricorn father has little to worry about in the form of a potential rebellion. Cancer needs approval and a sense of belonging, and it takes a lot for him or her to go against the grain. Also, the concept of family is so important to the crab that he would rather tie himself in knots than step outside it. So if both are to be happy, the goat must stop pushing his crab up the mountain. Crabs are very tenacious creatures and can find their own way!

Cancer Child with Aquarius Parent

Aquarius operates under the zany influences of Uranus, and Cancer picks up the shimmering rays of the Moon. Both signs are rather changeable, but Aquarius alters tack more suddenly and is therefore more unpredictable, while Cancerian moods are rarely in sharp focus, but tend to flow from one to another. The main difference between the water bearer and the crab is that Aquarius is known for the ability to detach himself. He can stand back and see the whole perspective from a rational point of view. Cancer, however, positions himself right in the middle and feels it all passing through him.

It is a challenge for Aquarius to understand the extreme sensitivity of the crab. Aquarius can explain everything away so easily, almost tell himself what he thinks he should feel in any given situation. Therefore, to be confronted with a child who lives, eats, and breathes feelings pulls him up short. It seems this child comes from another planet. He does! If the water bearer starts looking out for the changes in the Moon, he will get some idea of the rhythmical, cyclical phases that push Cancerians gently between bouts of inner reflection and outer expression. Aquarians love studying unusual things, and what could be more entrancing than this waxing and waning disc that can disappear into a pinprick and then light up the whole sky?

From his Aquarian mother, Cancer picks up a quality of aliveness that sizzles within his being. She is a live wire, and Cancer can assimilate this crackling energy that makes her willing to reach out into the unknown and try something new. By nature, Cancer would almost always go for the tried and tested rather than experiment, but being brought up by a water bearer mother, he or she will certainly have to expect the unexpected. There will be times when the challenge of this will make him want to retreat into his shell.

Aquarians refuse to stay with the safe option when there are so many ideas and courses out there in the world that can make life exciting. But Cancer would choose safety over excitement any day of the week. An Aquarian mother will soon learn that the best way to introduce new things into Cancer's life is *gradually.* If you push a crab, he or she will clam up and refuse to come out to play. Similarly, Cancerians can cling to their mothers, while Aquarians are keen to get their children mentally weaned. It's always best to let the crab keep his little claw in your hand until he's ready himself to let go.

Aquarius is a fixed sign, which means that these fathers can mentally set themselves in cement at times. For fixed, read stubborn, determined to get their own way. Despite all their humanitarian ideas and broad thinking, they can really dig their heels in. However, Cancerians need to be handled gently, and they are fragile even though they can do a good impersonation of not caring. But don't be fooled—inside, a crab can feel like jelly. And this needs to be appreciated as something delicious, an attribute rather than a failing.

Cancer Child with Pisces Parent

A crab child with a fish parent should basically be left alone to stroll along the seashore, build a few sand castles, and play in the water together. They are both water signs and have such a good understanding of each other that words are almost unnecessary. Their emotional attunement is so strong that much of their communication is carried out subliminally. It can be a little hard for other family members to understand this. The fish parent, however, feels completely comfortable swimming around in the world of intuition. It is the rational world that bothers him or her. Pisces can relate wonderfully easily to the Cancer child's dreams, fears, and hopes.

Although these two are bathed in the positive light of their mutual sympathy, they still have lessons to learn from each other. One is that Cancer is much more security-conscious than

Pisces. The fish is not attached to material things, or to particular outcomes in life. Pisceans know how to float with the tides, and they have a vision of spirituality that frees them from becoming imprisoned in material matter. Cancerians, however, carry the weight of their shells around with them and know the quality of attachment, which makes them more possessive than Pisces. When Cancer is feeling insecure, he can become obsessive about particular things, and the fish can teach him to have more faith in himself and in life.

Piscean mothers are cued in to spotting imagination and creativity in others. Cancer won't have to pretend to be more interested in playing football than dancing because Pisces places the highest value on being able to explore your dreams. A Piscean mother will just allow whatever is present in her child to emerge, and this gives permission for Cancer to discover and develop his or her innate sensitivity.

A Cancerian child will love to immerse himself in the stories that a Pisces father can tell. The fish can weave a magical tale that fires Cancer's imagination. But it is not only in the bedtime story that the crab finds himself drawn into the mysterious Piscean world. He is fascinated by his father's romantic spirit and refusal to see life purely in terms of what is in front of his nose. It encourages Cancer to explore beyond his shell, to reach out for his own dream.

Sun in Leo Child

24 July–23 August

THE LION

Qualities to Look for and Nurture in Your Leo Child

Self-confidence and radiance

LEO IS A CHILD WHO NEEDS TO SHINE. BECAUSE HIS OR HER planetary ruler is the Sun, which is at the center of our solar system, Leo likes to occupy center stage. The Sun is also linked to the psychological principle of the ego, so it is important that Leo develops a healthy respect for and confidence in himself, that he understands his own specialness, and is able to translate his own heroic vision into action. Leo naturally inhabits the world of princes and princesses—he has an enthusiasm and a zest for life that propels him toward finding his own leading role in his life story.

An ability to perform and express his or her own distinctive style

Leo is creative in the broadest sense. He is also to bring his unique touch to whatever he does and is looking for approval and appreciation for his efforts. Leo desperately needs feedback—other people to act as his own personal audience so that he can judge his performance in life. The lion needs to feel proud of himself: If he does not receive the reaction he desires, he can feel crushed and worthless. As a child it is essential that he is able to allow his creative spirit to flow freely. Later in life he will draw on this resource to express his flair for drama, color, and style. Leo has his or her own special signature.

Natural ability to lead others and reach for the best

Leo wants to be out there showing others how to do it, not copying or following. The lion is the king of the jungle and as such is an imperious and commanding beast. Even as a child, Leo can expect other people to bow to his or her greater magnificence. He cannot help aspiring to the position of top dog. He wants to be numero uno, not an also-ran, and he radiates the sort of natural authority and dignity that somehow draws attention. Second best will never do for Leo. He wants to give his utmost, and he appreciates all things that reflect this high-voltage energy. As an adult, he will always go for quality and excellence.

Giving of affection and attention to others

Because Leo enjoys being pampered, he knows how to make other people feel special. His warmly affectionate nature spreads light in such a way that he can appear to make the sun come out. Other people feel good in his presence because he gives out such a magnetic healing vibration. He has a life force within him that can transmit a sense of well-being.

Leo Boys

A playful male lion cub looks so sweet and cuddly that it is easy to forget he needs firm handling too. As a parent, you will be challenged to help this lion develop his power and channel it constructively. At times you will undoubtedly feel like a lion tamer yourself in the midst of a battle of wills, but when Leo turns his sunny smile on you he can melt your heart.

If he feels he is lacking attention, which is tantamount to neglect with this sign, then he will do everything he can to make you notice him. It's almost as if he doesn't feel he exists unless you are looking at him, better still if you are admiring him. He can't resist showing off a little and knows how to play to his audience. It is really important for this child to have some sort of arena where he can feel recognized. A Leo who is forced to live in the shadows will be forever looking for missing appreciation in later life and becoming more demanding of it by the minute.

Leo boys need to be able to let off steam, to be rambunctious and energetic. As a fire sign, Leo loves challenge, and he can be boisterous when he's got the bit between his teeth. His natural urge to dominate can make him seem overbearing at times, but really he is just testing to see how far he can go. And when he comes to the limit, he breathes a sigh of relief because he has a respect for authority.

Leo Girls

A baby lioness is rehearsing to be queen. In the meantime she will practice her regal wave and sometimes see if she can get you, her loyal subject, to run around after her! It can be easy to spoil a Leo daughter; she has such winning ways and really appreciates being pampered. Whenever events force her to realize that she is an ordinary human being, a storm cloud passes over her, and she can pout and sulk like a prima donna. But it doesn't last long; the sun always comes out again.

Give Leos plenty of praise, and flattery will get you everywhere. In fact it is the much-needed water for this young plant to blossom. And Leo girls who have been forced to hide their light under a bushel when young present a sad figure as adults. The courage of the lion is hidden behind a shy face and a tendency to hold herself in, as if she is in an imaginary cage. This proud little girl needs you to believe in her in order for her to believe in herself.

Her vitality and spontaneous all-singing, all-dancing pizazz can set the world alight. And you can be sure that if she makes you a daisy chain, it will be the very best you have ever seen, with a double row and perfectly formed. She will just give it to you—she's generous like that—and you will feel touched to the core and very special. Having a princess in the family somehow rubs off on the other members!

Leo at School

Leos excel whenever they are given an opportunity to express themselves. Writing essays, compositions, painting, playing music, and sports are all outlets for them to show what they can do, to put out their own ideas and capabilities. In subjects where they feel less confident, they will often give up before they have made much effort to succeed. This all-or-nothing approach reflects their own sense of pride—they either want to do something well or not at all.

With classmates, a Leo child can become a ringleader. Other children sense his strength of personality, and he is dynamic, open, and friendly. Things seem to happen around him, and this draws other people into his circle. He or she can be a bit bossy, expecting always to be the one to make the choices and not giving other people a chance. He or she needs help in understanding how to be fair and to stand back and allow others to have their turn too.

Leo children need a lot of praise if they are to give of their best. A little applause acts like a turbocharge on their ability to perform. If they feel unrecognized by a particular teacher, they will either play up to attract attention, or withdraw their efforts in this subject. Sometimes a round of applause on the home front can transform a Leo child's attitude and help him to shine in an area he has discounted. Basically, a Leo's natural theatricality stands him in good stead when he needs to pull out all the stops. He knows how to impress others when he has to!

Leo at Play

Leos have a fertile imagination, and in their imaginary world live all the monsters, heroes, and quests that challenge them to triumph. Small Leo children love listening to stories and dressing up as the characters they hear about. For them, fantasy can be more real than reality. Of course, they usually cast themselves in the role of prince or princess, with their friends playing bit parts and supporting them in the main adventure.

Lions really need to play, to be creative and self-expressive. It is a vital experience for them in discovering themselves. And unlike some other signs, Leos can get totally absorbed in play, completely immersed in what they are creating. It is magical to observe the kind of focused attention that they give to the creative process, and even as adults they never forget how to do this.

Leo Child with Aries Parent

These two firecrackers generate a lot of warmth and electricity between them. Aries is always quick off the mark and loves to be in the center of the action, and Leo is never far behind. As a parent, Aries will always encourage a child to move forward, and Leo possesses an enthusiasm that is easily kindled by this attitude. With a fiery ram parent, Leo is able to play with his own fire energy and get an idea of his own strength.

Rams do not take any notice of obstacles in their path. They believe that if you want something, then there is a way to get it, and if anything should block you, then you just charge at it in a show of force. But unlike Taureans, Ariens will rarely knock their heads against brick walls either—if the obstacle appears immovable, then Aries just turns his attention elsewhere. Under this parental guidance, Leo learns that he is master of his destiny, and, as a young lion cub, he is encouraged to flex his muscles as much as possible.

An Aries mother tends to call the shots in her household. She is the main mover and shaker, and she is not shy about moving and shaking you to get a reaction. However, a Leo child will never do as he is told just because you said so—he always chooses whether he will do it or not. So there can be a battle of power between an Aries mother and a Leo child. Sparks will fly! Yet the Aries mother knows how to deal with the willfulness of her Leo offspring. She enjoys seeing such decisive energy in her child, even if it is sometimes pitted against her. She is not afraid of Leo's mighty roar; in fact, she encourages Leo to affirm himself and speak his mind. So Leo grows up with a healthy ability to express his or her fire, a fundamental necessity for this sign.

Aries fathers need to make time to watch their young Leo's performance. Remember, this sign needs an audience. Ariens are so independent that they do not need the approval of others, so it is easy for them to forget that Leos seek response, reaction, recognition. Ariens can be so busy doing battle with the rest of the world that they overlook the importance of personal connection, but to a Leo child the Aries father *is* the world.

Leo Child with Taurus Parent

Taurus likes the simple things in life. The bull appreciates understatement and naturalness as indications that things are honest and down-to-earth. Leo, however, likes to make a big impact, to come in with trumpets blaring, banners waving. Leo likes things to be exciting, special, and eye-catching. So in this combination there is a meeting of the ordinary and the extraordinary. It is hard for Taurus to come to terms with the Leo need to make a song and dance because, in his book, making an exhibition and drawing attention to yourself is unnecessary. But Leo doesn't feel alive unless someone notices him.

In fact, sometimes any form of attention is better than none for a Leo. So he will go over the top and act up just to make you look at him. Short of waving a red flag there isn't a worse trick he could pull to irritate the normally placid bull. A Taurean parent may patiently wait for little Leo to outgrow this "show-off" stage, but he or she will wait forever because this need to perform is not something that Leo ever grows out of. Leo will still be doing his star turn in the old people's home, so Taurus had better just take a comfy seat and watch the entertainment—who knows, he might even enjoy it.

Leo enjoys the homey qualities of his or her Taurean mother. He loves to be cooked for, pampered, and looked after, and a Taurean mother knows just how to soothe a young lion cub when he has tired himself out being rambunctious and playful all day. It's hard work practicing to be king or queen of the jungle, and Leo needs time to rest and recuperate. In his relaxed mode he can putter around and be lazy. But Taurus usually has something sensible for him to do, such as putting away his shoes, hanging up his coat, and helping to lay the table. Living with a Taurean mother, Leo soon learns that he has to do his bit, banal though it may seem. He can live to be a hero another day, but for now he must be ordinary. Actually, this is good preparation for Leo, because if he is to realize his dream he must be able to live in the real world.

Bull fathers will have to watch their bank account. A young Leo usually has such an enormous desire for the biggest and the best that he is keen to have an overdraft with his pocket money. Taureans, with their careful approach to finance, have their work cut out with Leo. Even if it is just an ice cream, young Leo always wants the double scoop with the chocolate on top. But Taurus is firm—kind, but able to dig in his heels. If Leo watches carefully, he or she will learn a lot from his father's more cautious approach to life.

Leo Child with Gemini Parent

Both Leo and Gemini are capable of turning in a star performance. Gemini mesmerizes other people with words; Leo draws admiring glances simply for his or her radiance. The Leo child is so sunny that other people cannot help being attracted to him. He has a way of reaching out that invariably connects him to others. Gemini loves this, because the sign of the twins is a people sign. In fact, Gemini and Leo seem to make things happen around them—all the mother and toddler groups are heaving with sociable Gemini–Leo duos who are eager to "learn and meet people."

Because Gemini is a sign that concentrates to a large extent on the mind, he or she may miss Leo's all-around ability to express himself. Whether through drawing, painting, making things, or any other form of creativity, Leo is saying who he or she is. The written and spoken word is not enough to carry his message, which must be three-dimensional. The lion puts his heart and soul into what he produces. He cannot skip around like Gemini; he wants to show you a masterpiece.

Leos demand the time and attention of their parents, but Gemini is the type who usually has his mind on several things at once. This can be readily interpreted by Leo as a clear indication that he is not good enough. The lion appears to be so sure of himself, but inside he needs praise from other people. In the busy Gemini world, there is never enough time to look at everything, but if Leo feels overlooked he is utterly dejected. He needs to know that he rates in the first division of your interests.

Gemini mothers prefer to share their experience of motherhood with another mother. So you see them out in pairs in the park or strolling around the shops with their strollers. It feels pleasant for Leo, who loves a big audience—two mothers to impress is a bigger challenge than just one. As time goes on and Leo gets older, the house becomes overrun with his adoring fans. The lion is a popular crowd puller, because he is so spontaneous and playful.

Gemini fathers are always young at heart, prepared to roll up their sleeves and be a child again at the drop of a hat. Little Leo feels comfortable having a father with such a lively mind, and it is as if Gemini is feeding him ideas like tidbits—a constant flow of suggestions and thoughts that Leo can take away and play with. But really Leo would much prefer to have a game with the man himself, not his ideas. Gemini has to work on really giving himself wholeheartedly to this child, because nothing less will do.

Leo Child with Cancer Parent

Leo has a great deal to learn from Cancer's gentle ways. Although he may shake his magnificent mane and roar ferociously, the lion can still be cowed by a crab. Cancer has such a nonconfrontational style of confrontation that it takes Leo by surprise! He is caught on the hop, and if you have ever seen a dignified lion teetering off-balance, then you will know that the crab has approached him sideways and put him off his stroke. In fact, Cancer will only prompt the lion to pussyfoot around if he feels the beast has overstepped the mark. As a parent, Cancer knows that he must tame the lion if he is to help him develop the best in himself.

The crab is good at giving devoted attention to his offspring, and little Leo basks in the parental spotlight. Although Cancer and Leo are water and fire signs, respectively, and therefore a little like oil and water, they nonetheless wish to give and receive a great deal of affection, and that helps to break down any other barriers that may exist between them. Basically, any differences that rear their heads are the result of their being ruled by the two great luminaries of our solar system, the Sun and the Moon. So it is a case of night (the Moon) meeting day (the Sun). Moon-ruled Cancer is moodier, broodier, and loonier than Leo, who feeds off the bright light and heat of the Sun. The containing quality of Cancer reassures Leo that he always has a place at the center of his parent's universe. And a Leo child radiates a positive energy that lifts his or her Cancerian parent's lunar energy up an octave.

A Cancerian mother is not the sort to feel upstaged by her Leo child's sparkling exuberance. Cancer derives most pleasure from pouring energy into providing a rich family base that allows its members to shine. And this Sun child can outshine them all—Leo has a tendency to walk away with the honors. Watching her Leo child confidently taking the world by storm is quite an experience for a Cancerian mother, who remembers her own childhood sensitivities. But Leo is not as self-assured as he or she looks. He has the fiery energy that enables him to have to try at something, but he still needs you to watch his performance. Leo measures himself by "what other people think," and the greatest gift his Cancerian mother can give him is to think well of himself.

In response to Leo's dramatic thrust forward, his or her Cancer father will often present his protective face. To Leo it can feel that his father is retreating into his shell, not playing the game, but the crab is merely trying to defend his child from taking a knock. Leo is desperate to impress his father, show off what he can do. When he hears the Cancerian voice saying, "Quiet down, don't be silly," which is the crab's way of showing concern, not criticism, Leo is apt to take it all personally. He wants applause, not a wet blanket. But sometimes Leo does take things too far, and the best performers are the ones who take their cue from the audience. Leo would do well to learn to absorb from other people as well as give to them. His Cancerian father has a well-tuned listening ear, so he can teach him when to hold back a little and when to dazzle.

Leo Child with Leo Parent

It is always a tricky business putting together two people of the same sign. Even when nature has been the architect of two Leos sharing their lives together as parent and child, it is no less risky. On the plus side there is always a strong rapport between people of the same sign. They feel they understand each other on a deep level; the parent and child identify with each other and know what makes the other one tick. But Leo likes to be number one, and two people in the same house cannot both be center stage all the time. There has to be an element of give and take, which in time Leo learns, but they will often try to knock each other off the pedestal if they think the other one has occupied it for too long!

Leo is intimately linked with creative activity and the process of giving birth that is involved in all self-expression. This sign looks upon its progeny as the ultimate production, which of course it is. So a Leo parent is proud of bringing this little soul into the world and revels in being complimented on the magnificence of his or her genes. Purring and preening in sheer delight at such a creative coup, the parent lion sets about licking his or her offspring into shape. Which is when the trouble starts! Lion cubs are strong-willed creatures and eager to try their hand at big game, even if it means they bite off more than they can chew. It can be a full-time occupation for a parent lion to keep young Leo from running wild. And the annoying thing is that having a Leo parent automatically means that this lion cub can't wait to be living life to the full, which is what he sees his Leo parent doing.

A mother lioness can be indulgent with her children. Baby Leo laps it up and basks in her attention. But she also delivers a firm hand when she sees Leo transgressing the unwritten rule of respect for his mother. It is the Leonine version of tough love: plenty of affection, plenty of discipline. It is essential for all Leos to develop a very strong sense of themselves, to become their own authority, and in the early years brushing up against the law of the lioness does the lion cub no harm. He knows that she is always the first to reward him when he does well, and Leos show the most amazing loyalty to their own kith and kin.

Watching the prowess of his Leo father, the lion cub can feel that he is destined to spend the rest of his life in the shade by comparison. Because Leos naturally attract recognition, father has usually earned himself the admiring glances that comes his way. It can be a hard act to follow, but little Leo knows that he must search for his own place in the jungle. For his part, a Leo father does not feel the slightest twinge of competition in his veins when he looks proudly at his offspring. As top dog, or top lion, he doesn't need to stoop to conquer, but his generous, magnanimous nature ensures that he equips little Leo with the best start in life that he can possibly give him. And, by starting life in the lion's den, little Leo can't lose!

Leo Child with Virgo Parent

Virgos are essentially realists, although their perfectionist nature can make them look like idealists. In order to attain such a high level of excellence, Virgo feels he always has to be the first to spot the worm in the apple. Leo likes to impress other people; he has a larger-than-life countenance that never fails to make people look at him. But with a Virgo parent, Leo feels he has a difficult audience, one who is not taken in by the overall spectacle and who concentrates on the details instead. Virgo casts an appraising eye over every last aspect, while Leo would prefer just to have the praise!

While Virgo is primarily modest, unassuming, and more keen to get on with things quietly behind the scenes, the lion prowls around deliberately drawing attention to himself and determined to prove that he is special. Leo believes that he or she is born to be king or queen, and with a Virgo parent, he may believe that he is doing time in a humble background before he finally gets the recognition he deserves!

Mother Virgo is a thrifty soul (unless her own natal chart has several planets in Leo). She cannot bear flashiness or extravagance and will usually take the practical option. So little Leo may have to wear his clothes a size too big so he can grow into them, or a hand-me-down from an older child. This is simple common sense in Virgo's book, but a horror for Leo—where is his regal attire? Young Leos are every bit as conscious as adult lions about putting their best foot forward—preferably in new shoes!

Since Virgo actually likes to do things for other people and Leo loves to be pampered, it can seem that little Leo has got his mother wrapped around his little finger. But even a Virgo has her limits and detests arrogance, so the lion cub will have to pay his dues. The most important thing for these two to remember is to give each other credit. Virgo must applaud Leo for his dazzling performance, and Leo must appreciate the giving nature of his mother. If they insist on withholding their admiration for each other, things can get a little tense. Virgo will start carping and criticizing, and Leo will pout and sulk. They have the choice of producing a storm cloud or a sunny day between them!

A Virgo father is not normally the effusive type, but he might find life easier with Leo if he looked up a few positive adjectives in the dictionary and kept them up his sleeve. Leo always gives of his or her best when receiving the maximum encouragement. Telling him that you noticed his hands looked awkward when he was in the school play does absolutely nothing for his self-confidence. And a lion with his tail between his legs is a very dejected creature. He will either slink into the shadows, unable to radiate his fire, or will try to overcompensate. Letting Leo know how special you think he is helps him to believe in himself.

Leo Child with Libra Parent

A lion child usually ends up tipping a Libran's scales in a positive direction. Leo is not so interested in whether everything is fair and balanced; he is more extreme. He has a knack for pushing Libra off his habitual fence to come down on his side. Libra finds Leo's fire rather exhilarating, and he is warmed by Leo's affectionate nature and enthusiasm, but sometimes the heat gets a little too much for him. Libra needs to stand back and cool off.

A Libran parent often finds himself trying to put matters

into perspective for Leo, to offer explanations, reasons, and alternatives, because Leo always sees things from his own point of view. He or she simply doesn't know how to see them from any other angle. But that is an ability that comes naturally to Libra, so much so that he sometimes reaches the point of paralysis in the face of so many possibilities. So the judgment of Libra, coupled with the Leo spontaneity, makes a happy combination—if they are working together instead of opposing each other. But Libra normally likes to cooperate rather than stand in anyone's way.

It is highly gratifying for a Libran mother to have given birth to such a personable child. Leo beams his sunny smile and pulsates with an energy that makes him appear to be golden. Like a lion cub, his or her features have the innocence but budding magnificence of a baby big cat. And for Libra, who sets such store by creating a graceful and elegant appearance, a Leo child is the ultimate beautiful design.

As a child, Leo is already aware of his powerful desires and ability to get what he wants. He can appear to be very sure of himself and rather bossy in his methods of attaining his goals. Because his Libran mother possesses such charm and affability, he can make the mistake of assuming she is a pushover. Leo will take a strong stance, jump up and down, and make a scene that is worthy of the local amateur dramatic society. Surely, he thinks, after seeing how important it is for him to play on the swings for another half an hour, she can't possibly refuse. But Leo has reckoned without the famous Libran power of persuasion, tactical maneuvering, and diplomatic brinkmanship that is at his mother's fingertips, whether she is dealing with a truculent child or buying four fillet steaks. She will create a diversion for Leo that makes him think it was his idea to leave in the first place, and soon she has gotten him eating out of the palm of her hand.

Leo loves the laid-back artistry of his or her Libra father. In many ways it provides the perfect backdrop for his or her own more dramatic style to emerge. The Libran father will allow his Leo child to experiment with his own self-expression, which is such a vital part of his growth. And, better still, Libra is always so appreciative and disposed to finding the good in whatever Leo has to offer. Leo truly flourishes when he sees such a positive reflection in the mirror of his father's eyes.

Leo Child with Scorpio Parent

Leo and Scorpio learn to develop a healthy respect for each other. They are both powerful signs, but Leo is more outward in his or her self-expression, Scorpio more contained and mysterious. As a fire sign, Leo is active, warm-spirited, and enthusiastic, which contrasts with the more inwardly reflective, deeply sensitive, and watery sign of Scorpio. They are both very strong-willed, however, and capable of a clash that would put the Titans to shame.

Fixed signs want their own way, and both these signs are fixed—in cement, sometimes. However, if the lion is not to be stung by the scorpion and the scorpion is not to be trampled on by those big leonine paws, they must both learn to back off. Lions are not used to giving way to any other creature in the jungle, but with a Scorpio parent around, it is not just his jungle, and he must adapt to the environment in which he was born. Scorpios are not too keen on broadcasting their regulations, either. The rules are mostly unwritten, but they soon let you know if you step out of line. Leo is almost bound to overstep the mark—after all, he overdoes nearly everything. That fiery energy of his spills out, making him appear larger than life. And this is his birthright, so Scorpio had better be careful not to crush it completely, just learn to temper it.

Deep down, more than anything else a Scorpio mother wants her child to live honestly and truthfully. That means that he must be himself and not pretend to be anyone else. Scorpio detects any kind of sham and can spot it a mile off. As a performer, though, Leo relies on his props to enhance his showmanship. He loves to make things appear more dazzling than they really are—it is his speciality. If his mother is not to pour cold water on his fiery enthusiasm, she must allow Leo his grandeur and extravagance. His own distinctive style emerges from his ability to create a spectacle, which may be a little over the top, but is his own truth. Leo genuinely wants to be the biggest and the best.

A Scorpio father can be a little reticent with his praise. It is not that he doesn't admire Leo and wouldn't do anything for him, but he always holds some of his thoughts back in reserve. However, Leo is striving to catch his or her father's attention. It seems that little Leo is waving and calling out, "Look at me!" but Scorpio is deliberately looking the other way so as not to make the lion feel self-important. If Leo is to develop a healthy sense of self, he needs to win recognition from his father. So hang up your little Leo's pictures and give him or her a couple of gold stars—flattery begins at home!

Leo Child with Sagittarius Parent

Being presented with a Leo child can feel like Christmas for a Sagittarian parent because it seems he got just what he wanted—a playful, exuberant, miniature version of himself. Of course, when fire meets fire it always produces a glint in the eye, but before we get carried away and ride off into the sunset, let's make it clear that a lion is most definitely not a scaled-down replica of the archer. In fact, it is probably the single most important point that Leo has to make in his life—the fact that he is totally unique and unlike anyone else. "Okay, okay," I hear the archer sigh, "let's not get bogged down with all this heavy stuff, let's just enjoy . . ." and that is something the lion can understand.

Sagittarians believe in developing self-confidence. As parents, they normally encourage their children to reach out and make the most of any opportunities. And for Leo, this feels life-affirming. He or she gets the message that it is good to be outgoing, to say what you think and be who you are—in other words, not to hide your light under a bushel. And although Leo's light is not easily hidden, he can sometimes reduce himself to rather low voltage if he thinks other people would react badly to his brilliance. The archer, however, wants him to shine.

A Sagittarian mother will give little Leo plenty of space to find out who he or she is. She has a hale and hearty attitude and would rather risk a few bumps than mollycoddle her offspring. Admittedly, this does tend to emphasize the lion's roar rather than his cuddly, purry side. He grows up able to hunt and defend himself. In psychological terms, he learns to develop the will, which is an important tool; but the lion also has a softer streak, a devoted lovingness that he needs to bestow on others if he is to feel complete.

The thrill of following his archer father entices the young lion cub out into the heart of the action. Sagittarius and Leo are such an active combination that they rarely have time to sit still; they are always pursuing adventure together. And the archer is always urging the lion on, to have courage, to take his or her chance. It is a big lesson in developing faith in life and in himself—one that the lion needs to learn in order to fulfill his destiny.

Leo Child with Capricorn Parent

Not the easiest of combinations, this—but one of the most rewarding. Capricorns believe in self-discipline, keeping to the straight and narrow, with your nose to the grindstone. It sounds about as much fun as digging graves to a young lion cub. He is frisky, full of life, and raring and roaring to go. But it doesn't have to be the meeting of *joie de vivre* and jaundice—Leo has missed the point. In the Capricorn philosophy, working hard doesn't mean that you can't play hard, but you can't do one without the other. It's called paying your dues.

Now we are talking business with Leo; he knows all about this concept of winning your spurs. If you want him to go out and take the world by storm, he will be off at the drop of a hat. There he goes, overdramatizing everything as usual. You get the idea that Capricorn and Leo can easily misunderstand each other, misinterpret, misread, mistake . . . it takes a lot of careful clarification, but Capricorn usually has the time if Leo has the inclination.

When he was a child, Capricorn may have had difficulty in expressing himself. Often Capricorn has had to grow up quickly and feels that he was never given permission truly to be a child. So when little Leo arrives, it can touch a pretty sore spot in his psyche, especially as this child is bursting with the desire to play. In fact, Leo can offer Capricorn an opportunity to be a child again and go over all the parts he missed. If he lets down his defenses, he can enter into a child's world and re-create it, and Leo has that ability to take someone's hand, no matter what his age, and draw him into play.

A Capricorn mother is always ambitious for her children, not that she has it etched on her mind that little Leo has got to be a bank manager or a C.E.O. Rather, she has a plan that Leo will be able to apply himself properly to whatever he wants to do and can muster the level of effort required to reach his goal. The difficult thing for her to comprehend is that Leo likes to make everything look easy. He doesn't want everyone else to know that he had to stay up late like all the rest memorizing his French vocabulary. Leo likes to give the impression that he or she is naturally a cut above the masses. He cultivates an air of laziness like a basking lion in the long grass, but he is ready to pounce and catch his trophy.

The puritan work ethic underlies the Capricorn father's long hours spent in the line of duty. Time is short, but it is the most precious gift he can give to the young lion who craves his attention. Turning up for a sports event is not enough; Leo wants his father to share all the fun and games every day. The goat will have to learn to let his hair down if he isn't to miss out on what really makes his child tick. Leo can be excessive and outrageous in order to make his point, but if he doesn't feel the connection to his father, he will think there is no point to make.

Leo Child with Aquarius Parent

Leo and Aquarius see life through opposite ends of the telescope. Leo tends to magnify everything, and Aquarius often has an unusual perspective! The water bearer is in fact an air sign, which makes him or her identify with the mind. His ideas may hold water, but he doesn't live and breathe the stuff as do the emotional water signs of Cancer, Scorpio, and Pisces. As a parent, Aquarius believes in being a friend. His is the sign of friendship, and he understands this form of relationship more than any other. Being a touch unconventional, he will also refuse to adhere to anyone else's stereotype of what a parent should be. He prefers to make it up as he goes along, which is basically the way he approaches life—it makes it more interesting!

Leos, however, believe in leaders and followers, chiefs and Indians, and they need a hero or heroine to worship and model themselves upon. In adulthood, they naturally assume the starring role, but Leo children are in apprenticeship to be king or queen. From an Aquarian parent, Leo will learn the common touch, because Aquarius is not interested in being superior.

And although Leo won't be loved any less by an Aquarian parent, he or she won't be treated any differently from other children. In other words, he will be loved for his ordinariness as much as for his specialness, and this feels strange to Leo. He automatically assumes that he has to outdo everyone else in order to be acknowledged.

An Aquarian mother will refuse to be drawn into Leo's fire and brimstone. When Leo has got a bee in his bonnet, he hot-foots around and creates a drama that attempts to cast any innocent bystander as the villain of the piece. His Aquarian mother simply cannot understand what all the fuss is about, so she stands back and waits for him to cool down. Her detachment and logic helps Leo to come to his senses, and after all he doesn't want to look silly—every lion has his pride!

Leo is stunned by his or her Aquarian father's command

of life. The water bearer appears to be unflappable, and at times Leo will go overboard trying to get a response from him. You see, Leo needs a reaction. He wants you to enter into the fray with him, to become personally involved. This lion cub will get angry, throw a tantrum, then flash a sunny smile because he wears his heart on his sleeve. It is important for Leo to express how he feels at that moment. Aquarians usually have a time delay in their self-expression because they always think things through. Leo can learn a lot from this clear-headed approach, but still needs tangible proof of your love—a compliment, a squeeze, or a warm smile mean more to this child than a thousand explanations.

Leo Child with Pisces Parent

Although Leo and Pisces can be seen as embodying the self and selflessness, respectively, and are therefore at opposite ends of the spectrum, they do have a great deal in common. Probably no other sign understands so well Leo's yearning for life to be magical and special. Leo and Pisces both possess the kind of imagination that dreams are made of. They both refuse to live with their eyes fixed on the humdrum when they can spin so many fantasies and catch a glimpse of life on a higher level. Pisces encourages Leo to hitch his or her wagon to a star.

With this combination, the Pisces parent will often make some kind of personal sacrifice so that little Leo will not suffer. Whatever form this takes, Leo is given a head start in life. And the lion was always destined to walk the red carpet anyway—it's just that he may start a little younger with a Piscean parent. Pisces has to cultivate an idea of what the bottom line is with Leo, because the lion can take advantage—he just loves being spoiled and pampered. But too much fuss can make him autocratic and bossy and doesn't really serve the best interests of the little lion, who eventually has to learn to go out and hunt for himself.

A Piscean mother is not one to expend great effort in taming the beast. She doesn't want to enter into battle like an Amazon hell-bent on driving her principles home, and she figures that Leo will pass through phases and come out the other side without her nagging him. This is true, of course, and Leo appreciates being free to develop his own individuality without his mother pruning bits off here and there. But Leo also requires a sounding board, someone to measure how he is getting on. Although he loves appreciation, being deafened by applause dulls his ability to evaluate how to be on the cutting edge and truly give of his best. In other words, Leo needs standards because without them how can he be sure that he really is special?

However successful Pisceans are in reaching their goal, they usually feel that they have to give something back in return. Life is more than self-gratification. Leo is fascinated by his or her Piscean father's diffident attitude toward scoring points on the social Richter scale—Pisces really couldn't care less if he makes the earth move or not. It is a valuable lesson for Leo, who often feels he has to go through hoops to make people notice him. A Piscean father's modest attitude takes the heat off Leo, and makes the lion think about relinquishing the idea of life as a circus spectacle and just being himself instead.

Sun in Virgo Child

24 August–23 September

THE VIRGIN

Qualities to Look for and Nurture in Your Virgo Child

Mental alertness that both observes and discriminates

ALTHOUGH VIRGO IS AN EARTH SIGN, IT IS INEXTRICABLY CONnected with the air signs because Mercury, the planet of the mind, is the Virgo ruler (a position it also holds for Gemini). So, a Virgoan bases most of life's experience around what he thinks, because his mind is a powerful tool that shapes his understanding and organizes his reactions. The Virgoan mind never stops; the wheels are ever-turning, sifting through information, taking note of what is useful, and discarding the rest. Nothing much escapes this child's attention.

A natural efficiency and purposefulness

Virgo is an orderly soul, but not necessarily as physically tidy as is commonly presumed. The sense of wanting everything to be in its place is more of an idea than a reality with some Virgos. What they do possess, however, is an enormous desire to make use of themselves and of life. In other words, it is important for Virgos not to be wasteful and to find their own niche where they can be of service to others.

A kindly, considerate disposition and desire to help others

Virgos derive pleasure from doing things for other people. Because they are essentially earthy by nature, they often prefer giving to others in a practical way, and as adults like to be in a position where they can help or offer a service—in other words, to be useful! Virgos like to go about their business in a modest manner, preferring to be behind the scenes rather than at the forefront. But their quiet approach belies their great energy, which is always used constructively.

An ability to set high standards and aim for perfection

Virgos can readily spot faults and don't want to settle for second best in anything. Their eye for detail is outstanding, and undergoing their meticulous scrutiny is like trying to pass through the eye of a needle. As a child, young Virgo will not miss a trick and can tell you what is wrong immediately. His powers of observation enable him to judge the quality of anything and everything and cause him to set very high standards, both for himself and other people.

Virgo Boys

All Virgos are thinkers. In contrast to the fiery energetic boys, Virgo boys are steadied by their earth element, so they're happier exercizing their minds than their bodies. A Virgo boy will spend time planning and preparing something that he wants to do, rather than rushing in blindly. It is rare for parents of these children to have to warn them to be careful because Virgos are only too aware of the consequences of any action. Belligerence, bravado, and brawn are not characteristic of this sign because it values intelligence, consideration, and sensibility.

This is not to say that Master Virgo has gotten everything neatly signed, sealed, and delivered in his precise mind. He is apt to tie himself in knots at times and worry unnecessarily. This is the price he pays for being such an avid collector of information. His acute powers of observation can land him in trouble, making him refuse to turn a blind eye. For instance, he can become extremely fussy about the details—it must be the right brand of strawberry jam and fruit juice that is freshly squeezed (or not, according to his personal preference). He won't compromise. It can be infuriating for other people, but they don't have Virgo's ability to see life through a lens that magnifies the substance and quality of everything. There is no blurring of the edges for Virgo. And he can be misunderstood to be a fault-finder, when in truth he is sharply observant and mentally on the ball.

Virgo Girls

A desire to know, understand, and make some sort of order out of life is present in the smallest Virgo girl. She usually knows what she wants, not in the rather aggressive manner of the fire signs, but through an innate ability to observe and choose. Virgo is usually a good communicator, but this sign is also an excellent listener. Even when she is silent, her eyes are constantly measuring the world, taking in what other people are saying and doing and quietly analyzing it.

Because she seeks perfection, it is easy for her to feel inadequate herself. Virgos are often their own worst critics. In her mind she can visualize how to accomplish something perfectly, and so she feels that she can never live up to her own expectations. This is why she needs plenty of encouragement and praise and, most important, permission to get it wrong. The latter is vital if she is to get off the treadmill of setting such impossibly high standards for herself. Otherwise, inhibition will creep up on her. The inner voice that is always telling Miss Virgo to be "a good girl" can produce a reaction in adulthood. Either she lives her life within such tight constraints that enjoying herself is beyond the pale, or she does the opposite and longs to live wildly, recklessly, and with a liberating sense of abandonment. As a young girl, Virgo needs help in maintaining a balance between these two types of behavior so she can find a middle ground and a place of acceptance.

Virgo at School

A Virgo is in his or her natural habitat within a learning environment. He enjoys the order and rhythm of school, which gives him a sense of purpose—surprisingly, a young Virgo can be at a loss during the holidays when there is no set regimen. From a young age, Virgo likes to use his time constructively, to know what is expected of him, and where he is headed. Looking at the whole school system stretching ahead of him and having his future mapped out through the years suits him to a T.

He enjoys subjects that involve having to build up a fund of knowledge or develop a skill, but he feels less comfortable being asked to use his imagination. This brings out the worrier in Virgo—what kind of thing does the teacher have in mind? Will I be able to get it right? He or she needs guidelines and prefers creative activities that require practical talents—woodwork, needlework, or cooking rather than freehand drawing and poetry.

Because Virgo is an industrious soul, he doesn't need reminding to do his homework. As long as he can see the point in doing something, then he does it. He also loves to research and prepare, to gather information and sift it through, so he can take rather a long time to plow through assignments. He won't have a stab at something, or just throw it together and hope for the best. He works diligently and conscientiously, and almost like an elephant, he never forgets! He has a talent for writing—particularly those essays that require him to discuss or argue for and against something. Virgo has an inborn advantage over any other sign in the zodiac for this type of work!

Virgo at Play

Even at play, Virgos need to stimulate their minds or to be getting on with something. They are able to sit for hours painting a model airplane or decorating a doll's house because they have the capacity to become truly absorbed in what they are doing. They find it easy to concentrate—and this can make it hard for them when they don't have to focus on anything in particular. Virgos are not aimlessly playful, yet they can get exhausted if they don't get mental time off. They are like cars whose motors are constantly running, so, as a parent of a Virgo, you might have to intervene to switch the engine off every now and then!

Virgos need to be encouraged to make a mess, just let go, have fun, and behave childishly. Because they are so grown-up for their age, they like to help adults in whatever they are doing. They love to join in when you're cooking or washing the car. But Virgo is probably the child who needs the toy vacuum cleaner the least. It is really important for him to separate work and play, or he can land himself in the big Virgo workaholic syndrome later on in life.

A young Virgo really flourishes in the company of children who can introduce him or her to playing in other ways. Although he can be reticent, he makes friends easily because he is interested in other people and knows how to share and how to give and take.

Virgo Child with Aries Parent

Ariens cannot understand why Virgos need to spend so much time over things. For Ariens, life is about the quantity that can be achieved over a given period; for Virgos it is the quality that counts. A Virgo cannot be hurried, for fear of missing something. He is the sign of digestion, and he chews over life in the same way that he would carefully break down a piece of bread—no swallowing it whole. However, the ram will have to learn to swallow his words because, no matter how impatient he feels, he will not be able to get Virgo into the fast lane.

As a parent, Aries appreciates the stirrings of independence in a child, and, although a Virgo child is not itching to run his own life, he can certainly think for himself. Virgo does not exhibit a childlike dependency on others because his mind is too alert for that, and he is very much his own person right from the beginning. However, he is quiet about it, not wanting to make a song and dance to show off how clever he is. Because he is modest, Virgo often gets underestimated, and Aries in particular is a sign that often looks no further than the shop window. Having a Virgo child teaches the ram to be more careful about his or her assumptions.

The Aries mother is a doer, the Virgo child is a thinker. Both dislike wasting time, but Virgo can be fully engaged mentally while apparently standing still. It is the Virgo mind that is in perpetual motion, not his body. The need for busyness is present to such a high degree in Aries and Virgo that both signs find it hard to relax and take life as it comes. I can just picture the look of consternation on both their faces at these words. Take life as it comes? Aries wouldn't dream of being so lazy, and Virgo couldn't possibly let things ride without making a few plans, or shrewdly putting together some possible outcomes. So, really, an Aries mother and a Virgo child are partners in crime—or partners in time—and making the most of every moment!

The ram father is eager for his children to "get on in life." So naturally he is thrilled to pieces that Virgo needs little encouragement in applying himself wholeheartedly to whatever he does. But sooner or later Aries will find little Virgo with his nose in a book on a sunny day, or poring over a project that has occupied him for hours, and he will balk. In a flash, an Aries father can discount Virgo's efforts by making a suggestion that will save time, or tell him to get out and do something different. Having so little patience himself, the Aries father cannot understand how this child can be so stuck on something, so totally absorbed. He must realize it is the Virgo quality of dedication that is manifesting itself at an early age.

Virgo Child with Taurus Parent

These two earthbound souls feel very much at home with each other. Virgo is rather more finicky than Taurus, but they share an appreciation for all that is safe and solid in the world. Taurus is a traditionalist by nature, and as a parent, believes in providing security for the family above all else. The bull is often the rock that underpins the family unit and holds it together.

If you are the type who likes to be held in steady arms, then so much the better, but some signs feel the Taurean grip is made of iron and struggle to be free. Virgo, however, is not of this persuasion. Virgos are all for hanging on to what they know and value, and having a rock for a parent feels good to them. Although Virgo is an earth sign, and therefore cut from the same sensible, practical fabric as Taurus, these people can be nervous and skittish. Because of their link with Mercury, they mentally spin around at a million miles an hour and are prone to worrying and fretting. This is where the soothing influence of the Taurean parent stills the internal revolution within his or her Virgo child. The bull has the knack of being able to calm the most fevered of brows.

The tendency of a Virgo child to expect a lot of himself is calmed by the steady hand of a Taurean mother. She won't push Virgo into achieving the high standards he sets, but gently encourages him to approach things comfortably. This is nectar for Virgo, who can grow a little tense with his own belief that he has to get everything right and do it all perfectly. There is an enormous fear of failure with Virgo, which can lead to a defensive self-protection and withdrawal into being an observer, a bystander rather than a participant in life. But the bull believes in relaxing, not forcing anything, doing things at your own pace, and being kind to yourself. This is a precious gift for a Virgo child to receive early on in life. It enables Virgo to breathe.

Tapping into the formidable strength of a Taurean father feels like having an inexhaustible wellspring of stamina. There is something inherently reliable, dependable, and supportive about Taurus that feeds Virgo and makes this child feel that, no matter what, "everything will be all right in the end." A Taurus father will always bring matters back to basics—eating properly, sleeping, working, relaxing; all have their turn in his list of priorities. He provides Virgo with a framework for life founded on looking after yourself through a daily routine. Virgo needs to get the simple things in life straight, so that he or she doesn't burn himself out over the more complicated matters.

Virgo Child with Gemini Parent

Earthy Virgo and airy Gemini do not at first appear to have a lot in common, yet they are irresistibly attracted to each other because they share Mercury, the planet of communication, as their ruler. The result is that Virgo and Gemini have a meeting of minds that most people would envy, but even this does not guarantee that they will see eye to eye. In fact, they would both find such a thing terribly boring, because Virgo and Gemini thrive on exchanging differences rather than similarities.

Gemini has more of a trickster mind than Virgo. The twins can perform a dazzling display of mental acrobatics, twisting and turning their perceptions, ideas, and arguments, while Virgo stands on the sideline trying to analyze it all. So, it can seem that the Gemini parent has the dexterity of a child, and the Virgo child has the understanding of an adult. Gemini is the one who carries a certain naiveté and innocence, while Virgo possesses the kind of skepticism that makes it hard for him to believe in fairies. So, switching parent and child roles from time to time is often the case between these two signs.

For a Gemini mother who skips lightly from one thing to another, it can be hard to come to terms with a child who is naturally so precise, meticulous, and has such an eye for detail. Virgo will not let Gemini gloss over anything—he wants to know every single why and wherefore and have them presented in order of importance. Being a mother to a Virgo child can be an exacting occupation. Virgos demand their pound of flesh, and not an ounce more or less! But, at least, Gemini feels comfortable supplying information and commenting on life. The main focus of the relationship between Virgo and Gemini is communication, and because of this, the Gemini mother can find her child's preverbal years the least satisfying. But little Virgo finds his tongue almost before his feet, and once he's learned a few words, these two will have a mental rapport that lasts a lifetime.

The Gemini father will recognize the mental alertness of his Virgo child immediately. He is keyed into noticing whether other people's mental lights are switched on or off, so as soon as baby Virgo opens his or her eyes, the Gemini father will be congratulating himself on having produced such a clever child. Yet Virgo, as an earth sign, needs to be valued for more than his or her mind. His ability to spot what needs doing is second to none, but his real skill is in the way he carries it out—with dedication, attention to detail, and the sheer love of doing things properly.

Virgo Child with Cancer Parent

The crab understands the timidity of Virgo. After all, Cancer often ducks inside his shell when he doesn't feel safe or sure of himself. Therefore, he has the utmost sympathy for the modesty and shyness of Virgo. Both Cancer and Virgo are gentle souls, but their quiet manner belies their astounding capacity to make things happen.

Unlike the fire and air signs, who expend a great deal of energy talking about what they are going to do and how fantastic it is going to be, earthy and watery types like Virgo and Cancer just get on and do it. They don't need to gather an audience. A Cancerian parent will encourage Virgo to keep his own counsel and be his own judge. Unfortunately for Virgo, his internal judge often equals a critic—he always thinks he could have done better.

A Cancerian mother is the archetypal matriarch—empress of her home and family with a sensitivity that enables her to tune into the inner life of her child. Virgo emits a form of mental Morse code that sometimes bleeps with anxiety. And because Virgo never misses anything that goes on, he can easily become overloaded and simply be unable to digest all that he sees and thinks about. But he responds beautifully to the soothing nurturing and emotional support that his Cancerian mother gives him.

Virgo often simply needs to talk and get things off his or her chest. A Cancerian mother is only too happy to provide tea and sympathy—but she must always remember with this discerning child that it has to be exactly the right kind of tea! Getting things right can become a big issue for Virgo, and he can become so preoccupied with the details that he loses an overall sense of direction and priority. With Cancer's unerring ability to sense what other people need, this mother can help her little Virgo to maintain a balance between aiming high and allowing oneself to be imperfect and human.

Virgos always need someone to be on their side, because they are often their own worst enemies. A Cancerian father manages to give out this message of unconditional love to his family. Sure, he can turn crabby at times, but Virgo understands only too well that a little complaining now and again is only natural. Basically, a crab father is comforting and reassuring, and this child needs to know that he is loved without expectations, so that he can banish his inner worries about not being good enough to deserve love.

Virgo Child with Leo Parent

When Virgo and Leo are kith and kin, a particular kind of bonding takes place that involves them both in the deepest level of loyalty. Leo recognizes that this child possesses all the specialness of the lion but is modest about it, and Virgo looks up to the shining attributes of Leo with admiration. Precisely because Virgo is self-contained and unasking of applause, he never threatens the lion by appearing to want to take over his ground. Smart as he is, Virgo is quite happy to take a back seat and let someone else go to all the bother of driving. And so Leo can direct operations to his heart's content. Peace reigns between Virgo and Leo.

One could ask that if the parent is getting the lion's share of the attention, where does this leave young Virgo? Well, not skulking miserably in a corner, that's for sure. Virgo has other fish to fry; he doesn't need to keep looking in the mirror to see if he is the fairest of them all. And if Leo is happy with himself, he is a benign ruler, bestowing love, generosity, and a kindness that kindles a similar spark in those around him. So Virgo doesn't stand in the shade; he is just on the edge of Leo's footlights, receiving the warmth without having to perform.

When a Virgo child is brought up by a Leo mother, he has a constant ally in his striving for perfection. Leo appreciates the best—that means trying your best, surrounding yourself with the best, and aiming to be the best. Virgo aspires to the highest standards, but without the razzle-dazzle of Leo. For Virgo, it is just as important to tie shoelaces perfectly as it is to write the best essay. Throughout life, Virgo believes in devoting oneself to the task in hand, however mundane it may appear; and being an earth sign, Virgo will never reject the ordinary things that Leo considers to be beneath him.

The lion father needs to try to radiate a little of his own confidence to Virgo. It is so natural for Leos to slip into a position of authority, because they believe they have the answers. Virgo as a child, and even as an adult, will always mentally work things through to such an extent that he can't take the risk of just having a try or doing anything off the cuff. The Virgo brain likes to mull and chew, break down thoughts and possibilities, link them together, throw out the dead wood, and finally pigeonhole everything in its rightful place. A Leo father can give his Virgo child a little of his own spontaneity.

Virgo Child with Virgo Parent

Right from the word *go,* Virgo and Virgo are intent on dovetailing neatly together—this is a parent–child relationship where you can hardly see the seam in the joint. Virgos do tend to stick together anyway; they are drawn to each other's beady eyes and spark each other off in rounds of witty observations. At home, Virgos usually have some sort of precise routine, and a Virgo child will take to it like a duck to water. Each knows exactly what to expect and revels in the military execution of the rules.

It is not that Virgos are fanatically tidy—that is a myth. But they are obsessive about the details, things that no other sign would notice. Other members of the family may not appreciate it, but Virgo and Virgo know how important it is to make sure you have apple green soap, not strawberry pink, in the green bathroom. Such things matter to Virgos, who derive pleasure from perfect coordination, whatever their age.

A Virgo child can be a very picky eater, turning his or her nose up if something doesn't look or smell quite right. But luckily a Virgo mother has a memory like a computer, capable of storing away all the family's idiosyncracies and preferences, so she rarely produces something unacceptable, even for young Virgo. With this mother, a Virgo child feels his fussiness is totally acceptable. His mother would just call it discrimination, which in her eyes is a very important quality to possess and a sign of intelligence and good taste.

Living with a Virgo mother, one soon realizes that time is a precious commodity that must not be wasted—even her leisure time can be taken up with a list of things to do. For a young Virgo, this model of efficiency is taken as an example of how to squeeze the maximum usefulness out of life. So the puritan work ethic can be passed down from generation to generation, making it difficult for a small Virgo to justify having a really good time with absolutely no point to it whatsoever. Being an adult Virgo in the making, he is predisposed to notice his mother's busyness and adopt her ways, which confirm his own natural tendencies.

Virgo fathers are usually thoughtful about parenthood and eager to ensure they are creating the best possible early environment for their children. In particular, a Virgo father will try to filter out any influences that he deems unfit for his child and will avidly monitor television, reading material, and exposure to other children. It may sound like the Gestapo, but it isn't. In his kindly way, Virgo is only trying to give his child "the best," but he can have some pretty strong ideas about what is acceptable. For a Virgo child, who is born to grow up with the kind of mind that can spot a fault at fifty paces, it feels quite natural.

Virgo Child with Libra Parent

Because Libra follows Virgo on the astrological wheel, he or she embodies a different ethos. He can be just as picky as Virgo when it comes to appearances and presentation, but generally he glosses over many of the details and worries that trouble Virgo. The difference is that Virgo isn't happy unless he has something to chew over mentally, and Libra isn't happy unless the outlook is serene.

What this means within a parent–child relationship is that the Libran parent will tend to overlook many of the things that concern Virgo and be unable to comprehend why small things make such a big difference to this child. "Just forget it; put a smile on your face and relax," Libra will say, and Virgo will try to adjust his or her features accordingly (always willing to please) but inwardly stew over the matter. One can always tell when Virgo has gone quiet that his mind is ticking away on some inner issue.

Of course, a Libran mother will appreciate the way her little Virgo is thoughtful and considerate within the home. Virgo will not impose himself on people, so even as a child he won't create a bomb site in the living room, make camps in the kitchen, or mud pies in the bathroom unless it is absolutely okay with you. And there are no prizes for guessing whether this sort of thing is welcomed by Libra. Easygoing she may be in some ways, but when it comes to making a filthy mess, the scales tip pretty quickly!

Because Virgo is so sensitive to criticism, this child flourishes in the diplomatic world of Libra. Libra is ruled by Venus, the planet of appreciation and love, so this mother is unlikely to rule with a rod of iron. She manages to create around her a household that vibrates in harmony, and Virgo responds by becoming less anxious about himself and whether he is getting things right or not.

A Libran father tends to idealize his children. He is tuned into the sweetness-and-light dimension, and so as far as his children are concerned, he sees budding angels rather than little monsters. It would be fair to say that it is easier to pull the wool over his eyes than you can over Virgo's. Libra wants to see the good and tends to blanket things together. But Virgo is discriminating. He doesn't want his father to congratulate him on the master quality of each and every single one of his paintings, because Virgo knows himself that some are better than others and that there is always room for improvement. If you look for the details and comment on them, that will enable Virgo to feel his or her efforts have really been looked at, rather than just glanced at.

Virgo Child with Scorpio Parent

Virgo and Scorpio see eye to eye on many matters. They are great observers, putting people and life under the microscope to try to gain a better understanding. They are also realists, preferring to see the warts in order to get a truer picture. And as a parent, Scorpio is delighted that this child is so perceptive and receptive. So these signs feel comfortable with each other, and there is a special kind of honesty between them, which builds up trust and mutual respect.

Inside every Scorpio is an urge to transform. It is difficult for Scorpios to put up with the status quo because they cannot help having the desire to go one better and make it different. This applies to themselves, to other people, and to life itself. This yearning to go forward grates against some of the other Sun signs who like to stay with the way things are. But Virgo is also a member of the self-improvement society. A Virgo child loves to be encouraged to make the most of his or her talents. From the moment he is born, he is on the way to something better, but not in the sense that he wants to achieve fame and glory; he just wants to be the best version of himself—and that is really all anyone can aspire to.

The quiet but alert energy of the Virgo child sits well with a Scorpio mother. She has difficulty being around people who are blasting off with great physical energy; it disturbs her ability to think straight. Both she and Virgo need time to reflect. She is not fooled by Virgo's apparent composure, either. Scorpio is an expert at looking beyond the surface, so she can see that this child's extraordinary mental capacities make him or her unusually capable, and also at times a little tense. There is very little that Virgos cannot handle, but they need a lot of encouragement along the way.

A Scorpio father can communicate without words. It seems strange, but Scorpios can often say far more in a look than in a sentence, and even a young Virgo is able to pick up this language very easily. This is because Virgo never misses anything. He is always picking up clues; he notices people's facial expressions, the way they move their hands or their bodies, so he "just knows" what his Scorpio father is thinking. Just as well, because Scorpio is often not the greatest verbal communicator, and he can hold a lot in, but these two can find a level with each other.

Virgo Child with Sagittarius Parent

Virgo can be rather a serious child, because he is so busy taking notes he can forget to play. But having a Sagittarian parent will probably change all that—enjoying life is extremely high on the Sagittarian list of priorities. These people have an energy and sense of fun that is striving to burst out all over the place and contrasts strongly with Virgo's self-contained manner and carefulness.

The archer will encourage Virgo to have a try at many things he would avoid if left to his own devices. The spontaneity of Sagittarius blasts through Virgo's natural reticence, and the archer waves aside all Virgo's worries and doubts. He will undoubtedly be able to help Virgo express more of himself and be more confident, but he must remember that Virgo's life-script runs more like a game of consequences. He or she is born to think things through, take a practical stance, and err on the side of caution. Sagittarius may be the "mile-a-minute" plant of the zodiac, sprawling out and developing at the rate of knots, but Virgo is a tender biennial and worth waiting for.

A Sagittarian mother radiates enough optimism to seep through into her Virgo child. Not that Virgo is a pessimist, but he is a realist and needs to import a little of the Sagittarian faith in life. However, Virgo's finicky ways can drive an archer mother to distraction. "Why on earth is it so important to have a particular make of pencil to take to school? They're all the same, aren't they?" she asks. But Virgo has his own personal grading system for everything; he will always evaluate and classify objects because he is fascinated by the differences between things.

This child can stop his or her Sagittarian father dead in his tracks. As soon as he is able to talk, he is always drawing his father's attention to things he had never stopped to think about before. Virgos often make life more interesting for other people because being in their company is like having a commentator on the sport of life. An archer father would prefer to have his child out there as the tennis pro, but hearing him utter such intelligent observations makes him think twice. Virgo seems to have the world sewn up; he is nobody's fool, and his alertness is a gift what will always stand him in good stead.

Virgo Child with Capricorn Parent

Two such earthbound souls make wonderful companions in life. They walk along at the same rate, in step with each other. Virgo is one of the few signs that can live within the bounds set by Capricorn and feel comfortable with them. It is because Virgo doesn't need to chafe at the bit; he is not itching to dictate the terms of his life or stage a rebellion. Mentally he may turn a few tricks and consider a few alternatives to Capricorn's way of doing things, but generally he is content to stay within the system. And Capricorn offers security for Virgo; his sure-footedness and certainty soothes Virgo's fidgety nature.

Capricorn and Virgo both believe that if something is worth doing, then it should be done properly. That means making a plan beforehand, ensuring it is achievable, and then organizing it. Virgo would add a P.S.—clean up afterward! Together, they have the means to tackle most challenges, and both revel in creating order out of chaos. When they are in a parent–child relationship, they play things straight down the line, and everyone knows where they stand.

Capricorn mothers tend to view looking after their offspring as an organizational role and deal with it as if they are aiming to be chairwoman! They work like beavers to stay on top of things, implementing a routine that keeps life turning over with regularity and efficiency. Virgo loves this kind of approach—the rule that if-it's-Monday-it's-macaroni-and-cheese-and-hairwashing-night. He frets when he has to make life up as it goes along, feeling much safer when he knows what is coming.

One thing about Virgo that the Capricorn father appreciates immeasurably is the serious approach he or she has to life. Unlike fire-sign fathers, he won't try to get little Virgo to loosen up, take a risk, or rush forward. Capricorn has always been a grown-up, even in the cradle, and he believes that having a wise head on young shoulders is absolutely the best insurance against life's uncertainties that his child could possess. So Virgo's natural penchant for reliability, thoroughness, and industry is openly encouraged and gratefully received.

Virgo Child with Aquarius Parent

The Aquarian urge to experiment and try something new is not exactly music to the ears of little Virgo, who likes order in his universe. It can feel to Virgo that, just as he has gotten the measure of life, Aquarius can't help throwing a wrench into the works. The parameters of his or her understanding are permanently stretched to accommodate new things. It is really the Aquarian need for excitement that sends him in search of stimulation. But Virgo can always find enough to excite him in the details of what is already before him; he just examines it more closely. With Virgo and Aquarius, it is a matter of nearsightedness meeting farsightedness, and they both have to adjust to the other's vision.

There is no question about it, Virgo can sometimes get bogged down, and Aquarius is naturally gifted at coming up with new angles. While Virgo is intent on persevering with learning how to walk, read, or play tennis according to whatever stage he's at, Aquarius will take the heat out of the matter. It's unintentional, but somehow Aquarius gets Virgo to relax; he lets the steam out of the pressure cooker. It's because Aquarius rarely gets worked up about anything—when things get tense, he or she just turns the situation upside down and looks at it differently.

Virgo can give the impression of being as calm and rational as any air sign because his or her mind is so well developed. But he is a worrier, and in particular he worries that he is not good enough. This is where the Aquarian mother's nonjudgmental attitude gives Virgo a security blanket. The water bearer mother does not need her children to prove anything; she respects them as individuals in their own right. Aquarians don't want the people close to them to behave in any particular way, and if an Aquarian mother can convey her inner freedom to her little Virgo, she can let him off his own hook. He will receive the gold star just for being himself.

As the sign of friendship, Aquarius gathers people around him. The Aquarian father is seen by his Virgo child as possessing an ease with people, and a concern for others, that ties in with Virgo's own desire to give to other people. From the early years of his or her life, Virgo is mindful of others, thoughtful, and considerate. His is the opposite of the "me first" philosophy that often pushes the fire signs forward. In his father, Virgo can see the benefits of looking beyond himself and caring about other people—he is encouraged to make bridges, not islands.

Virgo Child with Pisces Parent

Having a Virgoan child invites Pisces to define himself more clearly. He must forget about floating along and must answer the question—and when he has finished, Virgo usually has another query to put to him. As an earth sign, Virgo often has the capacity to bring other people down to earth, even the fish who prefers to while away his time dreaming, imagining, and flowing with the tides. Because Virgo and Pisces occupy opposite positions in the zodiac, they are distinctively different and magnetically attracted.

Pisceans are very good at fudging the issue because they see all the nuances and shades that blend into each other. Virgoans, however, see everything with clarity and exactness, so they demand to know whether something is this or that, one thing or another. Never has Pisces felt so put on the spot as when a Virgo child is trying to build up his or her own personal encyclopedia of knowledge and wants some succinct information. And in the exchange, Virgo will have to add a new section to his internal book under the letter *S*—*S* for shades of gray!

Virgo needs the sort of order in his life that forces his Piscean mother to make plans and organize a routine. Not that she is normally a chaotic mess; in fact, many fish can be just as finicky as the average Virgo—it is surprising how often the opposite signs can steal qualities from the other. But she doesn't need her day to take on the ambience of a military operation; she likes to allow a little leeway for the unknowable.

She will ask little Virgo, "What do you feel like today?," meaning what sort of food does he want to eat, what clothes does he want to wear. She is introducing him to something other than life's being dictated by practical considerations. And it is a whole new world for Virgo—a magical one where one makes decisions intuitively, instead of looking purely at the facts. Pisceans possess a strong inner guidance that gives them faith in themselves and in life. Having a Piscean mother is a bit like swimming with a dolphin for Virgo—an experience that reaches beyond the ordinary things in life.

The father fish handles his children gently—not forcing or demanding—and Virgo feels totally accepted by him. He may puzzle over his father's rather *laissez-faire* approach, but he learns that it is just his way, and there is no point in Virgo getting miffed if a trip to the zoo turns out to be a trip to the museum. Having a Pisces father can seem to Virgo like being on a permanent magical mystery tour; he knows he is being led somewhere, but he will just have to be content to go along with things. With this father, Virgo will learn early that you don't have to be in control of everything all the time.

Sun in Libra Child

24 September–23 October

THE SCALES

Qualities to Look for and Nurture in Your Libra Child

A sense of fairness, justice, and equality

As THE SIGN OF THE SCALES, LIBRA IS CONCERNED WITH weighing and balancing before making judgments, and there is a tremendous need to be seen to be fair. As a child, Libra needs to be handled with fairness in order for him to maintain his own balance. It is commonly assumed that Libra is on an even keel because of his or her connection with the scales and therefore has an easy time of it, but internally he or she goes up and down in an effort to find the middle ground.

A drive to relate to other people and experience life through his or her connections with others

As an air sign, Libra is sociable, and in contrast to his opposite number Aries, who models the quality of independence, Libra is concerned with relating to others. In his or her early years, Libra needs plenty of companionship and the opportunity to experience different types of relationship on a variety of levels. However, it is important that Libra also learns to value himself because he can get lost in relationships when he adjusts too much to other people.

A charming, diplomatic manner and a talent for negotiation

Libra's desire for peace and harmony urges him or her to respond to others in as pleasant a way as possible. Libra wants to be liked, and so his behavior is never rough around the edges. He or she is well-mannered, considerate, and engaging. Even as a child he knows how to get around his parents without ruffling feathers, and he carries this talent forward into adulthood, where he becomes a skilled negotiator with the ability to make everyone feel pleased with their side of the bargain. His mind is naturally rational, and his charm smoothes his path in life.

A love of beauty and elegance and an appreciation of style and presentation

Libra's ruler is the planet Venus, which makes him aware of how things look. Ugliness strikes at his inner tranquillity, which is why he cares so much about style and form. Libra wants the world to be beautiful and is concerned with making a good impression on other people. Because of this, he or she can place a great deal of importance on surface appearances and sweep anything discordant under the carpet. Although his talent for making things look good is useful to him, he also needs to be encouraged to concentrate on more than presentation.

Libra Boys

Out of all the signs of the zodiac, Librans are probably the "easiest" children—in other words, the most pliant and adaptable within the family. However, although Libra is born to fit in, he must also tune into what he wants and needs if he is not to make a career out of letting other people call the shots. Libra is a cardinal sign and therefore requires a say in the action. As a parent of a Libran boy, it is important to listen for and respond when he feels like playing the director and calling "cut." Learning to say no is vital for Libra.

Because Libra is an air sign, and therefore lives more in his head than anywhere else, his main thrust of energy is mental rather than physical. Libra isn't the type to joust in the mud—he doesn't really enjoy getting messy, and there are far more interesting ways to spend his time. He loves people and companionship because he finds solitary pastimes rather dull—Libra is a great sharer. Of course, his charm and easygoing manner make him so popular that he finds himself in the midst of a social whirl before he can even walk.

As a child, Libra needs to be encouraged to make choices. He can get stuck on the fence of indecision, frequently delegating the responsibility of choosing to someone else and hiding behind an "I don't care" attitude. He gets caught up in what other people would like and the pros and cons of all the options. Parents can encourage Libra to state his desires regardless of what anyone else might think.

Libra Girls

From the cradle, Miss Libra knows how to flirt with anyone who catches her eye. Her smiles are guaranteed to entrance, and she revels in making other people feel good, which in turn makes her feel loved. It is natural for her to play the role of "good little girl" and, of course, natural for her parents to encourage her to play it; yet unless Librans come to terms with the fact that they don't always feel nice or want to be pleasant, they will end up repressing anything negative. So later on, the little girl who was always so good can have real trouble expressing anger, or going after what she wants, because she is trapped by the need to please other people.

A Libran girl is aware of her femininity from a young age. Being a tomboy is not her style. She oozes attractiveness and charm, practicing first by winding her father around her little finger before gravitating to other suitors in her play group.

In her teens she is the first to believe that love makes the world go around, but she has to be careful not to confuse love with the need for approval. It is important in the early years for her to value herself and be independent when she chooses, because Librans who spend their lives adjusting and compromising in order to keep the peace may be "loved" for their amiability, but secretly despise themselves. Helping her to develop her individuality means challenging her to stand up for herself.

Libra at School

The Libran mind is refined, objective, and skilled at comparing ideas and information. Librans love to put forward both sides of an argument, and therefore excel at writing essays that require a balanced viewpoint. Dressing up the facts to present a polished report is second nature, and Librans will always turn in work that is well presented. However, they can masquerade beneath their ability to make a good impression—Librans are clever at knowing what the teacher wants and knocking it out, but scratch the surface and you may discover their knowledge is only superficial.

Librans have a reputation for being lazy, which is for the most part undeserved. Their laid-back attitude contributes to this impression, and Librans don't make a big noise or get worked up when put to the test. They maintain a generally relaxed demeanor and are not hugely competitive, so it may be the parents rather than the Libran child whose blood is coursing with adrenaline on exam day.

Fitting into the school system rarely presents a problem for Libra. He likes the orderliness of school, and knowing what is expected of him brings out the best in Libra. He is not disruptive by nature, and because he respects authority and possesses a willingness to please, he gets along well with teachers and makes friends easily. He may, however, have trouble proving himself with the school bully, but Libra will try to win him over by flattery rather than force.

Libra at Play

Libra likes to feel he is part of something, so he loves group activities, clubs, or just having a friend over. As soon as he can talk, it is evident that he can chat to almost anyone because he is socially at ease. Loving parties, Libra throws himself into the whole event—the invitations, the getting ready, and the hosting. And it is not that he is even the life and soul of it—leave that to noisy Aries and Leo—but he likes the whole atmosphere of people getting together to enjoy themselves.

As a child, Libra is usually in touch with his own creative talents, and he likes to play with colors and make beautiful things. Yet he also possesses the sort of mind that enjoys playing games with other people. He has the mental alertness for chess, and the desire to get everyone together for Monopoly. With his friends he tends to join in rather than initiate the action—it is characteristic of Libra to assess the status quo and then react to it rather than demand that everyone else should do what he wants to do. Probably because he comes across as such a happy, contented child, he is welcome everywhere.

Libra Child with Aries Parent

Having a ram parent tips the scales of Libra one way or another. It is the magnetic energy of Aries that pulls other people along in a particular direction, and Libra is usually quite happy with this arrangement because he is so good at fitting in around other people.

Aries embodies the energy of the will—that which separates, motivates, activates—while Libra is always identified with the love energies of cooperation, peace, and harmony. So as long as Aries is in charge and Libra is following, all runs smoothly, but if Libra feels pushed too much, then his scales start to tip the other way. He won't play ball as the compliant child, but instead starts to prevaricate and procrastinate, which is Libra's way of saying, "Look, I'm not prepared to go along with this."

Pretty soon, the ram is having to look around for some method of placating Libra—sounds remarkably Libran, doesn't it? It is extraordinary how two signs living in close proximity move from opposites to togetherness and back again, but this is what happens when two signs are positioned directly across from each other on the astrological wheel—they exchange places sometimes!

An Aries mother wants her child to go for first place in life and cannot understand why Libra is so happy to be in the middle. But Libra considers occupying the middle ground to be the best possible position—from there he or she can see everyone. It's lonely being out in front, and Libra detests being on his or her own. No matter how much this Aries lady rams home the virtues of being a leader and winning, Libra will look at her quizzically as he inwardly weighs what he also stands to lose in such a situation. For Libra likes to keep his options open, and his game plan for life is not about getting through it as quickly as possible to see how many points he scores. Libra must be allowed to be Libran, not an imitation Aries. He needs time to consider things and an appreciation of his need for balance.

One thing that Aries can do, which serves a purpose for Libra (although he may not think so), is to goad him into speaking his mind. The fire of the Aries father ignites Libra and encourages him or her to "come out with it." Aries is so forcibly direct and straight to the point that Libra is put on the spot and learns how to make decisions. Of course, he may reverse them later, much to the chagrin of his ram father, who is a fervent believer in acting now and not regretting later. But being in such close connection with a "doer" gives Libra the opportunity to experiment.

Libra Child with Taurus Parent

Libra and Taurus are both Venusian types—that is, ruled by Venus, the planet of love, beauty, and harmony—so they have a great affinity with each other. But the Libran version of Venus has a much airier, lighter touch—Librans glide through life, but have you ever seen a bull gliding? Taurus is a solid earth sign and therefore rooted in material matter, but nonetheless executing the practicalities beautifully.

Of course a Libran child enjoys the aura of comfort that Taurus creates. Both insist on their little luxuries—some bubbles in the bath for Libra and really good food for Taurus. And being of Venusian origin, Taurus has no desire at all to make the home a war zone. In his or her book, conflict is a stupid waste of time, which is a sentiment echoed by Libra.

Why is it then that, despite his charm, Libra can push the bull's patience to the limit? Not because Libra is aggressive or testy, but simply because he or she will stand on the edge of the pavement doing the shoeshine shuffle and not getting on with things. The bull might amble along slowly, but he knows where he's going and why. Libra somehow dances along looking as if he might change direction at a moment's notice.

The Taurean mother is an eminently sensible soul. She keeps her feet on the ground, whereas little Libra can get lost in the clouds—he is more frivolous and liable to be carried away like a will-o'-the-wisp. He hears everyone's ideas and opinions and plays around with them, whereas his Taurean mother maintains her "I know what's best" attitude. Because she is so sure of what she believes in, Libra just has to play the devil's advocate, but he does it so sweetly, so charmingly, that he disarms rather than provokes. Incredibly, the immovable bull can be won over by little Libra's gentle persuasion.

The outward placidity of a Taurean father can be deceptive—in fact, he is rock-solid, strong as the ox that is the symbol of his sign. In the early years, Libra feels protected by his or her father's guiding hand, but later, when Libra has developed the rationality and reason that his sign is famous for, he needs to look at life in other ways. This can be when the relationship runs into trouble because Taurus is a traditionalist and sticks to his guns, and Libra is caught between his or her desire to please and a yearning to understand the other side of life's coin. Trying to box Libra in only unbalances his nature. If the bull can let go of his grip, he will find Libra comes back to his ideas anyway—he is after the middle ground, not the opposite extreme.

Libra Child with Gemini Parent

Gemini well understands Libra's need for other people because he is one of the air signs himself and therefore socially oriented. So he is more than happy to fix Libra up with an endless round of people to see and places to go. Yet when in the company of just each other, they are like two birds, constantly chattering away and flitting from one subject to another. Libra and Gemini will never run out of things to talk about.

The Gemini mother is psychologically predisposed to be a loose-hold mother—that is, one who retains her own identity and allows her child a lot of space to be himself or herself. It is the water sign mothers who tend toward tight-holding because they are by nature drawn toward very close relationships. Libra is the sign of relationship, yet because it belongs to the element of air, Librans want to experience communication rather than suffocating closeness, something a Gemini mother understands perfectly, so she is able to give this quality of mothering quite naturally.

She won't force her child to think or do things in any particular way, because she doesn't conform to any set behavior herself. Geminis absolutely dread to think that they are set in stone, that their actions are predictable—and on becoming a mother, this desire to create oneself anew every morning becomes even more important. The Gemini mother will not allow the physical routine involved in nurturing to detract from her free-ranging approach to life. She is open to change all the time, and so her child learns to be adaptable. Little Libra is in his element here—he is born to be adaptable and loves to respond appropriately, although too much change sets his scales in motion at such an alarming pace that it disturbs his equilibrium.

Libra is faced with a multitude of choices from his or her Gemini father, who flirts with many ideas and never dictates the status quo. For Libra, the stimulation is exciting, but it can also be confusing and sometimes unbalancing. Gemini may be used to darting between one thing and another, but Libra likes to feel that life is a beautiful pattern with everything weighed in equal measure. For this reason he or she needs continuity and symmetry.

Libra Child with Cancer Parent

Libra aims to please, while Cancer aims to meet other people's needs. So you can see here that Libra and Cancer can be so busy trying to fulfill these basic drives of their sign that they can end up missing each other in the middle! The serious point here is that the Cancer parent will make the child the focus of attention, and, although a Leo would love it, a Libran feels comfortable when someone else is holding the reins and guiding Libra into response.

With a Cancerian parent, little Libra can feel that he or she has a great deal of responsibility for making life happen, and that puts him in a twitch. Of course, Cancer is only doing his bit—putting his own needs aside so that he can tune into his child—to make him feel wanted and loved in the only way he knows how. But Libra reacts by feeling invaded and in danger of drowning in all the attention—he needs to come up for air.

Because the Cancerian mother is always able to feel intuitively what is going on emotionally, she will not automatically buy Libra's "I'm happy as a clam" attitude. Very often, Libra puts on a smiling face when he is feeling quite the opposite, and the crab mother will intuit his inner mood.

It's very disconcerting for Libra—he cannot hide behind his happy mask and pretend, even to himself, that everything is fine when his mother is saying to him, "I know there's something wrong." But Cancer can help Libra to become more in touch with his own feelings and to express himself authentically, without worrying about what everyone else thinks.

The Cancerian father matches Libra in his gentleness. When provoked, Cancer tends to withdraw into his shell rather than fight it out, and Libra always likes the amicable compromise rather than the battle. Understanding each other in this nonconfrontational manner, Cancer and Libra can live together in peaceable harmony. Nevertheless, they are both cardinal signs and therefore surprisingly eager to make their mark on life. They won't be wasting their energy swashbuckling and generally making a big noise, but Cancer and Libra have important personal goals to meet. And the crab father shows his small Libran how to make things happen without sacrificing the spirit of cooperation.

Libra Child with Leo Parent

Leo's verve and high-voltage energy make Libra appear to be more controlled than he or she really is. Leo gets so excited and wrapped up in his spontaneous childlike reactions, while Libra maintains his cool sitting on the sidelines. As long as Leo has the starring role, he is generous in helping newcomers. So, as a parent, Leo is like a benevolent ruler distributing gifts and raising morale among his subjects while maintaining his position as the supremo. Libra feels fine with this arrangement—it is not in his nature to vie for position, and his charm assures him the warmest rays of Leo's love.

Both Libra and Leo have a tremendous need for approval from other people. Libra is in the business of being as agreeable as possible, so pleasant and accommodating that it is not much wonder that other people like him. Leo, on the other hand, is not so much concerned with being liked as having his talents recognized; his style of delivery is designed to draw glances of admiration from other people.

Lionesses expect good behavior from their offspring, and Libra always produces the goods. He or she won't let the team down with sudden tantrums or high-spirited offensives and seems to take everything in stride. Libra has an incredible ability to look as though he is sailing through life—internally, though, his scales are dipping back and forth as he continually makes adjustments to new people and new situations. His easygoing manner can hide a lack of confidence in himself, and his sheer niceness means that he can easily be taken advantage of. People think, "Oh, Libra won't mind if we do this or that," and Libra carries on smiling regardless—but a Leo mother needs to read between the lines to understand this child.

Being a fire sign, a Leo father is in touch with his instincts and impulses—the lion cannot understand why Libra has to think so hard about everything, from the flavor of the ice cream he wants to which bedtime story he wants to hear. Being so considerate and willing to compromise slows down the decision-making process, and the more choices Libra has, the more difficult it is for him to make up his mind at all. Even though he is so eager to please, Libra can't make decisions to order. His is the sign of judgment, and he has to have time to listen to his own internal jury before he passes his verdict.

Libra Child with Virgo Parent

Virgo finds the company of Libra soothing and agreeable. There is something about the Libran equanimity that irons out the creases in Virgo's life. For Virgo cannot help noticing every detail, scouring life for a close-up view of each idiosyncracy, mismatch, or fault. So many of the things that drive Virgo to distraction simply don't matter to Libra, who looks at life's bigger picture and, as long as it is generally pleasing, accepts the bad with the good. After all, it keeps a balance.

Even as a parent, Virgo puts himself through his paces in an effort to reach his own high standards, and he continually monitors himself as if to ask, "Am I doing this right?" This "could do better/must try harder" attitude passes over a Libran child, who will not question the status quo unless it is very badly out of balance. He is relaxed about himself too, not feeling the need to put himself through the wringer, but staying open to whatever comes along and being pleasant about it. Libra will make the best of things, whereas Virgo won't put up with anything that is less than perfect.

As a mother, Virgo tends to put most of her energy into organizing the practicalities of life with the utmost efficiency. Clean sheets, pressed clothes, meals at the ready, advance tickets for movies, a school schedule that runs like clockwork—you name it, and Virgo has thought of it and, what's more, has done something about it! Libra's rather indolent attitude can irk her. He seems to dance through life—and not on his toes!

Because little Libra is so adaptable, he or she can fit into the Virgo mother's regimen without batting an eyelid. He will rarely refuse to cooperate because he gets enjoyment out of pleasing other people, and his idea of making a stand is to procrastinate—so the bedroom will be tidied tomorrow, and tomorrow, and tomorrow . . . By the time he gets around to it, he knows Virgo will have beaten him to it. Is it the Libran laziness or his flair for strategy showing itself in its early stages? Either way, he knows how to charm his mother into forgiving him.

A Libran child's mind gets a lot of exercise with his Virgoan father. Virgo's conversation is peppered with the kind of anecdotes, observations, and well-considered opinions that stimulate Libra's thought processes. So much so that he or she will often take the other point of view. But this is simply Libra's way—he has to balance the discussion, and he has a way of putting forward ideas that seldom aggravate the other person. But Virgo can be mentally intransigent—once he has put any idea through his sorting system, he will not change his mind, however much Libra tries to persuade him otherwise. And because Libra hates to be left out in the cold, he or she will follow the Virgo father's lead, saying that if you can't beat 'em, join 'em.

Libra Child with Libra Parent

One would think that with two sets of scales constantly moving back and forth, two Librans would feel out of sorts with each other. But what happens when you get two Librans together is that each pair of scales adjusts to balance the other one. Am I making myself clear? Clarity is everything with Libra. Maybe it would be best to leave them to their own finely tuned balancing act and say that a Libran duo of parent and child works in harmony and pleases most of the people most of the time—one cannot get fairer than that!

Libra hates to upset other people, which can involve him or her in the uncomfortable position of bending over backward to please someone else. Yet Libra is so lithe and agile that performing these contortions doesn't torment him in the slightest, and he can always justify them to himself—he needed the exercise, it was good to see things from another perspective, etc., etc.

Librans together can be so busy being nice and pleasant to each other that they find it impossible to voice their grievances, frustration, and annoyance—the normal emotions that crop up in any family. Anything difficult is automatically swept under the carpet, which buries the opportunity that family life presents to children to rehearse for the cut and thrust of the world out there.

Because Librans are so hooked into the sweetness-and-light side of life, they can exist in a kind of bubble where "nothing nasty ever happens in this family, and we all love each other all the time." Librans often need someone else to provoke the argument; so a Libran parent and child can form such a powerful alliance that they end up actually avoiding the intimacy that comes from confronting problems and working them through and lose the honesty of being real with each other.

Of course a Libran mother appreciates the fact that this child is so personable and easy. A Libran child will form himself into a hand that perfectly fits his parent's glove—no sagging or stretching here. This is his beauty and his gift, and it probably takes another Libran to truly perceive it.

It is from his or her Libran father that little Libra learns the art of negotiating and ensuring fair play. Of all the signs, Libran men are the ones who divide their time equally between family and work. So this child learns that his turn will always come, and that he will always be allowed to have his say. Librans mirror other people, so it is no wonder that in no time at all he has picked up the persuasive tactics, the charm, and the diplomacy of his father.

Libra Child with Scorpio Parent

It lifts the Scorpio heart to observe Libra with his sunny disposition, his glad eye for life. From the moment baby Libra melted Scorpio's tricky mother-in-law on her visit to the hospital, there was no doubting his mission to create harmony in life. Libra will stand between two disparate people and try to weave them together. More often than not, he succeeds in being able to find some common ground, in somehow taking the heat out of the situation. Nevertheless, it is a rare Scorpio who seeks out life at lukewarm level, because the scorpion tends toward extremes—he would rather stand near the fire and take what comes. When Scorpio and Libra are joined together by blood, there are bound to be some changes in temperature!

As a child, Libra is looking for clues to life from other people. There are so many questions he would like his mother to answer. Scorpio, however, believes that no one else can really give you the truth, and encourages Libra to look within himself. But that would only give one side of the story, and Libra needs to find out what other people think so that he can gauge things for himself. His starting point is to ask you your opinion, then he puts it on his scales, weighs it, counterbalances it with the opposite point of view, and measures his own thoughts against the equation. It is a complicated process, but it is Libra's way. He can see himself only in relation to someone else. He cannot picture what he is until he sees what he is not.

Aiming to please, Libra appears to be so affable, equable, and well behaved. He makes all the right noises and seems to know exactly what is expected of him. There is danger here in the long run for Libra—he can be too accommodating, which sets him up with a difficulty in having his own needs met later in life. Now, there is probably no other father in the zodiac who understands as well as Scorpio how important it is to be true to yourself. Scorpio's path is often strewn with situations that demand inner resources. Undoubtedly, he will have resisted joining the status quo several times in his life because he felt strongly that he must do otherwise. However, being able to make these kinds of choices and act on them is fundamental to Libra's ability to stand on his own two feet. He has such a talent for creating harmony and saying yes, yet he also needs to learn how to say no.

Libra Child with Sagittarius Parent

An archer parent scoops Libra up for a ride as he gallops along, and Libra is thrilled by all he sees but rather wishes he could slow down and take it at an easier pace. Although Libra will keep smiling, it doesn't take much to put him out of kilter. His is the sign of balance, and he needs life to be made up of equal measures in order to maintain his tranquillity.

Sagittarius can get carried away with the urge to do more and more, and he won't let being a parent deter him from his zestful desire to live life in the fast lane. Of course, Libra would prefer the middle lane (he is always looking for the middle ground); then he can speed up or slow down as the mood takes him. But he is so good at fitting in with other people's plans, and Sagittarius makes everything look so exciting, that he goes along with it.

The one thing a Sagittarian mother would do well to understand about her Libran child is that presentation matters to him or her. Sagittarians do not have enough time to spend hours on dressing things up and are not put off by a bit of dirt or things that are thrown together in haste, as long as everything meets their needs. They are simplistic in their ability to enjoy food, for example—if it tastes good, then it is good. But for Libra, if it doesn't look good, then he will have no truck with it. This is a child who will not wear practical shoes or his sister's old woolen hat to keep warm—Libra responds to style. That doesn't mean having to have whatever is most expensive, but certainly something pleasing to the eye.

When Libra starts hemming and hawing, his Sagittarian mother wishes he would just decide on one thing or another—quickly. And telling Libra, "This is make-up-your-mind time" doesn't help—little Libra simply doesn't possess his archer mother's ability to make instantaneous decisions. It is best to be patient with Libra and allow him or her to sit on the fence sometimes—there is something he needs to learn from this position, and when he is ready, he will jump down of his own accord.

Because both these signs look on the bright side of life, they create a positive atmosphere around them. The archer father always looks ahead with the expectation that opportunity is just around the corner, and Libra often coasts along believing everything to be sweetness and light and turning a blind eye to anything that isn't. So they feel cozy together—well, they would if Sagittarius wasn't always charging around firing his arrows all over the place. This father will never be the pipe and slippers type—he has adventure in his heart. And although Libra is more mentally than physically active, he or she loves the stimulation and enthusiasm of the Sagittarian father.

Libra Child with Capricorn Parent

Libra is made of much more pliable stuff than Capricorn. His elasticity around certain situations and people means that he adjusts easily and can slide in anywhere without causing disruption. Capricorn, on the other hand, has very definite ideas about what he will and won't do, and he has the resilience to stand firm. The goat doesn't need the approval of others that Libra so desperately seeks. If you could compare these two signs to parts of the body, Capricorn would be the stiff backbone and Libra a willing pair of hands. Capricorn believes in fortitude, self-control, and hard work, while Libra's *raison d'être* revolves around doing things for and with other people.

Librans and Capricorns are born to develop different qualities in themselves, as are all the signs, but these two are positioned in the astrological "square" aspect, which sometimes makes it difficult for them to see eye to eye. In fact, Libra rarely finds it hard to get on with people—he just adapts himself accordingly and finds a way to smooth a path between them. Particularly as a child, he or she is happy to follow the lead and dance to Capricorn's tune. As the years go by, however, he or she needs to be given the opportunity to hear other music—it's all about balance.

Libra appreciates the stability that is created by the Capricorn mother's routine in the home. She can be relied upon to keep the wheels turning, and her sense of timing and order creates a kind of practical harmony. She in turn can rely on Libra never to let her down in front of other people. Libra automatically knows how to behave appropriately in any situation—it is his particular talent, and he doesn't even need reminding of it. It is a source of wonderment to his mother, who has often had to restrain herself purposefully and keep herself in check, that this child doesn't need her to keep tugging on the reins.

When a Capricorn father lays down the law, Libra is quick to stand to attention. The male goat commands respect in his household, but Libra knows just how to soften him up. Charmingly, disarmingly, Libra can court his or her father into bending the rules without ever defying him—gentle persuasion, a smile, and a pleasing manner get Libra everywhere without putting anyone's nose out of joint. This child can make life look so easy that Capricorn wonders why he had ever thought it difficult.

Libra Child with Aquarius Parent

These two can fly on an airy breeze together. Being air signs, they are used to taking off mentally and turning a few loops before landing. It is the air signs' ability to rise above situations and see everything from a cool perspective that gives them the logic and rationality in their thinking. Air signs dislike being drawn into the heat generated by fire signs, the emotional depths of the water signs, and the heaviness of the earth signs. They prefer the lightness of air. Librans and Aquarians are able to feed each other with interesting thoughts and ideas; they have a special shorthand communication, and their minds move rapidly together.

A water bearer parent is very good at explaining things in a way that young Libra can understand. Aquarians can always think of a reason for everything and are not so attached to their own ideas that they cannot allow other people to have theirs. This creates fertile ground for a young Libran to consider and weigh and debate all the options, which is his way of reaching conclusions. Libra's mind is almost like the ball on a roulette wheel that has to go around and around all the points until it alights in a particular place, and Aquarius can give the space for this to happen.

Where Aquarius and Libra are poles apart is in their attitude toward individuality and relationships. The Aquarian mother will be on the lookout for indications that her child is different, unique, standing out from all the other children. This is because she is so bound up with the idea of individuality that she cannot bear to be the same as anyone else, and heaven forbid that her child should merge into the background. However, Libra's special gift is his or her ability to find common ground with others. He is a people person, and he is happiest when there is unity, peacefulness, and harmony. He has no wish to stick out like a sore thumb; he wants to be popular, accepted, and liked. Where Aquarius wants to do his own thing, Libra wants to join together—and in a way this is his uniqueness; he is especially good at being with other people.

Libra wants his or her father to be the same as everyone else's father. As a child, his urge is for conventionality, and he has a picture in his mind of what this looks like. But the water bearer father always has something a bit different about him—his car, his shoes, his ties . . . You may have to look closely, but he always bears some kind of statement that he chooses things for himself rather than following the pack. It brings a blush to Libra's cheeks—goodness, what will other people think? He may not follow in his father's footsteps, but Libra will benefit from having a father who shows him that the yardstick of acceptability should be oneself.

Libra Child with Pisces Parent

Although Libra is an air sign and Pisces a water sign, meaning that they belong to different astrological families, if they are linked by a blood relationship they have an opportunity to connect together. But, on the other hand, they are also very different. To a Libran this would make perfect sense. A Libran is more clear thinking, with his scales in permanent pursuit of levelheadedness, and Pisces is more dreamy and whimsical; but they are both bowled over by the concepts of love, peace, and togetherness. As parent and child, they have the urge to merge into perfect harmony.

Whatever the sex of the parent and child involved, Libra and Pisces are tuned into the feminine principles of passivity, beauty, and acceptance. They appreciate the small, delicate touches in life that add luster and enchantment—in fact, they are the great romantics, longing to be taken away from ordinariness and blandness. Together they share a special vision—perhaps it is because of the rose-colored spectacles they wear—but they certainly discern a dimension of beauty that less sensitive people may miss.

A young Libran can fully explore his or her artistic appreciation with a Piscean mother, and in fact she will probably help to awaken and develop it. Surroundings are so important to Libra, and Pisces loves to collect things that lift the soul. In the early years, Libra basks in the environment his Piscean mother provides—he sees and appreciates the music, the paintings, the flowers, and they give him an inner contentment that he is able to re-create for himself later. His mother's gentleness allows Libra to grow at his own pace, and Libra is the sort who likes to take a rest from the struggle of development and just "be." Without being prodded or pushed, Libra manages to unfold in his or her own time.

Sometimes Piscean fathers find it hard to accept their own sensitivity; then they flip into an opposite attitude that makes them look cold and cut off from their emotions. This is their own defense mechanism in action to stop their being swamped by their feelings. But with the appearance of little Libra, who is loving without being clingy, the Pisces father can relax and just enjoy the relationship with Libra, who is so undemanding and so giving.

Sun in Scorpio Child

24 October–22 November

THE SCORPION

Qualities to Look for and Nurture in Your Scorpio Child

An inner resourcefulness and strength, particularly in the midst of change and challenge

THE SYMBOL FOR SCORPIO IS NOT ONLY THE SCORPION BUT the phoenix rising from the ashes. Scorpios are born to experience transformation in their lives and to develop the inner strength to meet such changes. Not only do they possess an immense courage and resilience that help them through most personal challenges, but they can help others to find their feet again when they are tested in life.

A deep insight into and sensitivity toward other people

As a child, it is already evident that Scorpio seems to be able to look right inside other people. He has a depth that allows him to see beyond the surface and know what lies beneath it. This intuition and perceptive insight is already available to a Scorpio when quite young, and it is important that he or she grows up willing to trust it.

Determination and willpower to achieve

Scorpio has an ability to dedicate himself totally to whatever he wants to do. His power of concentration is enormous, so, if he sets his mind to something, very little will distract him. When Scorpio is young, his willpower makes itself evident to his parents as he tests out both himself and other people. He can be enormously resistant to being told what to do and also wholeheartedly behind his own choices. Handling him with sensitivity is important if he is to learn to use his own determination positively.

An intensity of feeling that enriches the voltage of life

As a water sign, Scorpio is attuned to the world of emotion, but unlike the other water signs of Cancer and Pisces, he does not wear his heart on his sleeve. He is self-protective and tends to keep his feelings under wraps, but they are nonetheless intense and powerful. It is important to help Scorpio to accept and express his emotional nature, which allows him to discover the passion he has for life.

Scorpio Boys

Scorpio wants other people to believe that he has everything under control and can handle anything. If you are the parent of a Scorpio boy, you might have to develop radar to anticipate what is going on beneath the surface of your child, because he hides the inner kernel of himself from view. He is acutely sensitive and at the same time afraid of showing that vulnerability, so he needs encouragement to express his feelings. When he goes quiet, he is often sending out a signal that he is struggling inside. He needs to know that he doesn't have to be strong and cope all the time.

Because Scorpio has such intense likes and dislikes, he will certainly let you know which side he is batting on. Once he has found an interest that captivates him, he finds it hard to turn his attention to anything else. Even as a young child, he can be consumed with a desire to involve himself with one particular thing, and in contrast he finds it difficult to bother with activities that do not spark the same level of enthusiasm.

A Scorpio boy is unfailingly loyal to those he loves, but he is also capable of delivering the truth (however hurtful). He is so aware of his own gut reactions to things that he finds it hard to dress them up to please other people. So he will often come out with the remarks that other people are afraid to say! Scorpio has a sense of togetherness that is almost tribal—and if anyone attacks the family or friends in his inner circle, he will be the first to rush in and defend them.

Scorpio Girls

Miss Scorpio is in touch with her feminine wiles as soon as she can walk and talk. She is practicing for when she's grown up and will be able to compel and magnetize people and situations in her life. Although she may be only four, she is definitely trying to seduce you into buying her an ice cream or reading another bedtime story. She knows exactly what she wants, and yet she is prone to feeling incredibly vulnerable—the combination is a complex one, and the source of her fascination.

There is almost always more to Scorpios than meets the eye, and when something is troubling them, they tend to bury it deep inside themselves, but their fears can emerge in bouts of bad dreams, or a withdrawal from other people. A Scorpio girl needs gentle understanding and a listening ear that encourages her to open up without feeling criticized or judged. She also needs to learn to trust other people, because Scorpio has an inner suspicion that can make it hard to reach out. It is amazing to watch this child laughing and exchanging intimacies with the grandmother she loves and then observe her with an aunt she doesn't like the look of—she will suddenly disappear inside herself.

She can be a force to be reckoned with, yet she is deeply loving. Depth is a continuing quality that Scorpio seeks in life, and as a child she needs to know that her parents' love for her is immeasurable.

Scorpio at School

Scorpio has a penetrating and incisive mind that is naturally able to assimilate great quantities of information and discern what is valuable to know. He or she has a great desire to investigate and research and is not satisfied with surface understanding—if Scorpios want to know about something, then they want to know every last detail about it.

The Scorpio tendency to take a black-and-white approach to life filters through into his or her learning capacity. Scorpio will either adore a particular subject or cannot muster enough interest to raise a little finger. This can cause problems if the "undesirable" subject is part of a compulsory school curriculum. It is not really a case of deliberate lack of interest; Scorpios are simply not the jack-of-all-trades types, but tend to display marked abilities in certain areas.

In exams they are usually able to summon up high levels of concentration and pull out all the stops. Scorpios like to be high achievers, to have a purpose and a challenge. In spite of all this, they can sometimes stumble on a block to their learning that they struggle against—and sometimes the block can be a particular teacher they do not feel is sympatico. Scorpios find it difficult to try hard for someone with whom they cannot establish a rapport. Similarly with school friends, Scorpios are either in their element or feel slightly on the outside, and that causes them enormous distress—they need to feel they belong.

Scorpio at Play

Scorpio is a sign of extremes, so these children will either adore particular activities and games or refuse to get involved. Sometimes it is really important to coax Scorpio into trying something he has set his heart against, because it is often his initial emotional response that has made him afraid of experimenting with an activity he will actually love. But gently, gently catch this monkey—ordering him to give it a try will certainly send him or her in the opposite direction!

Because Scorpio is a water sign, he or she has a creative imagination and likes to invent his own games. With other children he is often the leader and decides what will happen. Children as subconsciously in tune with their own levels of powerfulness, and Scorpio in particular is often looked on as the leader by his friends. He will never allow himself to be walked over, but of course his sensitivity means that he is often trying to prove he doesn't mind things that he actually cares about deeply.

He may find it difficult to share his toys—the famous Scorpio possessiveness extends in the early years to his favorite objects before transposing itself onto people. Scorpio is intensely loyal to friends and often keeps early childhood playmates for life. He is capable of forming immensely strong ties that connect him to others through the growing-up stages and beyond, sometimes loosening and then rekindling them again.

Scorpio Child with Aries Parent

In traditional astrology, Scorpio and Aries shares Mars as their planetary ruler. As the god of war, Mars presides over the impulse to get things done, to triumph over adversity, and achieve what one wants—all attributes that are commonly assigned to go-getting Aries. Although Scorpio's own ruler, Pluto, lends another vibration to those born under this sign that beckons them forward to personal transformation, Scorpio nonetheless possesses drive in equal amounts to

Aries—he is just a little quieter about it. However, when these two get together, they spark the Mars element in each other . . . battle stations!

They are not permanently poised with daggers drawn, but Scorpio and Aries can get into a battle royal when one crosses the other. It is hard for either of them to back down because they both tend to see things in terms of winning or losing. Except that with parent and child, neither really wins—they are united on a journey together that will last a lifetime, and the little skirmishes along the way are really neither here nor there.

It is from his Aries mother that Scorpio learns how to formulate a goal and set in motion his phenomenal drive to succeed. Ram mothers are often quite ambitious for their children, and Scorpio picks up the gauntlet and presses on with his mission to prove to her that he can do it. Implicit in this relationship is a high level of raw energy that needs a positive outlet. In many ways, an Aries mother is very good for her Scorpio child, who is capable of swallowing his energy unless he is able to express it. Ariens are so in tune with their own need for challenge that it is natural for them to keep Scorpios motivated and to ensure their vitality is flowing. With her around, this child is unlikely to bottle up his feelings, because the ram will always make him come out with what's bothering him.

Aries fathers will often encourage their children to be physically active. In general, fire signs don't mind high spirits and noise—they recognize the importance of letting off steam, and Aries has more steam to let off than most! With Scorpio, though, it is also important that he has time to be by himself and be private, because he needs to feed himself inwardly as well as give out his energy. Aries has a seemingly inexhaustible supply of stamina, but Scorpio is more delicately balanced, despite his show of strength.

Scorpio Child with Taurus Parent

These two are at opposite ends of the pole, eyeing each other from their differing perspectives. As with all opposing signs, there is a theme that runs between them of "I am like this, and you are like that." Yet although they take up their own corners, Scorpio and Taurus are remarkably similar. They are both willful, determined, and resourceful for a start and, dare we say, stubborn—they both believe they are right.

And if they were having a competition about who has the most staying power, neither would win—because they would both stick it out to the bitter end. They have so much in common, yet they persist in looking at their differences. Taurus sees him- or herself as eminently practical, realistic, and stable, and Scorpio carries the banner for overcoming obstacles, believing in things with passion, and always scratching the surface to see if what is underneath rings true. Still, opposites attract, so they say, so perhaps they prefer to see themselves as two halves rather than a whole.

It is probably because the Taurean mother is so enormously sensible that Scorpio feels lacking in this department. The bull mother is a great one for pointing out what is in front of her nose and being right, which irks Scorpio—maybe because he or she didn't think of it first. You see, Scorpio will often take the complicated route to something; it makes it more interesting—but of course, often more difficult, too. The Taurean mother will just go for being straightforward and cannot understand why Scorpio should want it to be otherwise. It also takes more to make Scorpio happy than just supplying creature comforts—sometimes his mother feels at a loss to know what to do, but little Scorpio is so sensitive that he can get upset over all sorts of things that Taureans would banish from their minds. The bull needs to look right inside Scorpio to see all the real and imagined hurts that accumulate when one takes life to heart as he does. But no one is better at soothing them away than the Taurus mother—she is the ultimate home comfort.

With a Taurus father, there is a rule, spoken or unspoken, that you do things by the book. Well, little Scorpio will often start out on chapters one and two, but very soon he wants to try another way, take a detour. It can make a bull father feel his child is waving a red flag at him. But it's not deliberate. Scorpio dislikes sameness—he wants to go out into the unknown, and of course his Taurus father is only trying to save him the trouble and make him more secure. But he is missing the point when he tries to deliver to Scorpio the way that is tried and tested, because as far as Scorpio is concerned, it must be tried and tested by him!

Scorpio Child with Gemini Parent

As an air sign, Gemini lives primarily in his head, while Scorpio lives in the domain of his feelings, which reflects his own element of water. What this means in terms of relating is that Gemini jumps into being rational, reasonable, and logical, which causes Scorpio to feel his emotions are unacceptable. He may very well try to deny his feelings and attempt to prove that he can be as objective as Gemini—presenting to his parent the depth of his mental abilities rather than the depth of his emotions. But it can make for a long, hard journey for Scorpio in later life to acknowledge and accept his passion, his sensitivity, and his imagination, if he has curtailed them all as a child.

Even as a child, Scorpio will take life more seriously than his or her Gemini parent—there are Important Questions for Scorpio to ponder, some of which are difficult to articulate. A Scorpio child will dare to grapple with profound issues such as life and death, God, and what is going on emotionally in his or her parents' relationship—thoughts that Gemini would banish because he squirms uncomfortably when he cannot tie up his life in neat, logical bundles. In his book, if it cannot be explained simply, then it is better to dismiss it from his mind and get on with more interesting things. The Gemini parent is really a child disguised as an adult. He skips lightly through life, almost imitating the child's game of stepping on the sidewalk and missing the cracks in case the bogeyman gets him. The Scorpio child wants to step on the cracks just to see what the bogeyman looks like—and maybe he doesn't exist!

Because Geminis have such a low threshold of boredom, they try to avoid getting trapped in domestic routine. Living with a Gemini mother, little Scorpio never knows what to expect next—plans change, new ideas happen, and there might be two or ten people for lunch. Geminis expect other people to enjoy change and be as adaptable as themselves. Now, Scorpio doesn't need a high level of constancy in a practical sense, but he does need permanent emotional nourishment. Intimacy and trust are important to him, and he cannot establish them on the hoof from a bevy of outsiders. Unless his relationship with his mother is totally secure, throwing him into contact with lots of other people only makes him more likely to withdraw.

Certainly, a Gemini father presents life to his child as an interesting conundrum. Through his father, Scorpio is brought into contact with many facets, many different types of people, and learns about the variety inherent in the world. He throws out a lot of food for thought, yet it can feel to Scorpio like being at a buffet where there are so many different things to choose from that he tastes a little of everything and still feels hungry for the main course. What he is searching for is contact with his Gemini father through the heart rather than the mind.

Scorpio Child with Cancer Parent

This is a combination that is emotionally well attuned. Cancer has such sensitivity and gentleness that he instinctively realizes Scorpio's tenderness as well as his strength. With Scorpio, the important thing is for him or her to trust another person, and Cancer exudes the assurance that he will always be there for his child, which creates a feeling of safety. Because they are both water signs, they understand each other on an emotional level, and the crab and the scorpion can exist in crustacean harmony!

The wonderful thing about having a Cancerian parent, as far as Scorpio is concerned, is that he doesn't have to pretend to be someone he's not. So often, Scorpio pushes down his emotions for fear of ridicule or attack, yet Cancer allows him to be himself and even encourages him to express his feelings. In so doing, he offers a great gift to Scorpio, who grows up with his emotional nature flowing—able to give and receive the kind of caring, passion, and love that is his birthright.

Incredibly, a Cancerian mother and a Scorpio child have a form of Morse code operating between them that dispenses with the need to tell each other things. Because they are both so highly intuitive and perceptive, they just pick up on each other and "know," without having to explain and discuss. They are also comfortable with the kind of closeness that makes air signs feel suffocated. Cancer and Scorpio can float along together in a state of unity and togetherness—until, of course, there comes a day when parent and child have to let go of each other, and the Cancer mother can find this stage difficult. But Scorpio is immensely loyal; he is unlikely to grow so far away that he cannot slip back into the emotional rapport that existed once before.

However active a Cancerian father is in the outside world, his home and family remain a central beacon in his life. And he loves to pull the drawbridge up and totally immerse himself in the stuff of his personal life, which feeds the public face he presents to the world. This makes perfect sense to Scorpio, who needs privacy and time alone. It is probably because the water signs get so involved with other people that being social can drain them of vitality, so they need to recharge their batteries. The Cancer father will recognize only too well how important it is to respect little Scorpio's "keep out" sign on his or her bedroom door.

Scorpio Child with Leo Parent

Leo and Scorpio are both very strong characters, although Leo is more noisy about it. Scorpio is more of the still-waters-run-deep type, but arouse his or her opposition, and you will know all about it. Where the lion and the scorpion are similar is in their ability to dramatize life. Leo does it because he is at heart a performer, so his life is a script with him in the starring role, all made in glorious Technicolor.

Scorpio, though, can be a secret drama queen—he or she is an extremist, and so it is very hard to persuade him not to make a mountain out of a molehill, because mountains are more spectacular.

When Scorpio and Leo live together as child and parent, the other members of the family have front row tickets to one of the most gripping productions they will ever see—it can be a thriller, a comedy, or a tragedy all in the space of ten minutes. When Leo and Scorpio can bring themselves to cool it a little, they get closer. The less they demand of each other, the more they get out of the relationship; and as they learn how to extricate themselves from the power struggles they will inevitably enter, they respectfully call a truce.

From the outset, a Leo mother knows that her Scorpio child cannot easily be coerced into doing anything he or she does not choose—she may not receive a barrage of protest, but one of his long, penetrating, and reproachful looks says a thousand words. Scorpio can outwardly go through the motions while inwardly performing the greatest act of defiance. He also withdraws from contact when he is cross, which is something his lioness mother finds hard to understand—she would rather have a quick bluster and then forget all about it. But her own warmth soon radiates out to him or her and pulls this child back into contact. Hopefully she can teach him to express his feelings rather than bottle them up.

With Scorpio, the level of his openness depends entirely on his or her level of inner confidence and trust. And a Leo father is devoted to building confidence by constantly communicating the message to his child that he or she is special. As a result, little Scorpio opens out like a flower.

Scorpio Child with Virgo Parent

Although Scorpio looks as though he is strong enough to withstand most things, a Virgo must remember that his or her natural tendency to criticize can eat away at Scorpio's confidence. The scorpion can look so self-assured that he fools most people into thinking that nothing touches him, but he is deeply sensitive and is quick to believe that the minor shortcoming, the tiny flaw, that Virgo has pointed out is of major significance. And Scorpio can dwell on something that has hurt him. For Virgo, it is essential that he try to bite his tongue with Scorpio—it's a case of least said, soonest mended.

However, a typical Virgo–Scorpio parent and child relationship is usually a fond and easy one. Virgo is so proficient at analyzing other people that he or she can get to the bottom of Scorpio without too much trouble. Painstakingly he will piece together the complex jigsaw that comprises Scorpio—the bravado and the silence, the intensity and the gentleness, the strong will and the sensitivity. Scorpio is a mysterious combination of qualities—that is what makes him or her so interesting, and Virgo admires this.

The Virgo mother admires the purposefulness of her Scorpio child. He does not often get bored and loll around asking her to make things happen. Once he is engaged in something, he is so single-minded that it is hard to drag him away, and she notices the Scorpio awareness and understanding of life on a level many adults never reach. So she is satisfied that he has the resources she considers valuable, and she can relax; she won't have to worry about him—but have you ever met a Virgo who doesn't worry?

A Virgo father tends to be a mine of information, and he can't believe the absorbency of young Scorpio's mind. He is able to soak it all up and is always thirsty for more. It as if Scorpio wants to get a grip on the world as soon as possible—in fact, he will grow up to believe that knowledge is power, so he will drink from the waters of his father endlessly. And Scorpio has the capacity to strike at the heart of the matter—in the face of all the details that Virgo files away, Scorpio will simply ask "And what is the point of that?"

Scorpio Child with Libra Parent

Libra is a very soothing parent for Scorpio. He is able to calm troubled waters and strike a happy medium whenever

Scorpio is going to extremes. It may be hard for Libra to understand why Scorpio gets so attached to things turning out a particular way, to having what he wants—Scorpio is a passionate soul at age three or sixty-three. When he wants something, it can feel like a matter of life or death. But Libra is a master at putting things in perspective, at somehow balancing things out. Because Libra weighs one thing against another, he can teach Scorpio that life is often a game of swings and roundabouts—you lose some, you win some; there are times to hang on and times to let go.

Psychologically, Libra and Scorpio tend to polarize. Libra wants to keep everyone happy, at whatever cost, to maintain the appearance that everything is sweetness and light, and Scorpio finds it hard to play ball with this approach. Scorpio is all for honesty, and if he cannot come out with the truth then he tends to swallow it down, but cannot help giving off the feeling that "something is not quite right." It can produce some rather tense undercurrents between Libra and Scorpio. But living together, they learn from each other how to blend their combination of charm and authenticity.

As a mother, Libra knows how to get the best out of her children. She has a box of tricks at her disposal that can coax truculence into willingness, and with Scorpio she realizes that pushing him or her often has the opposite effect of the one she desires. As a youngster, Scorpio can get really worked up at times and not know how to express himself until he explodes in a volcanic tantrum. His Libran mother is never one to appreciate unpleasant scenes—in fact, she will usually do her utmost to avoid them—so she soon learns to detect and defuse Scorpio's rise in temperature before it reaches boiling point.

Although Scorpio will find it hard to toe the line and pretend politely to Auntie Joan that her rice pudding was absolutely delicious when it wasn't, his Libran father is touched by the emotional honesty of Scorpio. Libra will often wear masks for himself and for other people, and it is refreshing for him to know exactly where he stands with this child. Although Libra is at the top of the tree in the popularity stakes because he is so good at saying what other people want to hear, Scorpio considers loyalty to his own heart to be the most important.

Scorpio Child with Scorpio Parent

Only another Scorpio would truly understand the outer calm and the inner turbulence that frequently characterizes this sign. Scorpios care so very deeply about everything that matters to them. In childhood particularly, when they are still learning to master the brilliant self-control that they use in later life to keep themselves in check, they can be thrown off balance by the intensity of their feelings. A Scorpio parent will recognize this stage and, if he has managed to make friends with his own emotional nature, will encourage little Scorpio to do likewise.

Far from bringing out the worst in each other, two Scorpios who are joined together in family life tend to have a special bond. They know how to avoid rubbing each other the wrong way so the Scorpio tail won't sting. One of the keys to their understanding is that they do not fear the depth of each other. An air sign parent can sometimes be at a complete loss trying to read a Scorpio child, but a Scorpio parent is tuned into this intense vibration.

Having a child brings an enormous desire to experience closeness and intimacy for a Scorpio mother. Although the potential for this is present to a degree with all the signs, Scorpio mothers can almost feel in love with their children—this is because when they care about someone deeply it activates their passion. A Scorpio child can receive this kind of love without feeling invaded, so an exceptionally close relationship between mother and child can develop. But it is important to have room in their lives for other people and not establish an exclusion zone that shuts others out and suffocates these two on the inside. While forming a supportive and empathic bond, a Scorpio mother and child also need to be able to let go of each other.

Scorpio fathers are secretly bowled over by the spiritual

dimension of creating a child. All Scorpios are fascinated by the mysteries of birth, life, and death, and having a child puts them in touch with a sense of their own purpose in life. Because he believes so passionately in making the most of your resources, a Scorpio father will try his hardest to make all the buds he can see in his child come into flower. His attitude can help little Scorpio over some rough patches, but it can also hinder him from finding his own way. This child needs to be the gardener of his or her own blooms!

Scorpio Child with Sagittarius Parent

Sagittarian parents usually feel good to be around—they have a sense of fun that children adore. The archer never grows so old that he forgets how to play, or would rather stay at home instead of having an adventure. As parents, Sagittarians urge on their children to "give it a try," and they would prefer high spirits to shyness any day of the week. In fact, the archer doesn't know what to do with sudden attacks of shyness or nerves—if a joke fails to do the trick, then the archer just hopes the problem will go away. And in many cases it does, but a Scorpio child is highly sensitive and needs careful handling.

In many ways, the archer's optimistic attitude helps Scorpio to take a lighter approach himself. Because he gets so attached to what he wants to happen, Scorpio is devastated when things don't turn out exactly as he hoped. But Sagittarius believes that life is like waiting for a bus—if you miss one, it really doesn't matter because another one is bound to come along soon.

Although a Sagittarian mother appears to be a hale and hearty type with no time for nonsense, she has a remarkable philosophy of life and an ability to see how things can work out in the future. Probably because of this, she refuses to get caught up in day-to-day irritations and problems. If she can transmit this vision and perspective to Scorpio, she will save him the agony of magnifying obstacles in his path. Scorpio can choose to have a positive or negative outlook, and with an archer mother, he will inevitably have the bright side pointed out to him at every opportunity.

Archer fathers tend to want their children to be active and outdoor types. Little boys are bought miniature baseball bats and football jerseys, and little girls are given tiny tennis rackets so that Daddy Sagittarius can teach them the joys of competition and challenge. It can be a source of great disappointment then when Scorpio literally refuses to play ball with his father. You see, Scorpio rarely chooses physical activity as his number one aim—unless he gets hooked into the psychological element of the game. He needs to feed his mind and emotions, and perhaps Sagittarius would be better off trying his other tacks of nature and travel.

Scorpio Child with Capricorn Parent

One of Capricorn's greatest qualities is his ability to steady other people. Confronted with turmoil, emotional upset, or a practical crisis, the goat picks his way evenly through the debris and finds a means of putting everything back together again. His solidity is comforting to a water sign such as Scorpio, and a Capricorn parent can seem like a raft that supports him while he navigates his way through the emotional currents of life.

Capricorn admires Scorpio's purposefulness—it reflects his own desire to climb mountains and achieve his goals. In many respects, the goat parent will view Scorpio as a reflection of himself—resilient and determined. Yet he must remember that Scorpio is a great one for holding in his feelings, particularly if he fears they will be met with disapproval. It must be said that Capricorn dislikes displays of emotion and sets great store by self-control, so he can communicate the message to Scorpio to stay strong and silent—not a healthy thing for this highly sensitive sign.

Because Scorpio does not constantly tug at his Capricorn mother to be let off the lead, she is relieved of the task of trying to pull him to heel. This is why Capricorn and Scorpio are easy in each other's company—because they do not set off the alarm bells. Scorpio won't charge around rambunctiously, embarrassing her with his antics—he seems far too grown-up for that. And Scorpio trusts that his mother won't turn up at the school gates dressed like the wild woman and making a spectacle of herself in front of his friends. They have a very traditional parent–child relationship, and they know where they stand. Scorpio needs a rock to rely on, and his Capricorn mother is always 100 percent behind him.

Capricorn fathers can appear to be a little stern. It doesn't feel comfortable when you have always felt like an adult yourself to be asked to enter into the world of a child. But Scorpio has a way of enabling Capricorn to turn back the clock because he comes halfway into the world of the adult. He has so much understanding for his age that he can form a bridge that doesn't threaten Capricorn and allows him to let the barriers down, maybe for the first time in his life. The experience of this creates a trust and loyalty between them that is totally unique.

Scorpio Child with Aquarius Parent

Scorpio and Aquarius are both fixed signs—for that, read very determined to have their own way. Neither of them find it easy to bend to meet the other's point of view, and yet family life offers them so many opportunities to do so. Notwithstanding a little bluster and contrariness, Scorpio and Aquarius have to admit that they admire each other for possessing strength—even if they both think they are right! And they are also fascinated by each other—the complexity and depth of Scorpio meets the objectivity and logic of Aquarius.

Fortunately, an Aquarian parent believes in cultivating the individuality of his or her child, but that doesn't necessarily mean that there is instant understanding. In fact, the water bearer is frequently confused by the intensity of little Scorpio—why do some things matter so much to him? Being an air sign, he is usually able to maintain a distance between himself and his feelings, but Scorpio seems to get caught up in his emotions to such an extent that he blows a minor happening out of all proportion. It is not that Scorpio will explode, because he wouldn't like you to see how much it mattered to him, but he is wounded, deeply aggrieved, and his Aquarian mother or father is just expected to read his mind. It can all seem a little wearing to Aquarians, who like things to be clear.

If the Aquarian mother can somehow enter into the emotional life of Scorpio, she will be able to establish a close bond with this child, but she must develop an understanding of his sensitivity—being rational cuts no ice when you are consumed with emotion as only a Scorpio child can be. And it does require patience and perception to circumvent the Scorpio tendency to set up guessing games complete with dialogue that runs along the lines of: "There's something wrong." "No, there isn't." With her Aquarian insight, she can tune into this child, and her flashes of inspiration help her to blast through the blocks that can deter Scorpio from making progress.

Aquarius and Scorpio are two of the most misunderstood signs in the zodiac. Although Aquarius is often to be found surrounded by other people, he or she still feels lonely, and Scorpio can appear to others to be absolutely fine when he or she is aching inside. By making a friend of this child, the water bearer father draws Scorpio out of his shell. Aquarius always finds a great deal to be excited about in life and maintains an interest in people. As a father, Aquarius carries a spark about him—something that refuses to be boxed and labeled into behaving in a particular way, and Scorpio finds his unpredictability enthralling.

Scorpio Child with Pisces Parent

Pisces releases the emotions in Scorpio. One of the reasons that Scorpio pretends to be so tough when he or she is so vulnerable is a fear of attack, but Pisces is so gentle, so undemanding, that this child feels absolutely safe in his hands. One of the greatest gifts that Pisces has to offer as a parent is the way that he allows the child to be himself without trying to mold him. Pisces' position as the last sign of the zodiac appears to equip him with a special understanding and respect for human nature.

However, these very qualities can sometimes backfire on a Pisces when he or she is dealing with people who have a bee in their bonnet about making a stand. For all the scorpion's sensitivity, he has the strength of an ox and the determination to prove something to himself—if not to you. Unless Pisces stands firm, at times he will find a Scorpio child is capable of running rings around him. Pisces needs to know when to adjust himself to the needs of his child and when Scorpio is served best by hearing a strong "no." It is not that Scorpio is a miniature tyrant, but he is a sure hand at subtly manipulating you into getting what he wants—and Pisces loves to give.

A Piscean mother is exceptionally well tuned into the emotional life of her child. She senses more than she needs to ask, and so it is hard to fool her because her antennae tell her if there is a disturbance in the vibration she picks up. Being understood on this feeling level enhances Scorpio's security, and he gets the message that it is perfectly all right to feel a little out of sorts at times—he doesn't have to pretend he is okay when he isn't. Experiencing this emotional cushion in childhood really helps Scorpio to accept his enormous sensitivity, which in turn encourages the richness of his emotional life, his insight, and his imagination when he is older.

There is no other father like a Piscean to show Scorpio how to flow with the currents of life. In the Piscean world, it is as natural to listen to your intuition and inner timing as it is to look at the clock, and a Piscean father can teach Scorpio to trust his inner knowledge of what is right for him. So often Scorpio gets stuck bashing his head against a brick wall and being unable to give up, but his father can help him to see that if he lets go, he can often find another way of getting to the same place.

Sun in Sagittarius Child

23 November–21 December

THE ARCHER

Qualities to Look for and Nurture in Your Sagittarius Child

An optimistic, happy-go-lucky approach to life

SAGITTARIUS IS ABLE TO INSPIRE OTHER PEOPLE WITH HIS OR her positive thinking. He is predisposed to looking on the bright side, and when something doesn't work out, he remains confident that there will be another opportunity. Allowing him to retain this benevolent world view is essential to his well-being, yet he also needs to be encouraged to create his own luck through effort as well.

An adventurous spirit, keen to take on challenge and move forward

The archer is continually aiming and shooting his arrows—and Sagittarius needs a target in life. He feels trapped in the confines of everyday matters and needs to believe that he is heading in a particular direction, that he has a goal. His sense of adventure makes him want to broaden his horizons both mentally and physically. Seeing and doing as much as possible comes naturally to him, yet he always wants to explore more. His itchy feet may take him traveling far afield when he is older, but wherever he is, he must have the feeling that his life is moving on in some way.

Having an open and friendly approach to other people

Sagittarius is outgoing and eager to make friends. His warmth is infectious, and he is able to make easy contact with people who respond to his relaxing manner. As a child, he disarms complete strangers with his ability to strike up a rapport and draw them in—he has a way of making other people drop their barriers. It is not that he is precociously extroverted, he just trusts that other people will like him, and so they do.

Being playful and wanting to have fun

Because Sagittarius is bounding with enthusiasm, he has a lot of energy to spare for making life as enjoyable as possible. He wants to laugh and play and clown around and cannot bear life to be too serious. He does possess a great sense of the ridiculous. He is also spontaneous and prone to exaggeration, all used to great comic effect. Of course, he has his down moments, but Sagittarius is a great believer in living life to the fullest, making the most of everything, and never losing the ability to play.

Sagittarius Boys

This child can do a wonderful impersonation of a boisterous puppy, leaping around, into everything, and disinclined to walk to heel. Yet his sheer energy and zest for life is to be valued. Nagging him to be sensible, to settle down, and sit still often has the reverse effect—he has to find ways to channel his need for action. Surprisingly, he doesn't even start to slow down when he gets tired. He is on full throttle one moment and flopped out the next.

He loves being outdoors in large, open spaces. This is where he feels free, and Sagittarius has a tremendous affinity with nature. He needs to run on the grass, climb trees, paddle in the pool, feel the wind and the rain, make mud pies, watch the campfire, roll down the hill. Having to dress up and be confined in any way goes against the grain—he is happiest when he can just be himself. As the parent of a child of this sign, you will soon become aware of how difficult it is for the archer to look clean and tidy for more than five minutes—he likes casual, comfortable clothes, and he can scuff new school shoes and tear off buttons in the blink of an eye (it was an accident, of course!).

Sagittarius has vision; he has big ideas about what he wants to do with his life. He needs help in sticking to his guns as a child because he is apt to start things with enthusiasm, but he gets bored quickly. Actually finishing something, however small, and feeling the resulting sense of achievement is vital for him so that he can really believe his bigger goals are attainable.

Sagittarius Girls

Miss Sagittarius is a girl with a mission—to enjoy life. She makes her presence felt within the family by doing her best to liven up the proceedings whenever possible. As her parent, you may find yourself wanting to tear your hair out when she is in one of her rowdy moods, but she soon has you smiling again—it is difficult not to get caught up in her enthusiasm. Although she seemingly has the capacity to put an electric charge into your life, she is remarkably easygoing too. Miss Sagittarius won't sulk if her birthday cake has burned to ashes in a too-hot oven. She'll probably find it more amusing than you, and anyway she reckons you will bake her another one, so what's the point in making a fuss?

She loves wildlife and animals—horses are her favorite—and she adores being in the countryside or in the park. It often seems that Sagittarius is absolutely fearless, and your heart will be in your mouth as you watch her throwing herself down the slide and aiming to make the swing go as high as possible. Sagittarius loves the thrill and excitement of pushing things to the limit, but particularly when young, she can misjudge her own capabilities and come up short. Even then, she is not to be deterred from having another try.

She is a giggler, and a practical joker. She may not be the quiet and demure image of the "good little girl," but she knows how to have a good time—and that is an asset in life.

Sagittarius at School

Sagittarius is the sign of learning, but before you have your little archer preregistered in the Ivy League you should hear the bad news—concentration is a rather elusive quality for this sign. Yes, Sagittarius has enormous potential, but the school report often reads "Must try harder." Sagittarius frequently puts in the amount required just to get by, to pass the exam by the skin of his teeth, simply because he thinks there are more interesting things in life than boning up on chemical formulas and Latin conjugations. His natural inclination to play means that he is constantly distracted by something that promises to be more fun.

For this reason, a Sagittarius child does need to be pushed a little, encouraged to reach the goal. There is no doubt about it, he has a good mind and plenty of enthusiasm, but he gets fed up when it comes to the grind of committing things to memory and churning out the information. The extraordinary thing is that Sagittarius goes on to be an inveterate learner—he or she is the one who signs up for the adult education classes, the Open University course, and who has an insatiable appetite for knowledge later in life.

Sagittarius is often to be found on the sports field letting off the steam that builds up in him whenever he is forced to sit still for long periods of time, and he is a natural athlete and good team player. He gets on well with people and is popular at school, but his high spirits sometimes clash with the system. Because he thinks all things are elastic, he will try to stretch the rules.

Sagittarius at Play

It has to be said that Sagittarius at play is operating within his natural habitat. In some ways life is a game to him, and that is why he doesn't take it too seriously. He is competitive, however, and will certainly aim to win. Especially as a child, the archer needs plenty of physical activity—his whole system seems to get clogged up indoors, and he needs a lot of fresh air. Having discovered mountain biking or camping, it is hard to persuade him or her to come back indoors.

Sagittarians are probably the least possessive sign when it comes to sharing their belongings and toys. They are naturally generous, but also a little careless with their possessions. Their nonattachment is to be admired, but Sagittarians do need to learn to appreciate the things that matter to them and to know how to look after special belongings, because items that have been lost or broken can't always be replaced.

Other children usually find Sagittarius exciting company, but maybe a little over the top at times. He or she is so kind, yet when he is caught up in a game, he doesn't know when to stop. Sagittarius can get overtired and overheated, and he needs to find some activities that stimulate his mind but give his body a rest.

Sagittarius Child with Aries Parent

A ram parent and an archer child egg each other on to do more and more. Two fire signs ignite each other into action, light each other's flame, and blaze a trail ever onward and upward—it can be exhausting for other members of the family! They, of course, feel good in one another's company, basking in the light and the heat and reveling in their enthusiasm and energy. It is wonderful for an Aries parent to have such a responsive child, so quick to react, so ready to jump into action. Loving to motivate others to do something, Aries calls the shots, but the archer is already raring to go.

Ariens share with Sagittarians the desire to start and the difficulty in finishing. They have tremendous drive, but not a great deal of staying power. The house may be littered with half-finished drawings, half-built cardboard castles, and a semi-assembled kite—all left behind when something else caught the eye. And Aries hasn't really the heart to remonstrate when he knows that he's not much better, and that only half the bathroom has been wallpapered and five out of ten rosebushes planted.

Sagittarius fits in easily with the Aries mother's way of life. No time for lounging around and ready at a moment's notice to take off somewhere—it might just be the corner store, but then again it could be Paris. The Aries lady does not believe in sitting around waiting for life to happen; she *makes* things happen. Picking up this energetic vibration enthralls the little archer and confirms his or her own optimism that there is always something good on the horizon. Because Sagittarius is not clued into needing order in his life, he doesn't notice if lunch isn't at the same time every day. He just enjoys whatever comes up, and that makes him a joy for an Aries mother, who feels the chains of restriction in domestic detail.

For an Aries father, a Sagittarius child fits the bill exactly—no whining and complaining, no tired and emotional tantrums. And it's just as well, because the ram father gets impatient when he has to spend hours soothing away the aftermath of things that go bump in the night. With the little archer, it is altogether different—the only thing that is likely to go bump in the night is him, suddenly awake and firing on all cylinders. This child is a delight to the Aries father, who is so proud of his ability to take life by the horns and make of it what he will.

Sagittarius Child with Taurus Parent

There are few Taurean parents who are not firmly rooted in providing a traditional family background. The bull believes in constancy, permanency, and stability, and he will tirelessly work to supply these qualities in his relationships. It is interesting when a little archer is born into this scene, because he has other plans—he is the bird that is itching to hatch out of the egg, is excited about flying the nest. And the more Taurus tries to hold him down, the more he longs to branch out. Sagittarius needs to have a lot of room to grow in his own way, and it won't be long before he bursts out of the safety of the Taurean container.

It boils down to the essential differences between Taurus and Sagittarius. The bull likes familiarity; the archer likes the unknown. Taurus implements routine, and Sagittarius thrives on change. There is no right and wrong, just two people who resonate on different levels. And it doesn't necessarily mean that they are locked in conflict about it, but simply that they want different things out of life. To begin with, the Taurus parent can organize life in his own way—although an archer, however small, is capable of upsetting the best laid plans. He is not willfully disruptive, yet he somehow manages to make everything go with a swing (watch out for the cut-glass vase!).

A Taurean mother tries very hard to make Sagittarius stop and think before he takes action. This is no easy task, as the archer is in permanent overdrive, and it takes a lot to slow him down. This really is the child who wants to run before he can walk, but he cannot help absorbing a *soupçon* of her common sense and practicality. She can help him to avoid some of the worst excesses. It comes down to being a case of his frequently biting off more than he can chew—and the Taurean mother is right in there with a knife and fork carving life up into manageable slices!

The Taurus father wants to show his archer how to do things "properly," not jumping in and making a mess. He is so patient and careful, and Sagittarius is so expansive and adventurous, that it is possible to make this a good team combination. We may not be able to choose the astrological signs of our family members, but we can be sure that we have a lot to learn from each other.

Sagittarius Child with Gemini Parent

Sagittarius and Gemini are both mutable signs—that means they enjoy change—so although they are diametrically opposed on the astrological wheel, they also have a great affinity. The pace of life is very fast around them both as they whiz around like jumping jacks—unpredictable movement and the occasional explosion! Their tendency to scatter their energy in many different directions can leave other people rather confused, but Sagittarius and Gemini have an uncomplicated approach to life—they just follow their noses regardless of the maze of tracks they leave behind. So the archer and the twins accept each other unconditionally, and understand their mutual need for excitement, interest, and diversity.

What the Gemini mother appreciates about her archer child is the way his eyes are open, constantly registering all the goings-on in the world. He may not be so consumed with the details as she is, but he is already searching for answers.

Sagittarians develop their personal philosophy of life over many years of watching the invisible laws of the world. Refusing to get drawn into mundane, material matters, they stand back from the vantage point of their farsighted vision and wish upon a star. It may sound rather ridiculous to the logical Gemini mind, but there it is—Sagittarius has a spiritual dimension that is tuned into believing that everything will turn out for the best and that there is a reason for everything, unfathomable thought it might seem at the time. Anyway, the little archer has a long way to go before he is really in touch with his own belief system, but a Gemini mother can nevertheless spot this child taking notes for future reference.

The archer loves the way his Gemini father appears to be

a walking encyclopedia of knowledge. As a child, there is a question mark at the end of nearly every Sagittarian sentence, but Gemini always has an answer, or an opinion at the very least. There is a terrific feeding of minds in this father–child relationship, which works both ways. Both dislike getting bogged down in such matters as having to clean shoes or wash plates, so they mentally wave a magic wand and turn chores into a game, a race, or a practical joke.

Sagittarius Child with Cancer Parent

Cancerian parents are all for cosseting their children, wrapping them up safely away from harm. But Sagittarius is a daredevil who loves taking risks—it is part of his or her *raison d'être.* He just can't resist seeing if he can jump over the wall, climb the gate, or wade across that pool of water—it gives him a thrill, and life without excitement is unbearably dull for him. Of course, he sometimes comes to grief, but even when subjected to a million "I told you so's," he would never regret taking his chance.

It is hard for sensitive Cancer to accept that his or her little archer is not racked with fear or doubt. He expects the worst every time, but Sagittarians do seem to be blessed with a benevolent guardian angel—or maybe it's because they *think* they have one that they are so lucky. Certainly the archer has no trepidation about venturing out from the nest—first Sagittarius wants to stay over with a friend, then take the hiking trip, and it's only a matter of time before bungee-jumping rears its head on his itinerary of pleasant pastimes. It's all enough to give the crab apoplexy. Remembering his own childhood, and the time it took him to summon up the courage to take his overnight bag and stay one step removed at his grandparents', the crab marvels at the outgoing nature of Sagittarius.

Because the Cancer mother is essentially a homebody, she feels that she has to stretch herself to accommodate Sagittarius and his voracious appetite for the great outdoors and his need to be "doing something." Sagittarians can't just putter, they have to be shooting their arrows at a particular target—whether they hit it or miss is rather irrelevant to them because what they want is a purpose and to be caught up in an activity. So the archer keeps his Cancerian mother on her toes, most likely chasing around after him.

Cancer is a sign that dances between being extroverted and introverted. Like the crab stepping onto the shore from the water and back again, Cancer needs to be able to go out there and then retreat whenever necessary. Sagittarius, however, is an entirely different kettle of fish. The Cancerian father realizes that this child has his own energy charge within himself and doesn't need to rebalance himself with equal amounts of quiet and activity. It is because Sagittarius is innately relaxed—he doesn't get wound up emotionally like Cancer and allow a feeling to gnaw at his equilibrium. And he *expresses* himself outwardly, not holding things inside himself like the crab.

Sagittarius Child with Leo Parent

The playfulness of Sagittarius and the exuberance of Leo come together to light up this relationship. Leo lovingly admires the *chutzpah* of the little archer, not affronted at all by his clowning and excesses. After all, the lion reckons, if you cannot express yourself, what is life about? So Sagittarius is free to indulge in his antics without fear of being confined to his room! As a parent, Leo wants to nurture the individuality of his child, and being a fire sign himself, he is particularly receptive to the emergence of high-spirited Sagittarian energy.

These two signs have different standards, however. Leo is all for making something as fine as it can possibly be, and Sagittarius has a more slapdash, haphazard approach. For Sagittarius, even as a child, it is the quantity more than the quality that counts. All the decoration and superlative presentation that is so important to Leo when he hands over his Easter egg is ripped off in a hurry to get to the edible part, which should be big if it is to score a hit with Sagittarius.

Because the Leo mother is aware of her own ability to assert herself, she is able to give the archer a long rein, knowing that she has the power to call him or her in whenever necessary. But basically she wants to see the qualities of confidence and courage in her child, and Sagittarius would be the last one to disappoint her! She believes in aiming for the top, and so she gives her archer *carte blanche* to shoot his arrows to the highest point.

As king of the jungle, the Leo father is an accomplished hunter. He knows how to get what he wants, and he is eager for his offspring to learn how to stand on their own two feet and be able to handle the challenges of life. Sagittarius responds by waltzing into life's fray without a backward glance and returning with tales of derring-do. Because this father and child are from the same fiery element, they are batting on the same team in life—holding the same vision of adventure, conquest, and glory and translating it into ordinary human existence.

Sagittarius Child with Virgo Parent

When a vibrant archer child has a meticulous Virgo parent, the two can appear to be set on a collision course. But surprisingly this is not the case. Despite their obvious differences, Virgo is not the type to skulk into a corner and take umbrage, and Sagittarius just laughs when the going gets tough. Undeniably they see life through entirely opposite perspectives—Virgo is looking at the nitty-gritty detail, and Sagittarius is gazing far into the distance. They value different things, yet somehow they are not at cross-purposes, just working on a different area of ground.

The careful and the careless meet in the Virgo–Sagittarius family, and when living under the same roof, as fast as Virgo makes everything neat and tidy, Sagittarius comes along like an avalanche of dishevelment. But it is impossible for the archer to adopt Virgo's level of organization as a way of life—left to his own chaotic devices, he is as happy as a clam and paradoxically free from the clutter of minutiae that surrounds Virgo. He just overlooks it, so it doesn't exist.

With a Virgo mother, Sagittarius is fed many morsels of interesting information. This lady likes to toss her child tidbits of knowledge to tempt and improve his mind, and the archer gobbles them up hungrily. He has a lively curiosity about life, but he is not a worrier like Virgo. He looks at it all, but just shrugs his shoulders over minor irritations that would bother Virgo. He is open to accepting things just as they are. Of course, with a Virgo mother running around after him, he can afford to be nonchalant!

Where a Virgo father will sometimes cross swords with the archer is over the Sagittarian attitude toward possessions. When the archer loves something, he wants to get as much out of it as possible. This is not the child who religiously puts his toys away and makes sure they are looked after. He will test their robustness to the limit and is also capable of making more disappearing acts happen than a top magician. It is trying for Virgo, who hates extravagance and wastefulness, and he doesn't want to behave like a Sagittarian himself, forever digging deeper and deeper into his pockets. Virgo inclines toward parsimony at the best of times—maybe the best toy he can give Sagittarius is an indestructible piggy bank!

Sagittarius Child with Libra Parent

Libra likes all things to be equal, while Sagittarius always wants to tip the scales and go for bust to make life more exciting. The archer is always to be found at one end of the scale, and Libra is looking for his or her place in the middle. But sometimes Libra doesn't know how to start, and Sagittarius doesn't know when to stop, so maybe they are evenly balanced between them! Libra has an innate tendency to weigh all the options before taking action, and the archer possesses a spontaneous desire to wade straight in regardless of the consequences.

For all that, Libra and Sagittarius get along together famously, probably because they are both easygoing people. Libra is always prepared to bend a little to accommodate someone else's wishes, and Sagittarius wants to have a good time and knows how to bring a smile to the situation—he soon has Libra sewn up in stitches. As a parent, Libra likes nothing better than the feeling of harmony around his or her home, and with the arrival of the archer, good humor abounds.

A Libran mother will have a hard time keeping up appearances when the archer is prone to riding roughshod around the place, leaving a trail of toys, books, and clothes in his or her wake. Sagittarius is not a great appreciator of tranquil beauty and graceful elegance—the half-horse part of him would be happy in a stable! He loathes formality and loves to be comfortable and casual, eschewing the idea of dressing up for events and occasions. As a mother, Libra will automatically seek out other mothers and children to give her a sense of belonging, and she doesn't function well in isolation. And Sagittarius is a social hit, having no shyness or timidity. Being so open and trusting of others, he makes friends at the drop of a hat, and it almost seems a crime to have him on his own at home when he generates so much spark among other people.

No one disrupts the Libran father's philosophy of all things in moderation more than an archer child. Even his impressive skills of bargaining and negotiation cut no ice with a Sagittarian in full throttle. If this child can't have it all, or do it now, then he or she will have no truck with it—what is a fair-minded Libran to do faced with a rampant archer swinging from one extreme to another? The only thing to remember is that all Sagittarian storm clouds blow over very quickly (nothing moves slowly in his or her life). And the archer is quite capable of making Everest out of a molehill, too, even when the problem isn't all that important to him. He will see the silly side if Libra retains his cool, so there is no point in jumping overboard with him.

Sagittarius Child with Scorpio Parent

The archer is usually in too much of a rush to examine life on the deep level that Scorpio operates on. As soon as Sagittarius has pointed his arrows and fired at something, he is off onto the next project, whether he has hit his target or not. With Sagittarius, there is always a sense of movement—he is on a journey somewhere, a whistle-stop tour, where he can't afford the time to stay, because there is still so much else to see. And while Scorpio is no slouch, he loves to concentrate his mind on issues that intrigue him, and he will delve and probe until he is sure he has gotten to the bottom of something and penetrated to the truth, at which point he is finally ready to move on.

The big test in this relationship is whether the Scorpio parent can allow Sagittarius to bounce around, ricocheting between one pursuit and the next, and resist the urge to turn him or her into stone. The archer is born to play with life. He is a jester and a free spirit, and he needs to be given a lot of rope in order to explore. Of course, he frequently looks as if he is veering dangerously out of control, which presses all the Scorpio buttons. The scorpion tries so hard to keep himself under control that the next step inevitably seems to be to keep a tight grip on other people. But who controls the controller part of Scorpio? By making a kind of inverse psychological flip, Scorpio can let himself and Sagittarius off the hook by allowing the archer a free rein in his self-expression.

In some ways, the Scorpio mother can understand how her archer child gets so fired up with enthusiasm because she always either wants to go whole hog or have nothing to do with something. Scorpio's passion inclines him or her toward extremes. However, the Sagittarian tendency to get carried away and swept up in excitement has a more indiscriminate flavor to it. Something catches his eye, and he jumps on the bandwagon without a second thought, propelled by his fiery impulsiveness. Scorpio can help the archer to *choose*, to exercise his will rather than acting on autopilot.

The Scorpio father is gladdened by the Sagittarian desire to go further and further because he realizes himself that life cannot be made to stand still. He knows that we are all engaged in a process of change that carries us into the future regardless of whether we wish it or not. Intuitively, he knows that his archer child is well equipped to handle whatever life throws at him, largely because his positive attitude enables him to make the best out of virtually any situation. So he can put out to Sagittarius the wisdom that this child already knows on some level—that it doesn't matter what happens, only what you think of it.

Sagittarius Child with Sagittarius Parent

A grown-up archer and a child archer are very similar—both want to have as much fun as possible. So with this as the main item on the agenda, you can be sure that a good time will be had by all. Certainly a Sagittarian parent won't try to constrain this child and delights in his outgoing nature and trusting openness . . . he just wishes that all people could be so positive.

As times goes by in the archer's life, he learns to tone down some of his excesses and to look before he leaps, because inevitably he will have had his fingers burned at some point. Sagittarius can channel his energy more constructively as he gets older, and he develops a philosophical wisdom that tempers his high-voltage vibrancy. But gazing at the little archer in front of him, bursting with excitement and raring to go, he smiles indulgently, remembering his own spiritedness that just had to be expressed when he was young.

A Sagittarian mother is broad-minded in her outlook and is not afraid to let this child into the mainstream of life. It is not permissiveness on her part, because Sagittarius has some pretty high moral ideals, but she doesn't want the archer to be kept on the edge of experience and receive all his information secondhand. Sagittarian parents are very "permissive," much to the chagrin of some of the earth signs! This mother would never dream of presuming she always knows what's best for her child; she believes in letting him find out for himself sometimes.

A Sagittarian father will expect to be more of a friend than an authority figure to his child, and this fits neatly with the little archer's picture of "what Daddy should look like." They can relate on the same level, play together, talk on the same wavelength, be interested in the same things. But, having a slight difficulty with boundaries, the archer father can at times not know when it is important to draw the line. Well, he can draw it, but sticking to it is another matter. And if the archer child grows up not seeing his father choosing to say no appropriately, he finds it more difficult to learn how to do this for himself. He needs practice in gauging when and how to stop!

Sagittarius Child with Capricorn Parent

The goat watches the archer flying wildly around and wonders how he can be so cavalier with his time and energy. Capricorn always feels that he must do something useful and worthwhile—frittering away his resources is grossly wasteful. Yet the spontaneous enjoyment the goat sees on this child's face is a delight to behold. Where Capricorn is tight, Sagittarius is loose; where Capricorn is correct, Sagittarius is casual. Can Capricorn bring himself to bend the rod he creates for his own back, so that Sagittarius can experience more elasticity?

Capricorn believes that if you want something, it usually requires effort and patience to get it, while the archer expects things to drop into his or her lap. The amazing thing is that while the goat is waiting patiently under the tree for the apples to ripen, the archer has fired off an arrow and caught one perfectly. But the goat will still maintain that food tastes better when you have worked up an appetite.

One of the things that the Capricorn mother notices about Sagittarius is that he or she finds it impossible to wait. If he wants something, he wants it now, this minute, and once he has achieved his desire, it is all over so quickly. It is hard for the archer to savor life; he swallows it whole. It is all such a contrast to the way his mother likes to plan ahead, preparing for every possible contingency and ensuring that she gets it exactly right. She can help the archer to understand about priorities and how good it feels to keep something in reserve. Her own self-discipline is bound to act as a bank manager for Sagittarius, encouraging him or her not to become mentally, physically, or emotionally overdrawn.

Because the Capricorn father can be somewhat self-contained in his expression, he gets a release from observing the archer's *joie de vivre.* But it is almost impossible not to join in when Sagittarius expects you to do so. You can be sure that the goat will try to avoid any situation that might run the risk of making him look silly, but this child can coax his father into letting his hair down. It is true that Capricorn gets younger as he gets older, but the process is certainly speeded up when there is a Sagittarian child around!

Sagittarius Child with Aquarian Parent

As a parent, Aquarius is not given to overreacting, even in the face of Sagittarius doing his best to whip everyone up into a state of hysteria. It is not that the archer is deliberately provocative, but he is prone to excess, and he easily goes over the top in his behavior. Now Aquarius may not be averse to taking people by surprise from time to time, but he is usually quite restrained and gentle, raising eyebrows through his words rather than his actions. So he needs to find a few well-chosen phrases to try to get Sagittarius to simmer down when he is doing his impersonation of the charge of the Light Brigade. And because Aquarius is the water bearer, he is usually able to pour enough cold water on the archer to cool his temperature!

In fact, Aquarius applauds the Sagittarian honesty because he likes to call a spade a spade himself. In this parent–child relationship, each one knows exactly where he or she stands, and nothing is hidden from view. Sagittarius is encouraged to be as open as he would like, and Aquarius does not believe in forcing round pegs into square holes—if little Sagittarius wants to be a round peg, so be it!

The Aquarian mother will accept that a little archeress is just as eager to rough and tumble as the boys. She won't imprison her in pretty dresses when all she wants to do is run around and get muddy. Similarly she gives the boy archer plenty of room to spread his wings. Sagittarians begin to feel incarcerated when they have to spend a lot of time indoors and can literally begin to climb the walls! Probably no other sign understands so well the need to be free to be yourself as the Aquarian mother. She knows that Sagittarius needs the stimulus of contact with other people and does not need to be stood over and given directions. She makes sure that she gives her child lots of opportunities, and the archer never misses a single one.

The Aquarian father can sometimes seem a little remote because he lives in the world of concepts and ideas rather than human relationships. He likes people *en masse* and is a sociable soul, but bring him into a one-to-one relationship, and he can quickly feel claustrophobic. His Sagittarian child, however, will have none of that—he wants a real live, walking, talking father, one who will gets his hands dirty, roll around with him on the floor, and playfully tickle him when he isn't looking. And the archer's enthusiasm is infectious and irresistible, sweeping up all in his path, so he'll probably get what he wants.

Sagittarius Child with Pisces Parent

Sagittarius and Pisces are tuned into different vibrations in life. The archer enthusiastically charges ahead, believing that if he wants something, then all he has to do is make it happen, while the fish flows along with the current, receiving and accepting what he finds along the way. Both, however, are inherently trusting in life and have a philosophy that everything happens for a reason and that something good is just around the corner. The Sagittarian and Piscean optimism and capacity to find meaning have an uplifting and encouraging influence on other people.

Of course, when Sagittarius and Pisces find themselves in a parent–child relationship, they unconsciously feed each other with positive energy. Being around an archer child injects a buoyancy into the atmosphere, and the Piscean parent is filled with hope for the future. It seems that this child really does carry the spark of life, that he has the zest and enthusiasm to make ideals a reality.

Because the Pisces mother is such a giver, there is always a danger that she polarizes her child into being a taker. There needs to be a two-way flow of energy about giving and receiving. Sagittarius is a generous spirit, but the fire signs can put themselves at the center of their own universe to such an extent that they become stuck in a "me first" syndrome. And if the Pisces mother becomes a satellite to this, she will be permanently picking up the pieces for Sagittarius, often literally—the archer is not the most neat and tidy child! Because the archer tends to act now and think later, he or she often rides across other people. His impulsiveness gets the better of him; this is why he has a reputation for being careless—it is not that he couldn't care less, just that he gets caught up in his own enthusiasm. Pisceans can martyr themselves on the altar of other people, thinking so much about others' feelings and needs that their own go unmet. So there is a great opportunity for a balance to be struck between Sagittarius and Pisces, with the archer child learning how to be thoughtful and the Pisces mother recognizing that she could do with a bit of the Sagittarian freedom to choose to have her own way.

The Piscean father can fire his archer child's imagination. Sagittarius loves to play in a fantasy world full of heroes and adventure, and Pisces is no stranger to this realm. He knows how to turn ordinary life into something extraordinary and magical, and he captivates the Sagittarian child with his ability to weave together the real and the unreal. Pisces won't constantly call Sagittarius to come down to earth, because he knows how important it is to dream a little.

Sun in Capricorn Child

22 December–20 January

THE GOAT

Qualities to Look for and Nurture in Your Capricorn Child

A sense of purpose, commitment, and loyalty

EVEN WHEN SMALL, CAPRICORN LIKES TO FEEL THAT HE IS doing something useful with his time, and once he is committed to someone or something, his loyalty is not easily shaken. He has a mature and serious approach to life that makes it hard for him to be carefree, which often means that he is treated as an adult rather than a child.

A talent for organizing and a practical way of handling things

As an earth sign, Capricorn shares in common with Taurus and Virgo the ability to stick to a routine, and to plan and build the things he wants to happen with care and efficiency. Once he or she has embarked on something, Capricorn will patiently see it through to the end. He has a reputation for reliability, and for this reason people tend to give him a great deal of responsibility, which he welcomes.

Wanting to be self-sufficient, strong, and self-controlled

Capricorn has a fear of being vulnerable and weak, so he takes great pains to develop self-reliance and disciplines himself to keep up the appearance of having everything under control. Even as a child, Capricorn will deliberately contain himself and keep emotional reactions to a minimum. Undoubtedly he is tremendously capable, yet he also needs to learn to trust other people and be more expressive, especially when he needs help.

Aiming to "climb a mountain" and get to the top

Capricorn is a sign that aims high; he sets standards and goals for himself that ensure he has to work hard to achieve the end result. And he is always prepared to put in a great deal of effort. No matter how long it takes, he will continue on his path, ignoring distractions and taking difficulties in his stride. Ultimately he wants recognition and respect. He is mindful of "doing things properly," and he wants to be taken seriously.

Capricorn Boys

Capricorn boys often seem more grown up than their fire sign friends, who charge around making an exhibition of themselves. In comparison, a boy goat will get on with what he wants to do without causing disruption and fuss. He often prefers the company of older people because he finds children his own age rather immature. It's not that he's a goody-goody, but he just can't see the point of running wild—he's got more interesting things to do.

He likes to have an agenda in life, to know what is happening and when, and he has a natural affinity for routine and order. Having firm guidelines and a solid foundation in his childhood helps him to find his feet as an adult. The more secure he is as a child, the more he can trust himself to open up with other people and let down his defense barriers. But if he hasn't experienced much stability in the early years, he will spend his life trying to compensate, building himself safe walls that can end up imprisoning him.

A Capricorn boy has a wise head on young shoulders, but his natural shyness means that he often hides his light under a bushel. Not exactly oozing with outgoing confidence, Capricorn will often wait to be asked rather than wading in with his ideas and opinions. And he is ever conscious of the need to behave appropriately.

Capricorn Girls

Because Capricorn admires the qualities of fortitude, independence, and self-control, girls born under this sign definitely know their own minds and are not about to be seen as frilly weaklings. The Capricorn girl is not "masculine," but she is practicing to take her place as an adult on equal terms with men. And she will never entertain the idea of not being able to do something just because she is a girl. She wants to have a try, and she possesses a great deal of pluck and resourcefulness.

The Capricorn girl wants to be helpful and be recognized within the family as possessing certain capabilities. Give her a special job to do that is hers alone, and she will take great pride in doing it well. This is the child who will remember to feed the fish and to bring the garden chairs in from the rain. Capricorns do not find mundane tasks dull and boring; they actually like to learn about how things work and how to accomplish practical tasks. This is where she excels.

However self-possessed she appears to be, she still needs a great deal of reassurance, because Capricorns can be very hard on themselves and always believe that they could have tried harder, or done better. The greatest gift you can give her as a parent is to let her know she doesn't have to make such a great big effort to win your approval and that you love her absolutely, regardless of anything she achieves.

Capricorn at School

In many respects, Capricorn is in his or her natural environment at school. He takes to the routine and the rules like a duck to water and feels absolutely content knowing exactly where he should be at any given time, and what is expected of him. The goat also likes the competitive challenge of school, and the chance to prove that he is capable. Winning the prize and scoring top marks in the exam are concrete achievements that he can aim and prepare for, and he likes the idea that he will be rewarded for his own efforts.

Capricorn is not the belligerent type, constantly looking for opportunities to transgress the rules. He has a great respect for authority, and stepping out of line is not his idea of fun. Because he is able to accept the structure of school life, he often gets ahead—his energy goes into working and achieving, which is his ultimate satisfaction. Capricorns love to be made class leader or monitor, and they take the responsibility very seriously.

The Capricorn mind is practical rather than imaginative, and the goat often takes his or her time in understanding something thoroughly. Although he may not appear quite so quick on the uptake as the air and fire signs, once he has learned something, he has a memory like an elephant. The standard of his work is consistent, he won't turn in half-finished essays thrown together at the last minute, and he rarely needs prodding to do his homework. Even if he finds a subject particularly difficult, he will persevere, but he often doesn't realize just how good he is at the things he is good at!

Capricorn at Play

It's not that Capricorn doesn't like playing, but he hates to waste his time in aimless activity. So he won't spend hours dreaming up great adventures or living in a fantasy world—the real world is the one that interests him. He likes to get involved in things that require practicality, like helping you wash the car or paint the walls.

As a sign, Capricorn is definitely more serious and controlled when younger. It is usually much later on in life that the goat feels he or she can ease up and play a little. In childhood, Capricorn is concerned with what people might think of him and whether he is "doing the right thing." His self-consciousness prevents him from being spontaneous and impulsive, so he will always try to work out what is acceptable behavior. Being a parent to Capricorn requires a great sensitivity toward his shyness and desire to please. He almost needs to be given permission to let his hair down and enter fully into playing.

Capricorn Child with Aries Parent

An Aries parent likes to live life on fast forward, while Capricorn feels far more comfortable at a sedate speed. So the ram is always trying to make the goat hurry up, and he gets impatient having to slow down to a sensible Capricorn walk. It can also be very disturbing for Capricorn to feel pulled along, with never enough time to catch his or her breath. The goat gets flustered when there is no definable pattern to his life. This is the child who likes order and routine—concepts that bore the ram out of his mind. Being a parent, Aries will try to organize his time better and take a responsible attitude, but sooner or later he is itching to feel the adrenaline that comes when he lives in his natural impulsive state.

Capricorn and Aries are both achievers who hate to waste time, and the ram admires this child's industriousness and independence. Capricorn is rarely bored and can occupy himself without constant entertainment from outside sources. And Aries literally marvels at the goat's long attention span, remembering how fidgety he used to be himself as a child.

Being so keen to do things by himself, Capricorn is remarkably self-sufficient and lets his mother's apron strings drop as soon as possible. Nothing could suit an Aries mother better than a child who demonstrates that he or she can get on without her. Aries is actually a warm and affectionate mother, but she believes that everyone should learn to stand on their own two feet, and she feels uncomfortable with clinginess. So she encourages her little Capricorn to get on with it, go off and stay at a friend's house, and run around and collect his sponsor money himself—she won't overprotect him from dipping his toe into the outside world.

The ram father also believes that courage and strength are essential ingredients for a young child to acquire. So he will support Capricorn in his or her struggle to overcome obstacles and emerge triumphant. He will always encourage him to go that extra bit further, and is never short of praise. The goat responds readily to his father's energy and aliveness—he may feel pushed, but there is a quality of vitality around his father that this child finds immensely exciting.

Capricorn Child with Taurus Parent

In many ways, a Taurean parent provides the kind of stable, ordered environment that makes Capricorn feel on cloud nine. Although some children react with rebelliousness in the face of the bull's firmness and insistence on conformity, the goat just feels comfortable and secure. He never has to worry about anticipating this parent's movements because Taurus likes his family life to run as regular as clockwork. The bull parent offers a big, dependable cushion for Capricorn, who can grow up at his own pace and with his feet on the ground.

Nevertheless, as Taurus and Capricorn jog along together with hardly a cross word, the goat is not confronted with the alternative self-expression of the fire, water, and air signs, and when he or she does come into contact with people who live within a completely different framework of reality, it comes as something of a shock. You mean not everyone tidies up after themselves and thinks things through before doing them? Capricorn can be in for a bit of a rude awakening.

The Taurus mother directs her energies into providing good food and a comfortable lifestyle for her family. She values relaxation, and wouldn't dream of hothousing young Capricorn into premature achievement. But the goat is a natural striver—he wants to get somewhere, and although he is not the type to make a big noise about it, he quietly walks his path, which most certainly is going to take him where he wants to be.

The Taurean father wants to get involved in doing things with his children and builds a relationship through giving them his time and attention. He is the type who will roll up his sleeves rather than bury his head in a newspaper when young Capricorn wants help unraveling the strings on his or her kite. And the goat is comforted by the Taurean father's practical approach to life and the sense of reliability that he exudes.

Capricorn Child with Gemini Parent

"What time is it?" cries the Capricorn child. "What does it matter?" replies the Gemini parent. Capricorn and Gemini have totally different approaches to life—Capricorn is ever conscious of using his or her time purposefully and organizing things to a schedule, whereas Gemini couldn't care less if he or she gets distracted from one thing because something more interesting comes along. Gemini is a butterfly dancing around the goat, who is always trying to pin him down.

There is a hint of role reversal going on here between Capricorn and Gemini, because the goat is born with the sort of mature outlook that takes years to distill in Gemini. In many respects Gemini is an eternal child, naive where Capricorn is wise, and frothy where the goat is serious. This child wants to do things properly and to get them right, and if the Gemini parent will not focus his mind on whatever it is that needs to be done, then Capricorn will do it for himself. It is so hard for the single-minded goat to comprehend Gemini's twists and turns and the capacity to think and do several things at once.

It's amazing how a Capricorn child can somehow manage to make a Gemini mother feel scatter-brained. "You've forgotten your purse and left your gloves behind," Capricorn points out to her as soon as they have left the house. It's because the goat's mind rarely strays from the practical dimension of life, which underpins everything for him, that he is so careful and orderly. And although he keeps his eyes fixed on the ground instead of gazing at the sky like Gemini, his gift is in walking a straight road from A to B and achieving his goal.

A Gemini father seems mentally skittish to Capricorn, who can't easily understand his explanations and darting intelligence. And Gemini can feel that the goat is a bit plodding and slow on the uptake. Nevertheless, they have to admire each other—the Gemini father is endlessly fascinating to Capricorn, and the goat has so much common sense and is so in command of life that Gemini is awed.

Capricorn Child with Cancer Parent

The opposite qualities of Capricorn and Cancer make them at first glance to be in direct contradiction. The goat is independent, practical, and disciplined, and the crab is dependent, emotional, and vulnerable. Yet they are both masters of retreat—the crab ducking into his shell, and the goat disappearing behind his barriers. And they are both a little shy and in need of a great deal of security. So a Cancerian parent can very well understand what lies behind Capricorn's stiff upper lip—a fear of rejection, uncertainty of others, and an anxious desire to appear in control.

In fact, Cancer is such a supportive and nurturing sign that the goat soon warms to this parent's acceptance and love. From time to time, he may defiantly push Cancer away and want to show that he "can do it all by himself," but this is just Capricorn's way . . . He wants to prove his capabilities both to himself and to other people. Only by learning things the hard way is the goat truly sure that he has the hang of them, so he will turn away from kindly advice that means to save him the agony. In Capricorn's book, the agony is the gateway to the ecstasy.

Although the Cancer mother longs to scoop up her child and tuck him safely out of harm's way, Capricorn is the original cat who walked by himself. She has to let go of him enough to allow him to discover himself. And being such an innately sensible soul, he is self-protective anyway and not inclined to take dangerous risks. Capricorn calculates the consequences before he takes action, a trait that governs him in adult life.

The goat senses a gentleness in his or her Cancerian father, but also respects his wisdom and tenacity. Like Capricorn, Cancer won't give up easily, and once he has gotten his claws into something, they remain entrenched. Looking at the softness and the strength lying side by side in his father, Capricorn dares to allow his own vulnerability to show, which is quite an achievement for him. Once he has opened up his heart in childhood, he will always be able to listen to it.

Capricorn Child with Leo Parent

Leo is an unshamed dazzler, stalking the limelight and giving all he's got. The lion is a magnificent beast and quite used to putting other creatures in the shade. In comparison to his radiant Leo parent, the goat may feel awkward and even a little dull, yet he can't quite bring himself to shed his self-consciousness. It all boils down to Leo's natural ability to express himself and his tremendous belief that he is able to give of his best and be appreciated for it. It takes Capricorn many years to come close to developing this self-confidence.

Yet the wonderful thing about being in Leo's company is that as long as he has an outlet for his own talents, he is fantastically generous at recognizing talent in other people.

So he is a great source of encouragement to the reticent goat, blowing his trumpet on his behalf whenever he gets the chance. The one thing that the lion has to remember with Capricorn is that he wants to make it on his own terms. Being thrust center stage to grab a bit of applause is unsatisfying to him—he wants to earn his respect and recognition when he is ready for it—and Capricorn is often rather a late developer, in keeping with his planetary ruler Saturn, the timekeeper, who often delights in putting the clocks back!

The Leo mother wants to feel that her children are absolutely unique and special—after all, they are her own creation! So she invites Capricorn to put his best foot forward, and this child is rather seduced by the amount of attention he receives for keeping up appearances. And the goat does care deeply about what other people think. He or she wouldn't dream of letting his Leo mother down by skulking in the corner when she wants him on parade. But Capricorn is never frivolous; his wish is to be taken seriously, to be respected, and as a child more than anything else he would like to be treated as an adult.

A Leo father had a big enough heart to convince Capricorn that the world is not such a bad place. Where the goat is naturally suspicious, Leo expects the sun to shine. This father is full of praise for Capricorn's efforts and thinks his child is wonderful regardless of whether he wins or loses. If this kind of love sinks into the goat, he can begin to let himself off his own hook early, and stop trying so very hard to gain approval.

Capricorn Child with Virgo Parent

Being earth signs, Capricorn and Virgo understand each other very well. They are both attuned to the practical dimension of life and the necessity to organize matters so they run smoothly. As far as Virgo is concerned, it is an absolute gift to have a child who doesn't drop his or her clothes all over the house and leave a trail of unfinished business. And the goat knows exactly where he or she stands in the Virgoan household—what is okay and what isn't okay, because Virgo is precise about such things.

The Virgo parent is a great one for encouraging the child to strive to do his or her best, and Capricorn is inwardly directed toward achievement, so this parent and child combination agree on maintaining a purposeful attitude in life. There isn't another sign in the zodiac that can hold a candle to Virgo in terms of sheer industriousness—Virgo is always occupied with something, however unimportant it might seem to other people. And Capricorn is not happy with too much relaxation—he quickly feels adrift if he doesn't know what he is supposed to be doing. Together, Virgo and Capricorn create the buzz of two busy bees.

Virgo mothers do tend to fuss and worry over their children—they can't help it, because fretting over details comes so naturally to them. Capricorn, however, refuses to be fussed over—he thinks it is undignified, and he likes to be considered as capable as a grown-up. He is also so sensible that he is the least likely child to take risks or go off the track in any way. Having said that, he likes to know that you are right behind him and going to be there for him if he needs you. So the Virgo mother had better bite her tongue if she isn't to ruffle the fur of her Capricorn child, and she had better trust the goat to climb his own path—he is surefooted and steady enough to get there without her constantly having to call out directions.

The Virgo father is touched by Capricorn's unassuming modesty. Being inclined toward behind-the-scenes work himself, he rather likes the fact that Capricorn isn't a noisy show-off. Virgo knows only too well how still waters can run deep and values the introvert, knowing that it is absolutely no indication of lack of strength. He is also such a good communicator and listener that he can draw Capricorn out of himself.

Capricorn Child with Libra Parent

Libra is never a pushy parent. He is unconcerned about competing in the mothers' and fathers' race for having the most brilliant child; all he asks is that Capricorn smiles and is happy. In fact, Capricorn is probably more ambitious than his parent—he actually wants Libra to see that he is capable, clever, and above average when he has committed himself to achieving something. It is Capricorn's way of feeling good about himself, and if Libra abstractedly tells him that he looked beautiful when he was putting his all into reaching the right notes in his solo, then he has sadly missed the point for little Capricorn.

Having schooled Capricorn in the level of politeness required to be invited somewhere again, the Libran mother feels that this child will have the social finesse necessary to glide through life. However, goats were not born to glide; they can be a bit gruff at times. And if they feel awkward in a situation, rather than jumping through hoops to please other people like Libra, they will withdraw into silent observation, too scared to put a foot anywhere in case it is wrong.

Really, Capricorn needs a lot of help in thawing out, rather than receiving a whole list of instructions from his Libran mother that are intended to show him how to win friends and influence people. This child needs to know that he can risk being spontaneous, can show other people who he is without fear of censure. He always has the voice inside him telling him that he could do better or must try harder, and what he desperately needs is an outside voice telling him that he is doing all right.

Where the Libra father and the Capricorn child feed into each other's expectations is that they are both concerned with doing the right thing. The Libran father wants more than anything to be able to present a picture of happy families to the outside world, and Capricorn has such a respect for his elders that he follows along with whatever they think is right. Further down the line, he may realize that he doesn't care at all what other people think, and he wishes to be free of contorting himself into a socially acceptable image, or saying yes when he would prefer to say no. His Libran father might be shocked that such a "nice" child can show such a defiant face, but he has to admit that there needs to be a balance!

Capricorn Child with Scorpio Parent

Capricorn and Scorpio have a special understanding of each other. The Scorpio parent would be the last one to try to draw Capricorn out of his self-protective defensiveness because he recognizes his own sensitivity is hidden from view by an impassive demeanor. It is not that Scorpio and Capricorn are trying to be something they are not, but they like other people to think they are in control. Even as a child, the goat will brazenly transmit fortitude, sensibility, and self-sufficiency rather than show an ounce of doubt or fragility. He is an expert at convincing others that it doesn't hurt, or that he doesn't mind. And Scorpio is an expert at seeing through it!

As a parent, Scorpio is glad that little Capricorn has such a mature attitude. He finds it hard work dealing with naiveté and juvenile high jinks, but the goat is far too sensible to wear him out on that front, and also possesses such a receptivity to learning that Scorpio adores his role as mentor. When he looks into this child's eyes, Scorpio is met with the understanding of one who wants to piece together a workable formula for life, and yet he already appears to know the answers from somewhere deep inside himself.

Capricorn almost embodies the puritan work ethic—he feels lost if there is nothing to occupy him. In childhood, Capricorn detests long lazy days with no set formula because he needs something he can sink his teeth into. And although the Scorpio mother may not share the earth signs' desire to get their hands into material matters, she believes passionately that life is about self-discovery. So if little Capricorn is learning about his capabilities, then she is thrilled that he is doing something so worthwhile. She detects such a quality of resourcefulness in this child that she feels he only has to dig inside himself to keep making the next step in life.

Rebellion can bring out the worst in a Scorpio father. He will meet defiance with his own steely strength and runs the danger of locking horns with his child or trampling over his spirit in the need to reassert his power. However, Capricorn is more than a match for him, because the goat will never contradict or go against his or her father just to score a point. The goat actually can't see the point in deliberately disobeying or staging a mutinous uprising—he or she is too calm and collected for that. He figures instead that if there is a rule, then there is usually a good reason for it, and if after a lot of careful thought he can't see the reason, then he will just refuse to cooperate—not by running amok, but by standing still. And when the Scorpio father meets this cool but immovable object, he is forced to open up negotiations!

Capricorn Child with Sagittarius Parent

The goat and the archer seem like opposites, even though they are placed next to each other on the astrological wheel. Sagittarius is raring to go, wanting to hurry up and get on, and Capricorn in contrast is dragging his heels, wishing to take his time and look over his shoulder. The archer's philosophy is that everything will be all right, and in the meantime one needs to have as much fun as possible, whereas Capricorn is not so convinced—surely life can't be as easy as that?

While the archer is looking for the shortcut, Capricorn is learning the hard way. As the parent and therefore supposedly the more grown-up of the two, the archer will have to stop riding so high, dismount, and walk at a steady pace to understand the inner workings of Capricorn. For a start he can try to understand that as a fire sign, he is bound to want to tackle things in an exuberant manner while this earthy child has a more measured approach. He cannot be rushed along because he likes to "do things properly."

The archer mother will always encourage her child to give something a try—the end result is not as important as the taking part. Yet Capricorn is desperately concerned that he should do well and imagines that his mother judges him on his success or failure. If she were to award points on sheer effort, Capricorn would come first every time, and Sagittarius marvels at the patience and commitment of this child—qualities that are not readily at her own disposal.

The one thing Capricorn yearns for is to feel safe in life, but the archer father couldn't disagree more. Safety and security are tantamount to predictability, which looms at him, trying to limit and restrict him. Sagittarius always likes to live a little dangerously, just a bit on the edge, so it is hard for him to understand Capricorn's fear of taking a risk. But if he tries to push the goat too far, Capricorn will suddenly dig in his heels and refuse to budge an inch—he is a great self-preservationist.

Capricorn Child with Capricorn Parent

By the time the goat has reached parenthood, he has mellowed somewhat. In fact, Capricorn is always more serious, more anxious and uptight when young; then gradually his shyness drops away and he eases up within himself. Having a Capricorn child touches the sore point in the goat, reminding him of his own self-consciousness when young. And he longs to be able to make this child's early years more joyful, carefree, and spontaneous than his own were.

You can lead a goat to water, but you cannot make him drink—however hard the parent tries to make frivolity replace this child's sense of responsibility, he cannot totally let go of his dutifulness. At times he looks merry, like trying on a fun outfit of clothes, but at the end of the day he takes them off and is stripped to his essential nature, which is deliberate, cautious, and prudent—all qualities that will stand him in good stead, but seem uncomfortable in a child. The parent goat can only be aware that this child will relax later in life—it is the fate of the Saturn-ruled to eat their cake at a later date than their peers!

For the Capricorn mother, a child of her own sign can feel like a dream. She doesn't have to organize him, pick up the pieces, or remind him of anything, because he has gotten himself together. And he fits into her own routine without a murmur of dissension. No fights over bedtime or pocket money—Capricorn readily accepts the status quo, knowing that he will progress in time.

In his Capricorn father, the little goat sees steadiness and reliability. He is quite certain that he wants to grow up just like Daddy, and, of course, he contains the same ingredients. All the dedication and self-discipline inherent in this young child will potentially come to fruition in constructive form, and Capricorn tends to measure himself by outward achievements. That is why, as soon as little Capricorn has won the egg-and-spoon race, his father recognizes the same ambition that has gotten him high up his own personal mountain.

Capricorn Child with Aquarius Parent

Because Aquarius is a fixed sign, and therefore very determined, the water bearer is not so skittishly unpredictable as is commonly presumed. In fact, when Aquarians dig their heels in, they can become so entrenched in a particular viewpoint that their famed open-mindedness seems to fly out of the window. So Capricorn won't find that his Aquarian parent is itching to initiate him into letting go of all that anchors this child in his own practical sense of reality. He might encourage him to experiment and break out of his habitual comfort zone, but ultimately, he understands the Capricorn need to play it safe.

As a social animal, Aquarius will naturally want to introduce Capricorn to a wide range of situations and many different types of people. Unquestionably, Aquarius is actually far happier within the sphere of friendship—he is a "more the merrier" type and easily feels cornered in close personal relationships. Needing a lot of room to breathe, he cannot handle other people's expectations of him, so he likes to lighten the load with an infusion of company. Capricorn, however, is rather shy and reticent, unless he knows someone really well and can trust them enough to open up. In the company of strangers, he withdraws until he is certain of his ground, a behavior pattern that perplexes Aquarius, who is in his element in the unknown.

Aquarian mothers need a breath of fresh air to wipe away the predictability of domestic routine, but Capricorn is just the opposite—he or she is never bored by familiarity and consistency.

The goat needs to feel that his feet are on solid ground, and sometimes the minutest change of plan can start to make him feel insecure. He needs plenty of reassurance to make him believe that the whole world won't collapse just because he will be having supper at Granny's tonight instead of at home. And forewarned is forearmed with Capricorn—be sure to give him as much notice as possible, because he adjusts slowly!

An Aquarian father is not the most practical type. Being an air sign, he tends to live in his head, in the world of ideas and communications. For all his vision, when little Capricorn needs help with his candle-making kit, the Aquarian father is reduced to reading and rereading the page of instructions. The laying on of hands is not his forte! Still, Capricorn usually possesses enough common sense for them both, and his Aquarian father provides the inspiration that lifts Capricorn up into new dimensions.

Capricorn Child with Pisces Parent

Pisces has a gentleness that dissolves the Capricorn fears and doubts. Yet this child, who is in need of rock-solid security, sometimes feels that his or her Piscean parent lives on a wing and a prayer. It is hard for Capricorn to translate security onto any other level than the material and physical. He is of the mind that if he can see something and touch it, then it exists, but abstract security such as love and understanding are harder for him to assimilate. Pisces is the opposite—physical reality is a poor substitute for the richness of feeling.

Really, Capricorn likes to feel that he has a measure of control over his environment. That means he knows what is going to happen and when, and he has planned out in his mind how it will take place. This child lives on a "need to know" basis; he feels completely adrift with the "wait and see" syndrome that guides the fish along the currents of life. Capricorn is afraid that if anything is left to chance, then he might be disappointed, and he desperately needs to absorb some of Pisces' faith in life.

In fact, because Pisces is such a highly intuitive sign, the Piscean mother instinctively knows what her little goat needs in order to feel comfortable in life. She oozes reassurance and a kind of soothing tranquillity, but even this is often not enough to quell the fear that rises in Capricorn if he somehow feels his ground is shaky. Pisceans often don't state the obvious because they live on such a subtle level where communication is picked up and transmitted nonverbally much of the time. But this Capricorn child needs to have a guideline—just expecting him to know something or assuming that it doesn't matter to him sets him up to feel small, and if there is one thing Capricorn is most eager to dispel, it is the idea that he is a small person.

The Capricorn child would really like to get involved in *doing* something with his Piscean father. Pisces can appear to be a slippery fish to the goat—he wants to engage him in activity, but although Pisces doesn't mean to be elusive, he finds it hard to be present for Capricorn in a way that meets this child's needs. Although he might be there in body, somehow he is floating away somewhere—there is always something dreamy about Pisceans. What Pisces really needs to communicate to this child is that he can trust in his love for him.

Sun in Aquarius Child

21 January–19 February

THE WATER BEARER

Qualities to Look for and Nurture in Your Aquarius Child

A strongly defined sense of individuality

AQUARIUS IS ESSENTIALLY A FREE SPIRIT. HE NEEDS TO DEvelop in his own way, without conforming to anyone else's idea of who he should be. From a young age he has a strong urge to be different, not to follow the herd, and although this can be construed as contrariness or rebellion, it is actually a search for the self. This child may develop at a different pace from other children, stopping, starting, and experiencing sudden breakthroughs that are typical of this sign.

An independent mind that is both logical and intuitive

As an air sign, Aquarius has a natural affinity with the mind. His or her thinking is clear, perceptive, and rational, combining the ingredients of logic and flashes of intuition. His thought processes are so fast that he appears to jump to conclusions, and ideas come to him like bolts of lightning. Aquarius needs to have room to develop free thinking and originality.

Wanting to make contact with other people yet retain freedom

The water bearer belongs to the sign of friendship. He or she loves to meet new people and is a kind and loyal friend. Aquarius also flourishes in groups, clubs, or teams where people get together for a common interest. Throughout his life he will have a knack of establishing friends wherever he goes, yet he always retains an element of detachment that makes him step back from getting too involved or dependent on other people.

Enjoying the stimulation of change and preferring excitement and unpredictability to constancy

Aquarius is easily bored by routine—once something has become familiar it no longer holds interest, and the water bearer wants to move on to fresh and stimulating pastures. He is excited by change, eager to experiment and explore something new. He loves surprises; they put a charge in his system and make him feel alive. He also tends to see routine as deadening, and it builds up tension that creates the desire to suddenly break free.

Aquarius Boys

Aquarians never take kindly to being told what to do and how to do it. Aquarian boys need to be given the opportunity to discover how to work things out for themselves. They have the kind of inquiring minds that enjoy experimenting, and their power of logic helps them to piece answers together quite easily. Don't expect your Aquarian son to come up with what you expect, though—he often looks at things from a different angle, and this is why Aquarius has a reputation for invention.

When he feels trapped or stifled by routine or an inflexible approach, he will attempt to test you by seeing how far he can go. With Aquarius one should always be prepared for the unexpected, even the outrageous, and this child can suddenly turn the tables in such a way that you will be caught off guard. He has a strong will and a tremendous resistance to doing things in the way everyone else does, so it is important to give him a lot of rope so he always has the opportunity to be individual. Given the Aquarian perversity, you may find that giving him permission to be unconventional sends him back into the fold!

Being an air sign, an Aquarian boy can cut off from his feelings and live in his head most of the time. He likes to think there is a logical explanation for everything, and he can have difficulty acknowledging feelings, although he is very sensitive. It is important to handle his emotions with care and to help him talk about what bothers him, so he can realize that feelings are natural.

Aquarius Girls

Your Aquarian daughter wants to be seen as a person rather than a little girl doll. She isn't necessarily a tomboy, but she doesn't want to be prettied up for parties just because that is what is expected. Later in life, she will develop her own individual style, but when she is growing up she will tend to reject being "made to wear" anything in particular, and although the water bearer is normally even-tempered, she is also defiant!

Right from an early age she adores the company of other people, and her curiosity propels her into making contact. Before you know it, her social life is the mainstay of *your* existence! Her temperament is usually calm and equable, and she adjusts easily to new situations and won't cling to your apron strings. In fact, she won't turn a hair if she has to be looked after by a variety of other people—she finds it exciting.

Aquarians are outstandingly thoughtful of others, because they care about people—they may have trouble expressing it in a consistent way, but they are the ones who turn up when needed. As long as your Aquarian daughter feels allowed to be herself, she is easy to live with. She isn't the type to throw temper tantrums or demand constant attention; in fact as long as she has something to interest her, then she is happy. Even as a young child, she has the rare ability to look beyond herself and show concern for other people. Aquarius has a humanitarian instinct—noticing what goes on in the world and seeing oneself a part of something bigger.

Aquarius at School

Because Aquarius is ruled by Uranus, the planet of lightning reflexes, intuition, and flashes of inspiration, an Aquarian child is destined to become a bit of a bright spark. The good news is that Aquarians are very quick on the uptake, original thinkers, and possess a rationality and logic that gives them a cool, clear head. The bad news is that Uranus is also the planet of erratic process, meaning that those born under this sign often exhibit a stop-start quality that impedes the consistency of their progress. Therefore, Aquarius may be way ahead in some subjects and appear to have blown a fuse in others.

Aquarius tends toward a scientific mind, one that can crunch numbers and facts and assemble them again with razor-sharp clarity. Those born under this sign also enjoy arguing the point in essay work, and putting forward reasons and explanations. They will not necessarily take the conventional viewpoint, however. Their memory is such that photographic recall is not beyond their limits, but on the other hand the unpredictable nature of their mental processes means that they can go completely blank on occasion or make mistakes by reading questions so quickly they get the wrong end of the stick. Aquarians unfortunately often can't be bothered with repetitious exercises, and they need to take things more slowly and put in some good groundwork so that they don't trip themselves up.

Aquarius at Play

Aquarius is a curious combination of being a loner and a good mixer; he or she is both social and antisocial. However many people he attracts—and there is often a crowd around him—he manages to stand out from it in some way. He likes a wide variety of people, prefers having a horde of buddies rather than clinging to "best friends," and adores any situation that involves teamwork or groups of people. Yet there is often something about Aquarius that looks a little lonely or as if he is out on a limb. He chooses to be this way at times; it is all part of his insistence on being his own person.

The attunement of Aquarius to sciences and communication means that he is fascinated by technology. He loves to play with machines—anything from a calculator to a computer game can keep him absorbed for hours. Being progressive by nature, he usually prefers anything that is new on the market or just invented, instead of traditional or old-fashioned games. The whole concept of space, extraterrestrials, and rockets excites the Aquarian mind—he finds Planet Earth a bit pedestrian at times! It is a good idea to encourage young Aquarius to become part of a club, but you might find he invents his own team or group that appeals to his sense of originality and being different. One thing is for sure, Aquarius is bound to surprise you. Left alone with his tricycle he produces a bike, tea trays become skateboards—be prepared for the unexpected!

Aquarius Child with Aries Parent

Aquarius has a coolness about him that keeps him from getting burned in the Arien flame of enthusiasm. As a parent, the ram is one of those "on your marks, get set, go" types, forever pressing on with a busy agenda of activities. He or she urges Aquarius to get on with life. Yet, the water bearer remains a little detached from the ram's vortex of energy, sometimes refusing to get drawn in at all. If he wants to do anything, it will always be done in his own way, because he wants to do it—not just to please Aries.

Although Aries can get a bee in his bonnet when he is contradicted, he has to admire the Aquarian ability not only to think on his feet, but to stand on them as well. When all is said and done, Aries is a great believer in the power of the self and the spirit of individuality. He really doesn't have much time for yes men, so he has to give Aquarius his due for knowing his own mind. And although Aquarius has a reputation for being unpredictable, he doesn't have the ram's drive for impulsive behavior, and therefore his actions are more considered.

Both Aquarius and Aries have a very low threshold of boredom, but the Aries mother is amazed to observe this child's total absorption in activities that stimulate his or her mind. Aries is more physically oriented and has to be *doing* something, whereas the water bearer child can entertain himself for hours without running around. The famous Aquarian detachment and objectivity also leave the Aries mother perplexed. In comparison to other children who throw tantrums over small concerns, he or she has the rare capacity to turn a mountain into a molehill. Aquarius is never small-minded—he can always see the larger perspective, and he considers selfish demands to be silly and unimportant. While the Aries mother is pushing her child forward to the front of the line, little Aquarius is allowing someone else to go first.

Because Aquarius refuses to get steamed up, he will often see his impatient Aries father getting all hot under the collar and be able to defuse the situation. For Aquarius, it really doesn't matter if you are half an hour late, have forgotten to defrost the supper, or the television set has broken down. This child is unerringly calm in such situations—but tell him he can't go out to play with a friend, and you will feel his feet itching and a nervous restlessness overtaking him. The

Aries father has to watch his somewhat dictatorial nature because the water bearer needs to be free.

Aquarius Child with Taurus Parent

If Taurus is sometimes rather like a wall, being solid and secure, Aquarius is off the wall—full of bright ideas and determined not to do what everyone else does. In many ways Taurus works with the ordinary things in life, getting pleasure from organizing them, yet Aquarius is attracted to the extraordinary and always searching for something a little bit different. It can be difficult for Taurus to understand the need for Aquarius to be free when the bull is content to live in a world of familiarity.

Yet there is a level where Taurus almost plants this child firmly into the ground, and even though Aquarius may be an unusual seed, he or she still needs this form of protective nurturing in order to grow. As the gardener, Taurus is fascinated by the development of little Aquarius, who invariably sprouts up in fits and starts, flowers at unusual times, and often turns out quite differently from the picture on the front of the packet! And the bull has to give Aquarius a very long rein, however much he feels like tugging it in, because Aquarius will have to live out some element of being a free spirit—even if it seems completely unnecessary to the practical Taurean mind.

Undoubtedly, Aquarius brings an enormous disruption into the smooth flowing of the Taurean mother's life. This is because his or her curiosity leads him astray, and she may feel drawn into a perpetual game of hide-and-seek. She never knows what to expect with him, which can be an upsetting experience for Taurus, who adores continuity. One day he likes peas, the next he loathes them—she will never get stuck in a rut with this one! It can be frustrating, but she has the strength to call him to heel when she needs to—and Aquarius knows when he has gone beyond the limit. It takes a lot to really rile the bull, and the water bearer can take her to the edge, but somehow he makes light of it at the last moment and avoids confrontation.

Because Aquarius is so quick on the uptake, he or she can't stand hanging around for other people to get the point. Now, the bull father finds it hard to trust his intuition, so he tends to deliberate before taking action. It makes Aquarius champ at the bit, but there is never any hurrying the bull. Often in the time lapse while his father is taking stock, Aquarius has gone off his original idea and done a complete about-face! They have much to learn from each other—Taurus to look at things from a new angle, and Aquarius to slow down and value the idea of seeing something through from beginning to end.

Aquarius Child with Gemini Parent

Aquarius and Gemini fire each other up with ideas and never stop talking! Because Gemini has a butterfly mind, he or she loves to consider new possibilities and play with different ways of doing things, and with an Aquarian child, the permutations are always endless. The water bearer is constantly on the lookout for something new and exciting because once he has got the hang of his current task, his interest is immediately attracted elsewhere. And Gemini will let him run because he believes in the goodness of breathing a lot of air into one's life and not sticking with the tried and tested.

It is not the Geminian nature to be suffocating in close personal relationships, because this sign gives to other people, and needs for itself a lot of room to maneuver. And Gemini has no preconceived idea of what qualities a child *should* possess, or driving desire to influence him in a particular direction, either. For Aquarius, this means he is granted a freedom to become himself, and, for this sign, individuality is of paramount importance.

The Gemini mother likes to intersperse her routine with little jaunts, and Aquarius laps up his introduction to plenty of new people and places. Being air signs, they both need a certain amount of changeability in the atmosphere and appreciate having their minds stimulated. So with this mother, Aquarius has little call to get into his itchy feet syndrome, and she doesn't squash his mind with a know-it-all attitude because she believes they are both learning about life together. The Gemini mother never loses touch with her childlike curiosity, and her lack of jadedness means that she remains open to what's new, so she really is on the same wavelength as her little water bearer and will be when she reaches eighty!

Because the Gemini father relates to being a child, he can treat Aquarius as an equal—their ages are irrelevant, and once they are talking about something, they get lost in the world of thoughts, opinions, and ideas. Gemini values the mind above all else, and he is delighted that Aquarius is such an original thinker and can use reason to cut through his personal feelings. Yet Aquarius does need to become more in tune with his emotions, because otherwise he has a tendency to disappear into his head to such an extent that he cuts off from feeling and reacts in a rather impersonal way. Gemini, too, can view emotions with suspicion, but even so, he can get the water bearer on a more friendly footing with his emotional life by *discussing* how he feels about things.

Aquarius Child with Cancer Parent

Aquarius and Cancer are attuned to very different levels of experience. Although Aquarius is the water bearer and commonly mistaken for being a water sign, his element is air—that of the mind and intellect. The crab, on the other hand, is a creature of the sea, venturing out onto the land at times, but always needing to be close to the watery realm of feelings. Therefore, Cancer strives to establish deeply emotionally connected family bonds, and Aquarius craves union of the mind, creating a relationship that allows independence and freedom yet connects through communication.

In the early years, the differences between Aquarius and

Cancer will be less obvious, because the young water bearer requires the sense of belonging that provides a solid bedrock in his childhood. But sooner or later he will surprise Cancer with his urge to do his own thing, and the crab needs to know that the Aquarian independence doesn't mean a lack of love for his family. But if Cancer tries to cling or overprotect, then Aquarius will try harder to pry himself away. More than any other sign, Aquarians require other people to "let go" of them, yet within their contrary nature they possess tremendous loyalty.

The Cancer mother will have to try to change her tack with little Aquarius, who finds it hard to be needy and dependent. As soon as he is able, he begins to rationalize his feelings and explain them away. His safety is gleaned through identifying with his mind—something that Cancer struggles with because the crab likes to swim around in his emotional life, empathizing and sharing feelings with other people. When the Cancer mother begins her homily of "I'm sure you feel worried about starting at a new school, but very soon you will feel you belong there," Aquarius looks her straight in the eye with a look of disbelief—for him, starting something new creates excitement, not fear. She will have to become more objective if she is not to attribute her own feelings to this child—she must take a leaf out of his book and start looking at people in a new way!

The Cancerian father is a traditionalist when it comes to family life. He likes everyone to cozy up together, and he pays homage to all the family rituals that keep everyone closely knit. But Aquarius will not play ball with this idea. Just because it's always been this way doesn't mean it has to stay the same, so he will come up with suggestions, new ideas, and alternatives to keep things from becoming boring and predictable. Aquarius also has an ability to feel a sense of family around his friends rather than being limited purely to biological bonding. He nearly always wants a friend to come too! Aquarius has an aura of surprise around him, and being his parent requires a degree of openness and flexibility.

Aquarius Child with Leo Parent

Because Aquarius is one of the cool, breezy air signs, he appears to stand back from the heat of the fire, whereas Leo visibly sizzles with the warmth and vitality of his fiery nature. Not that Aquarius is in the shade; he has his own electricity that crackles through him, but he refuses to get so personally involved in the dramas that are part and parcel of Leo's existence. Even in childhood, Aquarius appears to have some kind of overview, an ability to see the bigger picture that prevents him from magnifying small issues out of proportion.

The water bearer rarely loses his objectivity, so he views life with a rationale that frequently keeps him above the mire of human emotion. Leo minds so desperately about everything, and it can be a source of frustration to the Leo parent that this child apparently doesn't care what happens. In fact it is not that he doesn't care, but Aquarius has a certain detachment, which means he can almost flick a switch in himself that frees him from the pull of his wants and desires.

The Leo mother believes in being special and magnificent, and Aquarius has a need to be independent and individual. They are opposite signs of the zodiac and equally determined to maintain their own integrity, which sometimes means that neither will budge an inch on some issues. Both the Leo mother and the Aquarian child have a quality of fixity that makes both of them stick to their guns. Yet opposites always have a magnetism between them that is fascinating to them both, and they secretly admire each other's qualities even though they find it difficult to see life from the other's point of view.

The Leo father can have a tendency to think that he is always right, and at times Aquarius seems to be hell-bent on contradicting him. But before Leo rises to the bait, he needs to understand that Aquarius is often experimenting with ideas and actually enjoys stirring up a controversy because he hates to think that things get stuck in a groove. The

Aquarian child needs to be allowed space to be different, to do his own thing and express his own ideas—telling him what to do and how to do it crushes his spirit.

Aquarius Child with Virgo Parent

Aquarius is probably the least fussy sign of the zodiac—the details pass him by, making him appear easygoing and amenable. Yet if you try to box him in he will soon knock the door down. Virgo, however, appreciates the finer points of life—the little things are what consume Virgo and make the world go around for him. Virgo is usually involved in reading the small print in life, and their relationship is easy as long as he refrains from carping at Aquarius for not doing the same.

Of course, earth and air have to make some adjustment to each other, and the earthy Virgoan parent has practicality at his fingertips, while Uranus-ruled people are on a different wavelength. Their strength is not in keeping their feet on the ground, but in having their heads in the clouds and dreaming up original ideas. Yet Aquarius is not about to float away in space—incisive logic and clear thinking are some of his or her greatest attributes. His solutions and ideas can be inspired and so simple, and he arrives at them without pondering endless permutations like Virgo.

The Virgo mother is a great one for routine and ritual, which can send Aquarius flying off in the opposite direction. Aquarius thrives on surprise and unpredictability, so he balks at the Virgoan scheduling, list-making, and organizing, feeling limited and restricted by it. He can become deliberately disruptive and uncooperative just to stir up some excitement. Maybe the Virgo mother needs to direct her planning energy into some surprises for him in order to keep him happily on his toes. Yet Aquarius is the type who needs to become grounded if he is to make the most of his originality, and having a Virgo mother will certainly draw his attention to the practical dimensions of life.

Virgo is ruled by Mercury, the planet of communication,

and therefore is a sort of honorary air sign although unable to disassociate from its earthy roots. Because of the Mercurial connection, the Virgo father and Aquarian child enjoy a rapport of the mind. Aquarius is attracted to everything that is new, and Virgo loves to make something ordinary more perfect, so they are often thinking along different lines but nevertheless share an avid interest in life.

Aquarius Child with Libra Parent

Even though Aquarius and Libra are both air signs, and therefore two peas from the same pod, they do have their differences. Libra longs to fit in, to find the middle ground where all is peaceable and harmonious. He is happy if you are happy, whereas it can look as if Aquarius is happy when he has unsettled the status quo and caused you to rethink and embrace something new. Aquarius wanders on the edge, where he can belong yet still stand out. He can appear perverse and contrary just to make a point, changing his mind and direction in the blink of an eye and trying to ensure that no one can guess what he will do or say next—that way he remains uniquely individual.

Yet Libra and Aquarius are both people who need people, requiring the stimulating interchange that comes from meeting and relating to others. Although Libra may habitually say yes, and Aquarius no, they both desire connection with others. The strange thing is that Aquarius can often feel more crowded when there are just two people than when he is in the center of a large group. There is always safety in numbers for the water bearer; he or she needs a lot of space to pick and choose and come and go.

The Libran mother is a born diplomat and knows instinctively how to get on the right side of Aquarius—how to put things to him so that he doesn't feel railroaded and want to rebel. She understands his need to find his own way and make up his own mind even though she herself is a great compromiser. Some of her polish will inevitably rub off on Aquarius. Her insistence on manners and thoughtfulness toward others will make the water bearer better equipped to handle people rather than alienate them with his outré behavior.

Because Aquarius is such a champion of truth and honesty, he cannot bear whitewash. This child can sniff it out immediately if his Libran father is being economical with the truth so as to preserve appearances, or keep the peace. Libra never means to be dishonest, but he often wishes to avoid upsetting people—with Aquarius he learns to give him the straight facts, because Aquarius needs that kind of directness in order to trust other people. The water bearer is actually a great idealist, and he wants people to be true—later in life he will fight against deceit and hypocrisy—and he needs to have an openness with his father so they can both tell it like it is.

Aquarius Child with Scorpio Parent

One of the chief qualities associated with the sign of Scorpio is intensity. Scorpios are rarely indifferent about anyone or anything, and they tend to see things in black-and-white terms. It stems from their innate passion, which spills over into every aspect of their lives, so giving birth to Aquarius, who intellectualizes and rationalizes his feelings, is quite an experience for Scorpio. Scorpios hold a tight grip on life, and sometimes almost squeeze it to death, trying to extract all the juice from it. In contrast, Aquarius stands back from getting overinvolved and is able to reflect logically on the overall perspective.

When the water bearer is still very young, the Scorpio parent transmits his intense attitude by setting up a powerful bond between himself and the child, but at a later date this can actually feel very invasive to Aquarius, who needs his space. Scorpio needs to counter his possessiveness, which can sometimes amount to feeling that he owns his child's heart and soul, and just let him be. Although Aquarius is not easily ruffled, he will give Scorpio the slip emotionally by simply withdrawing into himself, pulling up the drawbridge as an act of defiance.

Through acknowledging the free-spiritedness of her Aquarian child, the Scorpio mother experiences a breath of fresh air in her own being. This child is undeniably exciting, and the relationship between them is never static and predictable. There is something about Aquarius that is destined to wake other people up to new ways of looking at things, and little Aquarius is a catalyst for Scorpio to dare to let go of the need to control and just allow individuality to speak for itself.

The Aquarian child has an openness to other people that challenges his father's rather suspicious nature. Scorpio can be quite circumspect in his dealings and becomes wary if he picks up distress signals; yet his Aquarian child is completely egalitarian in his attitude, hardly ever decides he doesn't like the look of somebody, and is prepared to give everyone a chance. Because Aquarius has a friendly but slightly detached approach, he feels quite safe to connect with all and sundry. He takes people as they come, and therefore they respond in kind. His Scorpio father would benefit by taking a leaf out of his book.

Aquarius Child with Sagittarius Parent

The archer understands very well the Aquarian need to keep his life fresh and interesting, and as a parent he is only too happy to supply an ever-challenging round of adventure. Yet he needs to remember that Aquarius is an air sign, and therefore does not need to be so physically active as his own fiery self, because in some respects, with Aquarius it is all in the mind. As long as an Aquarian's mind is engaged in something stimulating, he can stay in one place.

Aquarius is also a cooler customer than Sagittarius, who enthusiastically throws himself at life. The water bearer has his own inner sparkle born of his inspiration and intuition, but he doesn't wear his heart on his sleeve, and his subtle detachment allows him to maintain an aura of calm. As a young child, he is not bothered by changes around him and adjusts easily to new people and different situations. Unlike Libra, his equanimity is not designed to please you, but is a pure reflection of his ability to take life as it comes.

Sagittarius detests the overbearing mother syndrome, so the lady archer allows her little Aquarius to make up his own mind and do his own thing. With her philosophical nature, she believes that any mistakes little Aquarius may make are opportunities for him to learn something rather than posing a potential problem. This attitude is manna from heaven for Aquarius, who dislikes people breathing down his neck. He is itching to experiment and find things out for himself, which is the most direct road to his self-discovery.

On one level, the archer father and the water bearer are cast from the same mold. They both feel life is too short to spend time on boring practicalities when there is so much on offer out there. Sagittarius will always place pleasure high on his list of priorities, which allows Aquarius the freedom to rise above the mundane rituals of life. Because the archer is a great rule-bender, he believes that bedtimes are made to be broken, and Aquarius is delighted with this approach that allows the course of events to happen naturally rather than being restricted by a lot of oughts and shoulds.

Aquarius Child with Capricorn Parent

In traditional astrology, both Aquarius and Capricorn shared the planet Saturn as their ruler, and as a carryover, some Aquarians still resonate to the earthbound tones of Saturn rather than the high-voltage vibration of their new ruler, Uranus. And in fact, being brought up by a Capricorn parent certainly brings Aquarius into contact with this other layer of himself. Although the water bearer will still retain his quirkiness, he absorbs the Capricornian need for safety and order, and hides his outré light under a bushel in case it upsets the status quo.

The task for an Aquarian child who has embraced Capricorn principles is somehow to find a path in life that sheds new light on what has gone before. He must work with the old and the new and bring his originality forth without discarding tradition. The Capricorn parent can be entrenched in his values and rigid in his beliefs, but having an Aquarian child around is bound to challenge him to take a new look at life. Aquarius stirs up the situation so that everyone has to reevaluate their ideals. Why, why, why, he asks, making the goat examine himself and his views.

The Capricorn mother can usually think of plenty of practical reasons why something is impossible, but Aquarius loves to overthrow the limits and come up with a solution, however crazy it may seem. For every "no" she comes up with, the water bearer replies with an alternative. It can get quite wearing being challenged in this way, but Aquarius cannot lie back and accept other people's opinions without putting his or her oar in. It is a mark of his free spirit and independence, which are qualities that make him stand out from the crowd in later life.

The Capricorn father ultimately wants his child to be able to fit comfortably into the social system—which causes a problem for Aquarius, who really doesn't give two hoots about acceptability, even though he is a sociable soul. The water bearer will always notice where he is different from everyone else and magnify it as a sign of his individuality. When all is said and done, the goat cares far more than Aquarius about what other people think, and Capricorn when he is at his most conformist is a sitting target for Aquarius to spring his surprises—and Capricorn is only shocked because he is always so easily shocked!

Aquarius Child with Aquarius Parent

Two Uranian souls in the same household generate so much electricity it's surprising they don't blow the whole system—but then, maybe they do! Aquarians have a great affinity for one another, immediately recognizing the faraway look in each other's eyes that speaks of vision and originality rather than earthbound matters. An Aquarian parent has absolutely no expectation that a child will grow up in any particular way, and he can be sure that little Aquarius is going to surprise him anyway.

Because Aquarius is a sign that likes to have other people around, family life will not be restricted to the biological unit. To an Aquarian, if you are his friend then you are automatically part of the family, and he likes to spread his net as wide as possible to include many different types of people. So the small water bearer will grow up in an open house and get used to the throng—this is where he will learn to relate easily with other people, rather than clinging tightly to the Aquarian parent's apron strings. In fact, Aquarius develops a healthy disregard for putting all his emotional eggs in one basket, and this enables him to get his needs met from many different sources.

Picking up his mother's open-mindedness, little Aquarius gathers that he has permission to be himself. The Aquarian mother is careful always to treat her child as an equal—to ask him what he thinks and what he wants because she values his contribution and knows how important it is for him to feel he has a voice. It is only when Aquarians are boxed in that they fight to be free, so her tolerance takes the rebellious wind out of his sails. But the water bearer is never becalmed for long!

Talking and discussing are the fundamentals of relationships for the Aquarian father. He encourages his child to develop his mind and will always try to stand back from telling him the answer if it is going to inhibit his own free thinking. Of course, little Aquarius loves the opportunity to be inventive, whereas other children might prefer to listen to the voice of authority. From his Aquarian father he learns about friendship rather than control.

Aquarius Child with Pisces Parent

Although Aquarius and Pisces are air and water signs respectively, and therefore stand in their separate corners of head and heart, Pisces is the last sign of the zodiac and therefore able to accommodate all that has gone before. In other words, he is accepting of other people and has no wish to change them for his own purposes. Pisces is an all-seeing sign, with a remarkable perception of what motivates other people and what makes them tick, yet Pisces knows that it takes all types to make the world go around.

Aquarius can seem quite out of touch with his or her feelings even as a child. Emotions appear to be uncomfortable and somewhat alien to the Aquarian mind, and he or she prefers to keep them at bay, cut off from them if necessary in order to preserve a sense of well-being. It is little Aquarius who points out that another child is a crybaby. Yet if he has a Piscean parent, he will have to learn to accept emotions as a valuable dimension of life. Pisces is gentle and will never force the issue, but he is somehow able to dissolve the water bearer's fear of being dependent and needy, of showing his feelings.

Both Aquarius and Pisces are great idealists and concerned with the welfare of other people. The Pisces mother notices the water bearer's budding humanitarian instincts and encourages him to save for charity and think of what goes on in the world apart from his own personal concerns. For Pisceans it doesn't matter what their children achieve as long as they grow up to be caring individuals, and the Aquarian thoughtfulness toward others is apparent from a very young age and wisely nurtured by the Pisces mother.

The Piscean father has a creative spirit inside him even if he chooses not to use it. At the very least he shows Aquarius that there is more to life than logic and rationality—Pisces has the capacity to be swept away by music, beautiful scenery, and images. And although Aquarius might be embarrassed by his father's romanticism, it triggers his own creative spark.

Sun in Pisces Child

20 February–20 March

THE FISH

Qualities to Look for and Nurture in Your Pisces Child

An openness to, acceptance of, and trust in life

AS A WATER SIGN, PISCES EMBRACES THE FLOWINGNESS OF HIS element in his ability to swim with the current of life. He responds to changing situations by going with them rather than trying to resist them or assert a different path for himself. He also possesses a tremendous ability to take the rough with the smooth as part of his journey, while maintaining a sense of trust in life.

A compassion and tolerance toward other people that inclines him toward giving

From his position as the last sign of the zodiac, Pisces is able to identify with other people. He is essentially nonjudgmental of others and looks for the good in them, yet at the same time he has an empathy that allows him to reach a deep level of understanding and a desire to help others. Pisces naturally puts other people first and reaches out to give support and devoted attention to those in need.

A fertile imagination and innate creativity

Pisces is able to blur the line between the realm of the imagination and the real world and is therefore able to see life in a different light. The fish longs for magic and inspiration and finds that anything ordinary is rather bleak. He has enough vision to spread a little glamour around him and lift people out of their actual circumstances, and the poetry in his soul is deeply touched by beauty, music, and captivating images. Pisces is a born romantic.

A guiding intuition and sensitivity

Because Pisces does not put up protective barriers, he is uniquely open to his own inner wisdom, and has access to his intuition, which leads him through life. His sensitivity gives him a gentle touch in dealing with others, and he is always eager not to hurt their feelings. He often "just knows" how other people are, without being told, because he picks up much from the unconscious level.

Pisces Boys

Pisceans are so gentle and aware. In their evolution they are actually light years ahead of the souls who pass through a time of trying to prove their superiority by inflicting cruelty on others. Bullying other children or making concoctions to destroy colonies of ants is anathema to Pisces, who identifies with pain and therefore cannot find anything remotely interesting in observing suffering.

The boy fish is rarely the leader of the gang because he isn't one to give out orders and demand that his wishes be met. In childhood, the Pisces boy is not immediately in touch with his ego—Pisces is a sign that is associated with unselfishness, yet in order to prevent the possibility of being trampled on, he needs to strengthen his confidence in himself and his ability to assert his own needs and desires. As a parent to a Piscean boy, you must encourage him to stand up for himself and believe in himself—and it is important that his sensitivity is accepted and valued.

Because Pisces has such a vivid imagination, he can live in a world of make-believe when young. His mind is fired by fantasy, and he loves to invent characters or play out ones he knows. Unlike the earth signs, who can find it difficult to let their imaginations flow, Pisces can have a hard time trying to come back to the real world. Games of pretend merge with the real thing. Pisces is always wishing on a star, hoping that he will find a yellow brick road to take him away from Acacia Avenue, and in his mind he is able to make his own life larger and more enriching.

Pisces Girls

The Piscean qualities of sensitivity, imagination, and compassion sit well in the feminine world, and therefore Piscean girls can have an easier time of it than the boys, who have to work at finding a way of expressing themselves through a masculine channel. Girl fish encounter an acceptance of their gentleness from other people, and therefore swim free in their own world.

Her dreamy nature invites the Pisces girl into the arena of imagination. Pisces is the ultimate "wannabee," full of wishful thinking and longing, and if Miss Pisces can express herself creatively when young, she will open up a channel for her imagination that makes constructive use of her sensitivity. Her gift is her greatest ally, yet it also poses a potential danger if there is no legitimate outlet for it and her fantasy life becomes muddled with her real one. As adults, Pisceans can avoid reality, so solid boundaries in childhood can help her to discriminate and become adept at sorting out practicalities without losing her intuition and vision.

If you have a Piscean daughter, then you have a chameleon in the house. She becomes a nurse, a showjumper, and then a ballerina—all in the space of an hour! Pisces is so good at picking up subtleties that she can turn herself into anyone she chooses, and her impressionable nature allows her to reflect what she sees in other people. In many ways she is a mirror for the family because she will give out whatever she receives from you, but she needs to be encouraged to become herself—not a mirror.

Pisces at School

Pisceans excel at any subject where imagination and creativity are required and can also have a flair for languages because of their ability to "become" something else. It is in the area of logic and reasoning that they sometimes feel at a loss, because their minds are good at association rather than structure. This is not to say that all Pisceans are going to fail at math, but the subject needs to come alive for them through relating their calculations to life rather than pure numbers. In fact, Pisceans have a great appreciation for the nonverbal, such as color, music, and movement, and sometimes express great talent in these areas.

One of the greatest difficulties for Pisceans is in concentration and focusing, because their minds skip so easily from one subject to another—before they know it, the past imperfect tense has become a reverie about last week's visit to the circus. Like a fish, the Piscean mind finds it hard to stay in one place, and this sign can also experience periods of floating, dreaming, or drifting into space. Yet the odd thing about Pisces is that he often learns by just absorbing the atmosphere around him—even when he doesn't seem to be paying attention, the words are still going in.

He or she is not usually the ringleader, but is still very popular and has a tendency to be led into things and follow the crowd. Pisces is the type who goes along with his friends, so he needs to be encouraged to say no and exercise discrimination. But he or she is also the one who will help out the underdog.

Pisces at Play

Being a water sign, young Pisces adores water and often swims like a fish. He has a grace and elegance rather than grit and stamina, and his innate dislike of confrontation makes him want to avoid boisterous or highly competitive games. Put crayons or paints in front of him and his imagination flows, and he has the rhythm of a natural dancer and loves to hear and make music. He gets totally wrapped up in stories, especially old-fashioned fairy tales about dragons, princesses, and adventure—the more magical and fantastical the better. He is highly open to the power of suggestion, and he slips easily into the world of pretend and make-believe. Pisceans love to dress up as other people and create their own play.

Because he or she is so captivated by images and spectacle, Pisces is enchanted by pantomimes, magic shows, and films. Yet because he often finds it difficult to separate illusion from reality, he is more vulnerable to being upset than the thicker-skinned signs and may think that people have really died on stage or that he will be left in the scary haunted house forever. Pisceans do not enjoy gruesome scenes!

Pisces Child with Aries Parent

In the floating, faraway world of Pisces, all things are possible if you swim with the tide, and in the vibrant, heated world of Aries, all things are possible if you make them happen. With Pisces, life is all about acceptance and listening to the inner voice, whereas Ariens do battle with life and want to get caught up in a good challenge. So for the Aries parent, a fish child can appear to lack motivation, yet Pisces has a very subtle approach. Although he or she often seems to be lost in dreams, this child is really an idealist who always carries a torch for the highest outcome.

Because Pisces can be so acquiescent, he or she is a pushover when faced with the Aries drive, and if the ram is not careful, he can bulldoze Pisces into complying with his every wish. It takes a willed effort on Aries' part to allow Pisces to find his own way without his ram parent constantly pushing him along. Aries also values courage, strength, and independence—not qualities that are immediately visible in the fish child—but if he is looking for kindness, trust, and sensitivity, he will see them gleaming brightly out of Pisces' heart.

The Aries mother goes about her life at a cracking pace. She almost feels that she is in competition with the rest of the world and must achieve what she sets out to do as quickly as possible. If mothering is a job, she wants to do it as efficiently as she can. But there is something about Pisces that avoids this kind of direction. He can be a most slippery fish, never deliberately defiant, but nevertheless he is capable of sabotaging the best laid plans and somehow making his Aries mother adjust to a slower pace. Although the Aries mother may habitually set her watch five minutes fast, Pisces is the type whose watch stops so he completely forgets the time—and in his company time often appears to be irrelevant anyway because everyone is absorbed in enjoying the moment.

The Aries father can help to elicit clarity in his Pisces child. The fish is often swimming through muddy waters, and therefore can be confused about things. When he is in this state, he answers all questions with "don't knows," and this process can become a familiar pattern in his life. Often this paralysis is brought on by fear of the unknown, when suddenly all things loom large for Pisces, and he or she goes blank. But an Aries father is like a knight in shining armor, and he is capable of lending Pisces the courage to go on, simply by walking with him through the frightening parts until he reaches a clearer spot. Walking by his Aries father, the fish feels comforted in the knowledge that he will grow and move on.

Pisces Child with Taurus Parent

Although Taurus is a placid and kindly soul, he can have a problem dealing with other people's sensitivity. This is because the bull solves his problems by being practical rather than giving himself up to the world of emotional chaos. In Taurean terms, nearly all annoyances and turmoil can be assuaged by a good meal or some sleep, and he fails to realize that the Piscean fish sometimes ventures far out into deep water emotionally and cannot swim back to terra firma at the drop of a hat. He needs a lifeline, and the bull is able to stand on the shore and reel him in slowly and patiently.

While Taurus sets about organizing himself, Pisces drifts off into dreamland. His imagination is so strong that he can float away with his eyes open, and the bull needs to make sure he doesn't put his big feet on the fairies that Pisces can see at the end of the garden. And that is not all that Pisces sees—he "knows" about other people, tuning in with his finely developed intuition and slipping his hand into yours when he hears without words that your heart is lonely.

What the Taurean mother has to offer Pisces is an awareness of the importance of the practical aspects of life. She shows the fish how to look after himself and to value the body as the temple of the soul. And Pisces needs to absorb this knowledge if he is to be able to make his dreams come true. All his ideals and creative imaginings will come to nothing if he doesn't know how to ground them. Potentially she can teach Pisces how to balance his sensitive nature with sensibility, but she, too, needs to see the preciousness of both qualities.

The bull father feels as strong as an ox to lean against, and Pisces feels sheltered and protected by him. Taurus is a highly tactile sign, and Pisces sometimes reaches a point where words confuse him and touch is the best carrier of reassurance. There is safety and containment for Pisces within his father's orderly approach—and Taurus has time to listen to the fish. He is secretly enchanted by the magic Pisces sees in the world around him, even though he dismisses some of it as nonsense. Only Pisces can make sense of nonsense and translate it for others.

Pisces Child with Gemini Parent

For Pisces, the Gemini parent appears to orchestrate a never-ending excursion into the library of life. Gemini is so multifaceted, he spreads his interests far and wide, breezily skimming the surface so he picks up a passing acquaintance with most subjects. The Pisces child assimilates what he can and tunes out into his own dreamy world when he feels bombarded with too much information. The fish gets a glazed expression in his eyes, which means he has transported himself into his imagination. It is a great protection for him when the going gets difficult, like being able to switch on a film at will.

Because the element of air has the ability to detach from the emotions, the Gemini mother can sometimes feel at a loss in understanding her sensitive Piscean child. For Gemini, talking things out, explaining, discussing, and thinking about things is the means to relate to someone on a close level. The water element, however, lives in another dimension—that of the heart, not the mind. So Pisces experiences many feelings that are inexplicable, that cannot be defined and understood on a clear mental level. In other words, Pisces is at home with the nonrational, an area in which Gemini feels completely foreign.

And logic can be pretty dismissive of pure feeling, labeling it as silly, immature, or plain stupid—the mind likes to exercise a kind of one-upmanship. The Gemini mother can get caught in this because the mind is her friend and ally, yet if she uses it to alienate herself from her instincts and intuition, she will also alienate her Pisces child, who is brimming with feeling.

Pisces and Gemini share the quality of mutability that makes them adaptable, flexible, and appreciative of change. Therefore the Pisces child and Gemini father possess a mutual attraction for keeping things in the air. It is usually Gemini who ensures that family life never gets too settled and predictable, and the fish is able to float along with whatever comes up. The Gemini father has the energy of a kaleidoscope—the pieces keep changing and forming different pictures. Pisces is a child who can handle being in a state of movement; he doesn't demand a fixed routine, and that lets the Gemini father off the hook of expectation—from a young age, Pisces accepts others as they are and makes the best of what they have to offer.

Pisces Child with Cancer Parent

Both these signs bask in the fountain of the water element, constantly refreshed by the cascade of drops that symbolize the flowing of the emotions. With a Cancerian parent, Pisces is literally in his element and feels the great sense of connection that binds the water signs together in their search for unity of the heart. The crab is no stranger to the ebb and flow of the emotional tide. He understands that living through your feelings is a gift, a potential source of empathy with others, yet it also poses the danger of sweeping you away out to sea.

Because the crab is so aware of the vulnerability of a sensitive skin, he himself has developed a protective shell designed to throw others off the scent and to enable him to withstand the vicissitudes of life. The fish, however, has no such protection, but he or she is a fine swimmer and able to dart away. He also sometimes adopts a chameleon stance that enables him to fit in perfectly wherever he goes and therefore prevents him from being attacked. So whereas the crab parent may withdraw into his shell if he doesn't feel comfortable, little Pisces performs his magical trick that foxes everyone into believing he is one of them.

One of the Cancerian mother's greatest gifts if her capacity to create the bond of home and family. Cancer is the sign of the mother, and a female crab really comes into her own in this dimension of life. Pisces drinks up all her emotional support and feels totally understood by his mother, who can read the signals in the atmosphere around him and reach out to him without his having to explain himself. The fish receives her complete emotional attention, and this makes him feel valued. She is not pushing him to dive into life like a fire sign, do the mental high jinks of an air sign, or use the practical skills of an earth sign. Instead, she gently encourages his imagination and allows him to relate to life through his feelings, which is his natural mode.

Pisces appreciates the somewhat clannish attitude of the crab father. It makes him feel he belongs and has a special place in life, and Pisces stores away all the experiences that feed his later nostalgia for his childhood. Like a salmon, Pisces returns to his old spawning ground again and again, even if it is only in his mind, and it remains a source of inspiration to him. Even as an adult, Pisces will remember the way his Cancerian father showed him that he was loved unconditionally.

Pisces Child with Leo Parent

The fieriness of Leo and the floating cloud quality of Pisces makes the climate of this parent–child combination rather humid. The temperature is increased by Leo, who sometimes wants to push Pisces into action, yet this child still manages to evade the issue. The elusiveness of Pisces makes him or her rather like the disappearing Cheshire Cat—one minute you are having a conversation, and the next he is gone, but a smile lingers on. But Leo can go along with it for only so long, then he becomes feisty, and the storm erupts. Once it is over, the sun comes out and affection is restored between them, for Leo and Pisces are both very loving.

In fact, the lion and the fish idolize each other—Pisces is in awe of the Leonine creativity and self-expressiveness, and Leo sees in this child the specialness he craves. Leo sees the beauty of his Piscean child and desires the whole world to see it too—he has high hopes, and Pisces hooks into them because he, too, is looking for something magical and extraordinary in life. But the Leo parent has to restrain himself from expecting this little fish to fulfill his dreams, because Pisces is a great wish-fulfiller and quite capable of living out what another person wants for him, only to wake up later and discover that he is really someone else with different desires and needs.

The Leo mother can create a world of enchantment that the Piscean child wants to live in forever. There is no one like a Leo mother for wanting life to be rich, full, and experienced in glorious Technicolor, and no sign like Pisces who so much wants to believe that birthdays can come every day. Together, they can live in a sort of rarified atmosphere, although it may seem a little over the top to other people. Leo and Pisces feel hugely warmed by each other's presence, and Pisces in particular is made to feel confident and secure when he sees himself reflected in the proud look in the lioness' eyes.

When he or she hears the growl of the lion, Pisces scurries into the right place at the right time. The Leo father has such strong presence that he demands a certain following of protocol in his household. Pisces is a great one for thinking he can get away with things, that just this once someone won't mind . . . or that he forgot what he was supposed to do. But Leo will have none of this—when he commands, he expects people to jump, and the fish takes a great leap back into reality where there are limits and boundaries. It is a great lesson for him to learn, and Leo is a kindly teacher, but the father lion will ensure his little fish knows the rules. . . .

Pisces Child with Virgo Parent

These two sit on opposite ends of the astrological scale, but of course the parent weighs heavier than the child and tips the balance in favor of Virgo precision and orderliness. Even so, as fast as Virgo is tying up Pisces' shoelaces, they will come undone again! The otherworldliness of the fish means he appears to walk around in a dream, and Virgo is constantly calling him to pay attention.

But the fish can be so slippery, somehow he is never quite with it in the Virgo dimension of things. This is because his attention is elsewhere—that faraway look in his eyes says that he is absorbed in his own dreams and imagination, and he finds all the details that fascinate Virgo really rather unimportant. Still, these two are unlikely to cross swords and draw blood. Of course, they have the odd skirmish—life wouldn't be quite the same for Virgo if he couldn't say his piece—but gentleness prevails. Virgo isn't cut out to be a drill sergeant, and Pisces is no renegade.

Although the Virgo mother has her feet firmly on the ground, she is a great appreciator of beauty and creativity. When Pisces is letting his imagination flow, she is mesmerized by its vividness. The ability of the fish to slip into fantasy touches a longing in the Virgo mother because she can never really lose herself—she always has her agendas and lists of things to be doing—yet Pisces is capable of blanking out everything other than what absorbs him at the time. For him the story he is reading or the painting he is making is real, and having to get in a bath or have supper is irrelevant and unreal. However much the Virgo mother might feel like yanking Pisces back to the task in hand, she must guide and not pull, because his creative spirit is so tender, as fragile as a flower, and he needs to value it and nurture it, not feel guilty about it.

Because Virgo is a modest sign, the mindfulness of others that Pisces shows is highly valued by the Virgo father. Both Virgo and Pisces believe that there is more to life than looking after oneself—this is why they are great sharers and givers. So the Virgo father, although he is enormously proud of Pisces, won't make him stand up there in front of other people and blow his own trumpet; he shows him how to listen to his own internal applause. Yet no one applauds louder than this father when Pisces demonstrates how much he has to give other people.

Pisces Child with Libra Parent

Pisces and Libra are more than happy to live in a bubble where everything is beautiful and serene, because the reality of the world often appears appallingly harsh and stark to them. Both Pisces and Libra like to dress up the truth—they are not liars, but they see life with a little poetic licence that dilutes the mundane and magnifies the magic. So the little fish born to a Libran parent starts his life in an ornamental pond rather than the muddy waters downstream, and it certainly brings out his artistic streak and appreciation for the good life.

As a refined air sign, Libra doesn't like to get his hands dirty with the messy aspects of relationships. Loving people, but loathing conflict, aggression, and untoward behavior, Libra rises above such things and just smooths them all over. This often means he doesn't get involved—he's too busy making the bed look beautiful to actually lie in it. However, as a sensitive water sign, Pisces needs to be able to express his feelings, and Libra will have to dip his toe in Pisces' water if he is to allow this child to develop as he should. Otherwise, this fish will learn to avoid and escape his feelings—and that is a pattern that is detrimental to his growth.

Mirroring other people, Pisces picks up and expresses what he finds in his Libran mother, especially her politeness and polish. And Libra is so used to adapting to other people herself, she is stunned that someone else is actually taking cues from her! She feels like a ballet teacher with Pisces at the barre performing a perfect pirouette with confidence. But Pisces is naturally graceful and elegant; he has a gentle touch with people and a kindness that shines out. All the Libran mother does is create the right environment for his best qualities to come to the fore.

The only problem with Libra and Pisces is that they both find it difficult to make decisions. So the Libran father will ask his Pisces child what he or she would like to eat, do, or watch, and Pisces isn't sure, and Libra doesn't mind, and so it goes on—and on! Sometimes Pisces needs to be fished out, or he will swim in circles, or just float. Although there are times when it is useful to be able to do this, Pisces can get stuck, and he needs a prod to move him forward. So if Libra can turn the other scale and be very direct with Pisces, he will help this child to elicit his own clarity.

Pisces Child with Scorpio Parent

Scorpios have such a controlled exterior that many people do not realize the extent of their inner sensitivity. The scorpion wears a mask that hides his vulnerability, letting it drop only when he feels he can really trust someone. In fact, one of the greatest tricks Scorpio can master is to trust in life itself, and this implicit belief and openness is found in the Piscean child.

At once, Scorpio recognizes that he has found a soulmate in the fish, but he is so worried that Pisces will get burned and bruised by life that he cannot help hoping that the fish will learn how to cover himself up. Pisces, in fact, does not know how to get out of trouble by adopting a guise, but he chooses to wear the same one as other people so he can blend in, whereas Scorpio just retreats behind his dark glasses, keeping everyone guessing. Pisces is the most fluid of the water signs, and therefore less afraid of getting caught.

Qualities of feeling are valued highly by the Scorpio mother, who will help to elicit the compassion, sensitivity, and intuition that she knows is the essence of her Piscean child. While some of the fire and air signs may feel embarrassed by the overflow of feeling in Pisces—too many tears, too much emotion, and a sense of water, water everywhere—the Scorpio mother welcomes it and understands why her child is the way he or she is. She considers logic, rationality, and competition to be as dry as the desert, and she values feelings as providing nourishment in life. So she allows Pisces to revel in his imagination—he can believe in the tooth fairy and Santa Claus for as long as he likes. She knows that Pisces has a great gift to offer other people in his hopes and dreams, and she is not about to nip them in the bud. In his naiveté lies wisdom.

The Piscean child has the ability to reach right into the heart of his or her Scorpio father. His questions cause the Scorpio soul to search. Little Pisces wants to know whether his father talks to God, and why he doesn't talk to Auntie Vera. The Scorpio father might feel more comfortable revealing what he discusses with his banker compared to this, but he has to hand it to Pisces, who isn't much interested in material matters but instead in what goes on inside and between people. This is the stuff of life to him, and actually the real core interest for Scorpio too—if only he would admit it.

Pisces Child with Sagittarius Parent

The archer and the fish are always on the move. Being mutable signs, they are both adaptable enough to accommodate change and prefer adjusting to something new rather than staying stuck in the mud of a routine. The Sagittarian motto is "Ever onward and upward," and he or she does his or her best to keep going forward toward his or her goal. But the fish has a mysterious movement; he or she often doesn't want to go anywhere in particular but just to swim around and see what happens. Pisces is happy to go along with the Sagittarian sense of adventure, but he is not naturally as willful or outgoing as his parent.

Because Sagittarius tends to live life on a larger scale than other people, he can have a problem knowing when to stop, and in particular in recognizing where Pisces' comfortable limits are. Pisces is so aware of what other people expect of him that he tries his best not to disappoint them, and therefore won't say when he is flagging, insecure, or just plain scared. And therefore it is up to the archer to step down from his high horse, take stock of the situation, and allow Pisces to have his vulnerability.

The Sagittarian mother believes that life always has a nice surprise waiting just around the corner, and her optimism connects with Pisces' innate capacity to trust. She encourages the fish to look for the good in others and to make the best of whatever situation he finds himself in. She also nudges him into taking opportunities that he might otherwise have let slip. Pisces sometimes does miss out by being in a state of confusion; not knowing whether he wants something means it can pass him by before he makes up his mind. But the archer mother has already got the fish lined up with his target in sight, so he cannot miss. And although she may push him, he also benefits from having a little turbocharge in his life and will ultimately find the same spur from within.

Sagittarius is associated with learning and teaching—not the nitty-gritty fundamentals of education, but in the form of putting together your own philosophy of life, understanding yourself and other people, and encouraging others to develop themselves. So the archer father is a natural mentor for the Pisces child, especially as the fish possesses such broad vision and a talent for giving people hope. What passes between the Sagittarian father and the Piscean child is a spiritual gift that is found in the essence of their attitude toward life.

Pisces Child with Capricorn Parent

They are so different—yet they have so many things to teach each other that somewhere in the middle is the perfect balance. The goat is naturally suspicious. Being a realist, he believes in what he can see and touch and is doubtful about everything else. Capricorn will do everything in his power to protect himself from disappointment, and anything vaguely wishy-washy such as feelings, intuition, and imagination puts him in a dangerous, unknown place. If it looks at all likely that he might get let down, he puts the barriers up.

Coming face to face with the openness of the Piscean child, the goat is shocked right out of his socks—how can he wear his heart on his sleeve like that? Yet something begins to melt in Capricorn, and he is connected with his own longings and hopes and dreams, things that he has defended himself against for so long. Yet the goat knows how to say no, how to make things happen, and how to keep his feet on the ground—skills that Pisces would do well to assimilate. And because the Piscean skin is so permeable, this child picks it up beautifully.

The Capricorn mother has a rather "do you or don't

you?" approach—not wanting to waste a second, she tends to put people in the hot seat where they have to make choices. This all feels rather uncomfortable for Pisces, who could float around forever, and the Capricorn mother has to resist a temptation to make up his mind for him. But she can really sling him a line that teaches him to come up with his own answers, and once Pisces has got the knack, he is in possession of a valuable tool for life. But sometimes she needs to let him swim, because this is when Pisces is in his element. It looks as if he disappears, but he is just deep-sea diving and revitalizing himself with his imagination and vision.

The Capricorn father represents an anchor for this child. The fish can get lost in a world of make-believe and confuse himself with his own red herrings. But Capricorn is very good at being clear, and he remains stable and protective in his affections. Pisces knows how to let go, and Capricorn knows how to hold on, and in the crossing of their purposes they show each other another way of doing things.

Pisces Child with Aquarius Parent

Because the natural habitat of Aquarius is air, the Pisces child of this sign can feel like a fish out of water. Aquarius is interested in communication between people, discovering new ideas, and maintaining an objective overview. Although he may bear water, he still prefers not to get his feet wet while he is pouring. In contrast, Pisces lives in the sea of emotions and feelings—he often doesn't know what he thinks, but he always knows how he feels. Yet Aquarius and Pisces are both essentially creative idealists, and they possess great concern for other people rather than focusing life around themselves. They share a vision of a world that is less selfish.

The logic of Aquarius can slice through Pisces' romanticism. Even as a child, Pisces devoutly wears his rose-colored glasses that illuminate the starkness of what he sees and makes the world seem magical and glowing. For Aquarius to tell him not to be silly is missing the point entirely—

Pisces believes what he wants to believe, which is in fact true of all of us, but no one does it with as much openness as Pisces. His imaginary friend and talking tree are absolutely real, and rationality doesn't come into it.

Rebelling and doing your own thing *à la* Aquarius is simply not Pisces' style. He is inclined toward tolerating and accepting, so he appears to have less of a struggle. Yet Pisces can sometimes feel browbeaten when he or she has swallowed too much from others. This is where his Aquarian mother can help him to stand back and take a look at what he wants, rather than wade straight in because he "feels" what is expected of him. From her airy perspective, she can teach him how to take a breath, which is vital if he is not to feel green about the gills!

The Aquarian male is rather suspicious of anything that cannot be logically explained. As a father, he can come up with many sensible solutions for the reason why things go bump in the night, but he is actually pouring cold water on little Pisces, who is distressed and fearful because of what he or she is feeling, not what is happening. Above all else, Pisces needs his or her feelings to be taken seriously, which requires quite a shift in attitude for Aquarius, who believes that the key to life is in the mind.

Pisces Child with Pisces Parent

The Piscean symbol shows two fish, so when a Pisces parent produces a Pisces child he or she feels a sense of total completeness—the parent has found his or her twin. Symbolically they swim in opposite directions, and they may feel that this is the case because fish are never predictable in their movements. However, two Pisceans feel at one with each other, whatever they are doing, because they link deeply at a soul level.

There is a sense with Pisces of somehow knowing everything, but not with a smug "know-it-all" attitude. Piscean babies are born with a look that says they have been here before, and therefore they can allow and accept rather than resist what happens. Pisces does not have to hit his head against a brick wall, because when he recognizes something familiar, it is as if he is connecting with something he once knew, rather than discovering it for the first time. And who better to gently remind him than a Piscean parent, who is not predisposed to pushing and shoving?

A Pisces mother embraces life rather than carving it up into categories, rules, and regulations. She allows the family to knit together in its own way rather than dictating who does what and when. And her ability to go with the flow feels wonderfully nurturing to little Pisces—like being back in the fluid waters of the womb where he or she can trust that she will be looked after without having to force anything. Of course, her intuition tells her immediately how Pisces is feeling, and her ability to read him and respond accordingly makes their relationship especially close. And she encourages him to keep wishing and hoping because she still does it herself. This mother actively encourages little Pisces to express himself creatively, so he is free to indulge his imagination without thinking there are more important things to do.

The sensitivity of the Piscean father toward his little fish means that he is not constantly trying to propel him or her into a bigger pond. He lets Pisces develop at his own pace without heaping huge expectations on him. And Pisces can become easily crushed by getting out of his depth, so he appreciates having time to enjoy his achievements without being rushed on to the next thing. What good is wisdom if we don't value it?

Further Information

THIS BOOK CONCENTRATES ON THE SUN AND MOON SIGNS, AND while they form the core of a person's birth chart, they are nevertheless only part of the astrological jigsaw. There are eight other planets to be considered, as well as other important factors such as the Ascendant; so you may want to explore your child's birth chart in more detail.